# Performance Evaluation of Financial Holding Companies

Xiao Ning

# Performance Evaluation of Financial Holding Companies

Springer

Xiao Ning
Beijing, China

ISBN 978-981-97-8127-0 ISBN 978-981-97-8128-7 (eBook)
https://doi.org/10.1007/978-981-97-8128-7



This Springer imprint is published by the registered company Springer Nature Singapore Pte Ltd.
The registered company address is: 152 Beach Road, #21-01/04 Gateway East, Singapore 189721, Singapore

# Contents

**1 Overview of Financial Holding Group Performance Evaluation** ..... 1
1.1 Research Background and Significance ..... 1
1.2 Research Problems ..... 7
1.3 Research Approach and Methods ..... 9
1.3.1 Research Approach ..... 9
1.3.2 Analysis Methods ..... 9
1.4 Research Framework ..... 10

**2 Literature Review** ..... 13
2.1 Brief Introduction to Financial Holding Groups ..... 13
2.1.1 Separate Operations and Integrated Operations ..... 13
2.1.2 The Concept of Holding Companies ..... 14
2.1.3 The Concept of Financial Holding Groups ..... 14
2.2 Types and Characteristics of Financial Holding Groups ..... 15
2.2.1 Main Types of Financial Holding Groups ..... 15
2.2.2 Characteristics of a Financial Holding Group ..... 18
2.3 Economic Analysis of a Financial Holding Group's Operating Performance ..... 20
2.3.1 Scale Economy Effect of Financial Holding Groups ..... 20
2.3.2 Economies of Scope Effect of Financial Holding Groups ..... 25
2.3.3 The Synergy Effect in a Financial Holding Group ..... 29
2.3.4 Decentralized Risk Effects of a Financial Holding Group ..... 34
2.3.5 The Operating Performance Improved by a Financial Holding Group ..... 40
2.4 Summary of This Chapter ..... 44

**3 The Development of China's Financial Holding Groups** ..... 45
3.1 Environment for the Development of Financial Holding Groups ..... 45
3.1.1 Macroeconomic Situation ..... 45

3.1.2 Interest Rate Marketization Reform ..................... 46
3.1.3 Capital Market Reform ..................... 47
3.1.4 Financial Technology Development ..................... 48
3.2 Development History of China's Financial Holding Groups ....... 49
3.3 Classification of China's Financial Holding Groups .............. 50
3.4 Introduction to Typical Financial Holding Groups ............... 51
3.4.1 I Bank ..................... 51
3.4.2 E Bank ..................... 54
3.4.3 M Bank ..................... 57
3.5 Research Questions About Financial Holding Groups ............ 59
3.5.1 Before Transition: How to Promote Business Performance Through Transition? ..................... 59
3.5.2 How to Evaluate the Performance of China's Financial Holding Groups? ..................... 60
3.5.3 After Transformation: How to Continuously Improve Business Performance? ..................... 61
3.6 Summary of This Chapter ..................... 63

**4 Innovative Methods for Evaluating Operational Performance of Financial Holding Groups** ..................... 65
4.1 Main Methods for Evaluating the Operating Performance of Financial Holding Groups ..................... 65
4.1.1 The Concept of Performance Evaluation ................ 65
4.1.2 Introduction to the Main Performance Evaluation Methods ..................... 66
4.2 Selection of Operating Performance Methods for Financial Holding Groups ..................... 69
4.2.1 Introduction to the Factor Analysis Method .............. 69
4.2.2 Comparative Analysis of Main Management Performance Evaluation Methods ..................... 69
4.2.3 Reasons for Selecting the Factor Analysis Method ........ 71
4.3 Selection of Performance Evaluation Indicators for Financial Holding Groups ..................... 74
4.3.1 Sample Selection of Financial Holding Groups ........... 74
4.3.2 Principles for Selecting Performance Evaluation Indicators ..................... 77
4.3.3 Selection of Performance Evaluation Indicators .......... 79
4.3.4 Performance Evaluation Indicator Analysis .............. 80
4.3.5 Differences from Traditional Commercial Bank Evaluation ..................... 84
4.4 Performance Evaluation Introducing the Economic Value Added EVA Model ..................... 86
4.4.1 Economic Value Added ..................... 86
4.4.2 Return on Economic Value Added ..................... 87

4.4.3 Comparison of the Economic Value Added Model and Traditional Performance Evaluation Indicators ........ 87
4.5 Steps to Implement Business Performance Evaluation ........... 89
4.5.1 Research Hypotheis Setting ........................... 89
4.5.2 Conduct Performance Evaluation Data Analysis .......... 89
4.5.3 Reliability and Validity of Questionnaire ................ 89
4.5.4 The Empirical Analysis Process of Performance Evaluation of Financial Holding Groups ................. 90
4.6 Summary of This Chapter .................................... 90

**5 Research Results and Analysis** .................................. 93
5.1 Research Hypotheses .......................................... 93
5.1.1 Hypothesis of Integrated Operation and Profitability ...... 93
5.1.2 Hypothesis of Integrated Operation and Solvency ......... 94
5.1.3 Hypothesis of Integrated Operation and Cost Control ...... 94
5.1.4 Hypothesis of Integrated Operation and Business Performance ......................................... 95
5.1.5 Summary of Research Hypotheses ...................... 95
5.2 Conduct Performance Evaluation Data Analysis ................ 96
5.2.1 Index Forward Processing of Performance Evaluation ..... 97
5.2.2 Standardization of Raw Data for Performance Evaluation ........................................... 98
5.3 Reliability Analysis and Validity Analysis ...................... 98
5.3.1 Reliability Analysis .................................. 98
5.3.2 Validity Analysis ..................................... 100
5.3.3 Commonalities Test of the Original Variables ............ 101
5.4 The Empirical Analysis Process of Performance Evaluation of Financial Holding Groups ................................ 102
5.4.1 Factor Extraction .................................... 103
5.4.2 Economic Significance of Rotating Component Load Matrix and Factors .................................. 105
5.4.3 Score Coefficient Matrix of Common Factors ............ 110
5.4.4 Scoring of Common Factors ........................... 112
5.4.5 Ranking of Comprehensive Performance Evaluation Scores ............................................. 112
5.5 Verification of Empirical Results of Performance Evaluation ...... 113
5.5.1 Introduction to Cluster Analysis ........................ 114
5.5.2 Evaluation Indicators and Sample Data Adopted .......... 115
5.5.3 Results of the Cluster Analysis ......................... 115
5.6 Conclusions and Implications of the Study on Performance Evaluation of Financial Holding Groups ...................... 119
5.6.1 Grouping of Performance Evaluation of Financial Holding Groups ....................................... 119
5.6.2 Analysis of Comprehensive Performance Evaluation Scores of Financial Holding Groups .................... 120

5.6.3 Analysis of Solvency Evaluation Index Scores ........... 123
5.6.4 Analysis of Profitability Evaluation Index Scores ......... 125
5.6.5 Analysis of Asset Quality Evaluation Index Scores ........ 127
5.6.6 Analysis of Cost Control Evaluation Index Scores ........ 128
5.7 Verification of Hypotheses in Performance Evaluation Research ........ 130
5.7.1 Analysis on the Chi-Square Test Model of Integrated Management and Solvency ........ 130
5.7.2 Analysis on the Chi-Square Test Model of Integrated Management and Profitability ........ 131
5.7.3 Analysis on the Chi-Square Test Model of Integrated Operation and Cost Control ........ 132
5.7.4 Analysis on Chi-Square Model Test of Integrated Operation and Business Performance ........ 132
5.7.5 Summary of Performance Evaluation Research Hypotheses ........ 133
5.8 Summary ........ 133

**6 Conclusions and Suggestions for Performance Evaluation Research of Financial Holding Groups** ........ 135
6.1 Conclusions of Performance Evaluation Research on Financial Holding Groups ........ 135
6.2 Academic Significance of Performance Evaluation of Financial Holding Groups ........ 136
6.3 Suggestions for Performance Evaluation Management of Financial Holding Groups ........ 138
6.4 Research Limitations ........ 147
6.5 Prospects for Future Research ........ 148

**Annexes** ........ 151

**Bibliography** ........ 187

# List of Figures


Fig. 2.1 Structure diagram of a universal banking financial holding group. *Source* China financial stability report in 2018 (PBOC 2019) . . . . 16
Fig. 2.2 Structure diagram of a public financial holding group. *Source* China financial stability report in 2018 (PBOC 2019) . . . . 18
Fig. 3.1 The proportion of direct financing in China from 2013 to 2018. *Source* Website of the People's Bank of China . . . . 48
Fig. 3.2 Main research questions . . . . 59
Fig. 3.3 The first research question . . . . 60
Fig. 3.4 The second research question . . . . 61
Fig. 3.5 The third research question . . . . 62
Fig. 4.1 Flow chart of empirical research . . . . 74
Fig. 4.2 For the process diagram of factor analysis . . . . 91
Fig. 5.1 Cluster analysis results of performance data of financial holding groups in 2018 . . . . 116

# List of Tables


Table 5.1 Summary of research hypotheses ........................ 95
Table 5.2 Communalities table .................................... 102
Table 5.3 Communalities range .................................. 102
Table 5.4 The total variance table ............................... 104
Table 5.5 Total explanation of variance ........................... 104
Table 5.6 The rotation matrix of the different components ............ 106
Table 5.7 The transformation matrix table ......................... 109
Table 5.8 Matrix table of component score coefficient ................ 111
Table 5.9 Groups of the 13 financial holding groups ................. 120
Table 5.10 Grouping analysis on comprehensive scoring of business performance in 2018 ................................. 121
Table 5.11 Group scores from 2014 to 2018 ......................... 122
Table 5.12 Overall group scores from 2014 to 2018 .................. 123
Table 5.13 Summary of research hypotheses and test results ............ 134

# Chapter 1
# Overview of Financial Holding Group Performance Evaluation

This chapter first introduces the research background of this book. Secondly, the research question is put forward, that is, the performance evaluation of China's traditional commercial banks after they are transformed into financial holding groups. Thirdly, the purpose and significance of the study are clarified. Fourthly, the research ideas and analysis methods of this study are expounded. Finally, the research framework is described.

## 1.1 Research Background and Significance

Due to the different degrees of economic and financial development in different countries and regions, the development stages of integrated management are also different. Under this background, countries such as Europe and America started earlier in the theoretical and practical research of financial holding groups, while China's research on financial holding groups has just started. This section mainly describes the theoretical background and the current situation of China.

1. Theoretical background

Financial holding groups are originated and developed along with the financial industry from separate operations to integrated operations (People's Bank of China [PBOC] 2019). In 1999, the congress of the United States deliberated and passed the Financial Services Modernization Act (Liu 2017), which first expounded the legal category of "Financial Holding Group". At present, due to the massive gap in financial market development and legal systems in different countries and regions, the international community has not yet formed a clear consensus on the definition of a financial holding group. According to the actual situation of the financial industry, major countries and regions classify local financial holding groups into different types and define the identification standards. In July 2019, the People's Bank of China issued

 
X. Ning, *Performance Evaluation of Financial Holding Companies*,
https://doi.org/10.1007/978-981-97-8128-7_1

the Proposed Measures for the Supervision and Management of Financial holding groups (PBOC 2020) which clarified the accreditation standards of financial holding groups in China. China's financial holding groups are established in accordance with laws and regulations, investing in and holding two or more different types of professional financial institutions. Holding companies only carry out equity investment and management, and do not directly engage in commercial business activities, while holding financial institutions engage in commercial business activities. To facilitate the following discussion, the Chinese financial holding group referred to in this research is defined in accordance with the Proposed Measures for Supervision and Management of Financial holding groups. Since the financial holding group's own operating data has not been released, this research uses the operating data of the financial holding group and its subordinate financial institutions.

The early research on financial holding groups abroad mainly focused on the advantages and disadvantages of separate operations and integrated operations, while the mid-term research focused on the economies of scale, economies of scope, synergy effect and decentralized risk effect of integrated operations. In the later period, it mainly focused on the management efficiency, supervision system and risk control of financial holding groups. Most foreign experts and scholars believe that financial holding groups have economies of scale, economies of scope, synergy effect and decentralized risk effect, which can promote the improvement of business performance. However, some scholars' research findings do not support the above conclusions. Among them, the supporting conclusions are as follows.

As for the benefits of economies of scope, Chen (2014) state that universal banks can allocate the fixed costs of customers to diversified financial products, and then obtain scope economy. Kanatas and Qi (2003) argue that after commercial banks obtain securities underwriting business qualification, enterprise customers can handle securities issuance services more conveniently through commercial banks, and commercial banks can expand profit sources, keep profit growth, and realize scope economy. In terms of economies of scale, Fei (2014) indicates that universal banks have more advantages in economies of scale and scope than other financial institutions. Fei (2014) also believes that financial institutions can achieve economies of scale by carrying out diversified operations.

In terms of synergy effect, Lin (2016) points out that financial holding groups can strengthen business synergy among subsidiaries by implementing diversified operations and obtain efficient internal synergy effect. Conducting comparative study on financial holding groups and professional financial companies in the Netherlands and Belgium, Vander (1999) considers that financial holding groups can make use of the capital market to achieve more financial synergy than professional financial companies. In terms of decentralized risk effect, Yue (2005) thinks that commercial banks can achieve the purpose of risk diversification through business diversification after implementing diversified operations and adapting the environment changes in the market.

In terms of improving business performance, Wang (2017) have studied financial institutions in nine countries and conclude that commercial banks can set up financial holding groups through diversified operations to enhance profitability and market value. Chronopoulos et al. (2011) took the financial holding groups and professional commercial banks in 10 European countries as samples and conducted an empirical study on the operating conditions from 2001 to 2007, arguing that the operating efficiency of financial holding groups is higher than that of professional banks.

Due to the late start of China's financial system reform, the development of China's financial holding groups has just begun. Domestic research mainly focusses on discussing the advantages and disadvantages of separate operations and integrated operations in the financial sector, the development mode of integrated operations, risks, and the supervision system. There are very few theoretical and empirical studies on economies of scale, economies of scope, synergy effect and decentralized risk effect of China's existing financial holding groups, and even less on the management performance evaluation methods and empirical studies of China's financial holding groups. Wan (2018) believes that commercial banks, security companies and insurance companies subordinated to financial holding groups can provide loan services for enterprises, direct financing services for enterprises and comprehensive insurance services respectively, and businesses among subsidiaries can complement each other to maximize the benefit of economy of scale. Fan and Yin (2019) believe that financial holding groups can reduce search costs, transaction costs and risk premium costs by providing customers with one-stop financial services, which will attract more financial consumers and exert scope economy effect.

The PBOC (2019) believes that financial holding groups can realize the sharing of various financial infrastructures, avoid the repeated establishment of institutions among subsidiaries, and play a synergistic role through cross-selling among subsidiaries. Han (2019) believes that implementing integrated operation will bring some risks, such as opaque information, complicated risks, and moral hazard, and that it is necessary to strengthen supervision of major transactions, affiliate transactions and risk firewalls within financial holding groups. Han and Liu (2019) think that financial holding groups not only have conventional risks such as credit risk, market risk and operational risk owned by professional financial institutions, but also have special risks such as high conductivity, strong correlation, high repeatability, and strong monopoly. Conducting research on financial holding groups in Taiwan, Shao et al. (2019) find that the subsidiaries of financial holding groups in Taiwan outperformed professional financial institutions.

2. Current situation in China

In recent years, with the slowdown of China's economic growth, the substantial advancement of the financial reform and the rapid development of financial technology, the profitability of traditional commercial banks has declined. According to the development experience of financial institutions in developed countries in Europe and America, the integrated operation of financial institutions is an important way to cope with macroeconomic changes, diversified customer needs, and enhance profitability and risk resistance. Some domestic financial institutions have transformed into financial holding groups by holding various financial licenses in the manner of establishing new companies, mergers and acquisitions.

In recent years, China's economy has changed from high-speed growth to medium–high-speed growth, and the growth rate of the Gross Domestic Product (GDP) has dropped to single digits (National Bureau of Statistics of China [NBSC] 2019). After the interest rate marketization reform, the customer needs of traditional commercial banks have changed, the market competition has become more intense, and the profitability has shown a downward trend. With the intensification of capital market reform, the development of financing structure is constantly diversified, and financial disintermediation is further accelerated, which is mainly manifested in the following aspects: diversified investment needs of enterprises and residents, and increased proportion of direct financing (PBOC 2020). The deep integration of finance and technology will increase the competitive pressure of commercial banks. The booming of third-party mobile payment, cloud computing, blockchain, artificial intelligence will divert customers from banks and reduce the income of traditional banks in related business fees and commissions, and the profit growth rate of traditional banks will decline.

Since 2000, with the accelerated pace of globalization of the financial industry and the rapid development of financial market innovation, China's financial industry has gradually developed integrated operations based on the original separate operations. In 2002, the State Council of China took three holding groups, namely China CITIC Group, Everbright Group and Ping An Group, as pilot projects to carry out integrated operation of the financial industry, which marked China's financial industry entering the stage of integrated operation. Since then, the regulatory authorities have relaxed supervision over wealth management products, asset management and asset securitization. Also, financial institutions have accelerated innovation in related fields. The pace of business cooperation between commercial banks and securities firms has accelerated. At the same time, the pace of commercial banks entering the insurance industry and the acquisition of trust companies by commercial banks has been sped up. Since February 2005, the State Council of China has allowed commercial banks to set up fund management companies. Therefore, commercial banks such as the Industrial and Commercial Bank of China, the Bank of China, the China Construction Bank, and the Bank of Communications have successively approved the establishment of fund management companies, accelerating the pace of financial institutions' integrated operation.

After more than 10 years of development, some integrated financial holding groups have been established in China's financial industry. According to the different investing and holding subjects, the People's Bank of China classifies China's financial holding groups into five categories, namely, financial holding groups, central government owned holding companies, local government owned holding companies, private holding companies and Internet holding companies. For example, financial holding groups such as the Industrial and Commercial Bank of China, the Bank of China, the China Construction Bank, the Ping An Insurance Group of China, have covered banking, insurance, trust, and other businesses. Financial holding groups of central enterprises such as the China Merchants Financial Group, the Yingda International Holding Group and the Huaneng Capital Services Group hold controlling shares of financial institutions such as commercial banks, trust companies, securities companies, property insurance companies and fund companies. TEDA Investment Holding Group, Shanghai International Group and other local government owned financial holding groups have invested and controlled local commercial banks, trust companies, securities companies, and life insurance companies. Private and Internet companies such as the Alibaba Group, the Tencent Technology Group and the Suning Holding Group hold two or more financial institutions (PBOC 2019).

Banking financial holding groups take banks as the core holding platform. For example, the Industrial and Commercial Bank of China, and other large banks have already owned subsidiaries such as funds, financial leasing, and insurance, and basically formed a pattern of holding relatively complete financial licenses. At present, domestic financing is still dominated by indirect financing, and banks occupy a prominent position in the financial system. Bank-controlled financial holding groups have gained sustainable development among Chinese financial holding groups and bank subsidiaries play a significant role in financial holding groups, which are still in a basic position in China. In this book, 13 banking financial holding groups and three typical banking financial holding groups, are analyzed in detail in the section of case analysis.1.1.2 Significance of the research.

1. Purpose of the research

At present, China's financial holding groups are still in the initial stage of development, and there are still gaps in the research on the performance evaluation of financial holding groups. This book takes Chinese banking financial holding groups as the research object, summarizes, and draws lessons from the latest research of financial holding groups based on relevant theories of financial holding groups, adopts factor analysis method as the research method of operating performance of Chinese banking financial holding groups, and carries out modeling analysis and data analysis with the corresponding discussion on the results obtained. Specific research purposes are as follows.

Put forward research questions. In recent years, with the slowdown of China's economic growth, the deepening of interest rate marketization reform and capital marketization reform, the net interest margin of commercial banks has been narrowing and the growth rate of net profit has slowed down. Combining with three typical cases of China's banking financial holding groups, this study puts forward three problems that need urgent research. Firstly, how do traditional commercial Banks maintain profit advantage through transformation and reform? Secondly, how to evaluate the operating performance of financial holding groups seeing that many financial institutions in China have transformed into financial holding groups. Thirdly, after transforming into financial holding groups, some financial holding groups do not improve their operating performance in an obvious manner, and their profitability is weak. How to promote the evaluation of operating performance?

Explore the evaluation method of business performance. In this book, the annual reports of 13 listed banking financial holding groups in recent five years (2014–2018) are selected as the research objects, and 15 important indicators are selected as the performance evaluation indicators of financial holding groups. The factor analysis method is used to evaluate the business performance, risk compensation ability, profitability, asset quality and cost control ability. According to the number of financial licenses held by the financial holdings, they are divided into three groups for comparative study. The empirical results are verified by cluster analysis and the Chi-square test model is used to verify the four research hypotheses of integrated management and solvency, profitability, cost control ability and business performance, which are supported by empirical tests.

Put forward management suggestions after summarization. This book summarizes the main conclusions of the research on the performance evaluation of China's financial holding groups. Implementing diversified operation has a positive impact on the performance, solvency, profitability, cost control and asset quality. The transformation of traditional banks has become a more urgent choice, and integrated operation is an option for the direction of transformation. In addition, promoting the governance at the group level and subsidiary level, establishing business collaboration mechanism within the group and among subsidiaries and a comprehensive risk management system are conducive to increase business performance.

2. Research significance

Conducting empirical studies on financial holding groups in Europe and America, some foreign experts, and scholars (Bergor 1999; Levine 2000; Qi 2003; Han et al. 2019) think that financial holding groups can obtain economies of scale, economies of scope, synergy effects and decentralized risk effects by implementing integrated operation. However, no scholars have done empirical research on the existence of economies of scale, economies of scope, synergy effects and decentralized risk effects in China's financial holding groups. This book is groundbreaking research in this field.

Due to the late start of China's financial system reform, the financial holding group, an organizational model of financial institutions, is still in its infancy in China. In recent years, although the domestic literature on financial holding groups has gradually increased, many literatures focus on the necessity of financial reform, mode selection and supervision system reform of China's financial industry. Because of the short history of the development of China's financial holding groups, there are very few studies on the comprehensive management of China's financial holding groups, especially the performance evaluation. This book discusses the performance evaluation index system, management performance evaluation methods, classification, and comparison of performance evaluation of financial holding groups in China.

3. Practical significance

Based on theoretical research, combined with the actual situation of China's banking financial holding groups, this book establishes a business performance evaluation model to verify the research hypotheses and puts forward management suggestions according to the analysis of the results obtained.

It is an important strategic choice for traditional banks to transform into integrated operation. The gradual opening of the financial industry, the deepening of interest rate marketization reform, the prosperity and development of the capital market, the increase in the proportion of direct financing, the rapid development of financial technology, and the acceleration of the trend of "financial disintermediation" have brought great pressure on the profitability and survival of the banking industry. Commercial banks provide customers with one-stop integrated financial services by carrying out integrated operations, realize stable and sustainable growth of profits.

Promote corporate governance at both group and subsidiary levels. In recent years, the integration and collectivization of commercial banks have developed rapidly, and financial holding groups own many branches and complicated administrative relationships. It is necessary to continuously optimize corporate governance, clarify the division of responsibilities between financial holding groups and subsidiaries, and stimulate vitality through mechanism innovation. At the group level, it is urgent to establish and improve the corporate governance system and promote the construction of an integrated financial service system. At the subsidiary level, what we need to do is to promote the establishment of a unified authorization management system, to implement of the Group's strategic planning, and to form a distinctive development model for each business segment.

Establish business collaboration mechanism within the group and among subsidiaries. By promoting the establishment of management mechanisms such as business collaboration and benefit distribution among subsidiaries of the Group, the cross-selling and business collaboration among subsidiaries are strengthened, the integration and utilization of resources within the Group are deepened, and the effect of comprehensive financial services is promoted. Moreover, establishing a management mechanism such as benefit distribution of business collaboration among subsidiaries within the group can promote the provision of comprehensive financial services. Strengthening cross-selling and business collaboration among subsidiaries can build an integrated financial service platform.

This book also puts forward some management suggestions for establishing a comprehensive risk management system for the group and its subsidiaries, improving the management level of financial technology and digital intelligence, and speeding up the training of comprehensive financial talents.

## 1.2 Research Problems

The management challenges and specific problems of this book are as follows.

By the end of December 2018, the number of banking financial institutions in China had reached 4588 (China Banking Regulatory Commission [CBRC] 2019). In recent years, China's economy has been transformed and upgraded, financial market reform has been intensified, finance and technology have been deeply integrated, businesses and residents have diversified their wealth management and investments, and the profit growth rate of traditional banks has declined.

Elsas (2010), Chronopoulos (2011), Chavas (2012), Wang (2018) and other foreign experts and scholars think that financial holding groups themselves have many institutional advantages such as economies of scale, economies of scope, synergy and decentralized risk effect. The empirical research on foreign financial holding groups shows that the integrated operation of financial holding groups can promote the improvement of business performance.

Some traditional commercial banks in China have been transformed into financial holding groups. Due to the short history of China's financial holding groups, a large part of financial companies in China are still facing the problem of loose and superficial structure. Most of them just simply invest into other companies. Although the structure of financial holding groups has been formed, the integrated operation and management of the financial institutions they hold have not been realized. It is widely recognized that being a financial holding groups contains more institutional advantages such as scale economy, scope economy, synergy effect and diminishing risks in integrated operation, but few Chinese financial holding groups have really brought into play the institutional advantages of group integration and separation of subsidiaries. At present, no financial holding group in real sense that meets international standards has been formed, and the overall business performance of the group is relatively weak.

In view of the above, it has become a management problem to maintain sustained improvement in the operational performance of traditional commercial banks in the face of declining earnings growth.

According to the above macro-economic background, the development process and trend of China's integrated financial management, typical enterprises of China's financial holding groups, and in combination with the previous literature review, the following research questions are put forward:

1. Before transition: How to promote business performance through transition?

Under the background of economic slowdown and structural adjustment, deepening of interest rate marketization, financial disintermediation, comprehensive management and rapid development of Internet finance, bank interest margin space is narrowing, homogeneous management is becoming increasingly serious, profitability is declining, and the impact on traditional banks is rising. Referring to the development process of China's integrated financial management and the transformation experience of benchmark financial enterprises, how to transform and reform to increase business performance of commercial bank has become an urgent problem to study.

2. How to evaluate the performance of China's financial holding groups?

Wu (2010) and Yamori (2003) evaluated the operating performance of foreign financial holding groups by means of comparative studies. Some foreign scholars (Bergor 1999; Levine 2000; Qi 2008; Kanter 2003) have studied the samples of financial holding groups in Europe and America, and the research shows that the financial holding groups in relevant countries have economies of scale and scope, risk decentralization effect, and their business performance is improved. There is very little research on the performance evaluation of China's financial holding groups in China, so it is necessary to study and explore how to build a performance evaluation model based on the actual situation of China's banking financial holding groups. We should consider that whether diversification plays a positive role in improving the profitability of China's banking financial holding groups and whether it promotes the improvement of business performance, this needs to be verified.

3. After transformation: How to continuously improve business performance?

As matters stand, after some financial institutions are transformed into financial holding groups, their overall profitability is relatively weak, and their inherent advantages have not yet been brought into play. As for a large part of financial holding groups, they have not formed coordinated development among subsidiaries, their subsidiaries and group implement integrated operation and service mode. The overall operating performance of financial holding groups is weak, so it is necessary to summarize and analyze in depth which aspects have a significant impact on the promotion of operating performance of Chinese financial holding groups. Through in-depth summary and analysis of typical cases, some management and control suggestionαs to improve the operating performance of Chinese financial holding groups can be put forward.

## 1.3 Research Approach and Methods

### *1.3.1 Research Approach*

Based on sorting out the existing literature, this book firstly discusses the concept of financial holding groups, describes its connotation and characteristics, and expounds the economic theoretical basis involved in the operation performance evaluation of financial holding groups. Secondly, combined with the domestic macroeconomic development, the development process and trend of China's comprehensive operation are studied, and typical cases of Chinas' financial holding groups are analyzed. Thirdly, the main business performance evaluation methods are sorted out and compared, the factor analysis method is used to build the model, and sample data and evaluation indicators are selected. Lastly, it makes an empirical analysis on the operating performance of financial holding groups and puts forward management suggestions.

### *1.3.2 Analysis Methods*

This book adopts the methods of combining theoretical research with empirical research, while also combining quantitative research with qualitative research.

In this book, scale economy theory, scope economy theory, synergy effect theory and risk decentralization theory are adopted, and the research literature of previous scholars is sorted out, and the research hypotheses are put forward. Based on summarizing the evaluation methods of business performance, the factor analysis method is used to evaluate business performance. This book selects 13 banking financial holding groups as the research objects, and focuses on three representative banking financial holding groups, and puts forward research problems. According to the results of the business performance evaluation, combined with management practice, this book classifies and analyzes 13 banking financial holding groups, and puts forward management suggestions to improve business performance.

In addition, the annual reports of five-year listing disclosure of banking financial holding groups are selected as the research objects, and 15 important indicators are selected as the performance evaluation indicators of financial holding groups. The KMO test, Bartlett sphere test and other data tests show that it is suitable for factor analysis, and the business performance evaluation is carried out using the factor analysis method. The accuracy of the factor analysis results is verified by cluster analysis. And the research hypotheses are verified by the Chi-square test. We conduct studies on the financial and business development, risk management, capital management, corporate governance, and board of directors' reports of 13 banking financial holding groups in the past five years (2014–2018, both inclusive). On this basis, qualitative research is carried out, which is combined with five-year quantitative research on business performance evaluation.

## 1.4 Research Framework

The structure of this book is as follows.

Chapter one is the introduction. This part describes the research background of this book, puts forward management challenges and research problems, introduces the purpose and significance of the research, and expounds the research ideas and main research and analysis methods.

Chapter two is the literature review. This chapter summarizes the concept of financial holding groups, studies the main types and characteristics of financial holding groups, and analyzes the economic theories of financial holding groups' business performance, such as economies of scale, risk decentralization effect and business performance.

Chapter three describes the development of financial holding groups in China. This part firstly introduces the macroeconomic background financial holding groups in China, describes the history and trend of the development of Chinese financial integrated management, and then analyzes three typical cases of the Chinese financial holding groups, and thus puts forward three specific problems in promoting the performance improvement of China's financial holding groups.

Chapter four is the research method. This chapter first introduces the main methods of evaluating business performance and carries out comparative analysis. Factor analysis method is also adopted for the research. Then it introduces the collection method of the data needed for the study, describes the selection of evaluation indexes, and takes non-interest income and other indexes as the difference between financial holding groups and traditional commercial banks, and finally introduces the EVA model in the evaluation indexes.

Chapter five is the results and analyses of research data. In this chapter, the hypotheses of the research are set based on the literature of the previous study. The reliability and validity analysis of the collected data is carried out, and the data test indicates that it is suitable for factor analysis. Secondly, the empirical analysis is carried out, the common factors are extracted, and the scores of common factors, business performance scores and rankings are calculated. The empirical results are verified by cluster analysis. Thirdly, the comprehensive score and ranking of business performance, risk offset, profitability, asset quality and cost control ability are summarized and analyzed. Finally, the four hypotheses are verified by the Chi-square test model, which is supported by empirical test.

Chapter six is the conclusion and outlook. This chapter summarizes the main conclusions of the research on the performance evaluation of China's financial holding groups, discusses the contribution of this book to the theory, sums up the management significance in practice, points out the limitations of this research, and looks forward to the future research direction.

# Chapter 2
# Literature Review

The connotation and concept of financial holding groups are discussed in this chapter, the main types and characteristics are sorted out, the supporting theories of financial holding groups, including economies of scale, economies of scope, synergy effect and decentralized risk effect are reviewed and the recent research on business performance are introduced. These theories will be used for empirical research and analysis of the business performance of Chinese banking financial holding groups.

## 2.1 Brief Introduction to Financial Holding Groups

The separate operation among different financial sub-sectors changed into integrated operation, and the financial holding group emerged and gradually developed ([PBOC] 2019). In different countries and regions, the development processes and levels of financial industry are various. Therefore, the laws, regulations and supervision systems of the financial industry are different, and the definitions of financial holding groups are also different. Before defining financial holding groups, the connotation of holding companies needs to be clarified.

### *2.1.1 Separate Operations and Integrated Operations*

The financial industry is mainly composed of banking, security, insurance, trust, fund, and other industries. Separate operation means that the financial supervision and administration department of a country or region only permits a financial institution to operate a financial sub-industry, that is, commercial banks, securities companies and insurance companies can only operate commercial banking, securities business, and insurance business respectively. Integrated operation means that



X. Ning, *Performance Evaluation of Financial Holding Companies*,
https://doi.org/10.1007/978-981-97-8128-7_2

the financial supervision department allows a financial institution to operate two or more financial sub-sectors at the same time. For example, commercial banks are allowed to operate securities and insurance business, while trust companies are allowed to operate commercial banks, securities companies, fund companies and other businesses (Han 2019).

At present, the financial industry in most countries in the world has adopted an integrated business mode. After 11 years' development, the market share of comprehensive financial groups in banking, securities and insurance increased from 53%, 54% and 41% in 1990 to 71%, 71% and 70% in 2001, respectively, and the market share exceeded 70%. The market share has increased by 18% points, 17% points, and 29% points respectively, maintaining a rapid growth. According to the development practice of financial industry in countries and regions around the world, there are many ways for financial institutions to realize comprehensive management, among which financial holding groups are one of the main organizational ways (Qi and Wang 2007).

### 2.1.2 The Concept of Holding Companies

A holding company is a property ownership mode often adopted by enterprises, which is established according to laws and regulations. By holding the shares of one or more enterprises with voting rights, and the number of shares held exceeds a certain proportion, it can achieve the actual control right of the enterprise. Holding companies can be divided into two types, pure holding company and mixed holding company, according to different business modes (Han 2019).

The parent company of a pure holding company does not carry out specific commercial activities, but only carries out equity investment management and capital operation according to the company shares it holds. Based on the responsibilities of pure holding companies, mixed holding companies can directly engage in commercial business activities. The holding company has the right to decide on strategic planning and design, personnel management, finance, and fund management of its subsidiaries, and can appoint senior executives to manage daily operations. A financial holding group is a manifestation of property right organization of holding group in the financial industry (Hao et al. 2018).

### 2.1.3 The Concept of Financial Holding Groups

In essence, a financial holding group is an important application of a holding group mode in the financial industry. Financial holding groups have the characteristics of collectivization in management mode and operation mode. As a comprehensive financial enterprise group, a financial holding group is different from enterprises operating a single business. From the perspective of operating, it has the characteristics of wide business scope and diversified business types, and its financing channels are wider, resources are richer, and funds are more abundant. From the legal point of view, the financial group and its subsidiaries are independent legal entities of enterprises, which need to carry out accounting such as bookkeeping, and are responsible for their profits and losses, and there is no direct relationship between their profits and losses. Also, the group and its financial institutions are interrelated through equity, and the group can control the rights of financial management, personnel management, and foreign investment of its subsidiaries (Tian et al. 2004).

At present, because of the different degree and stage of economic and financial development in different countries and regions, the judgment and classification of financial holding groups are somewhat different; The international community has not reached a clear and unanimous opinion on the definition of a financial holding group, nor has it formulated a unified management standard for a financial holding group.

## 2.2 Types and Characteristics of Financial Holding Groups

As can be seen from the above, the types and characteristics of financial holding groups in different countries and regions are different because of the different definitions given by the laws and regulations and financial supervision in different countries and regions.

### *2.2.1 Main Types of Financial Holding Groups*

In 1999, Principles for Supervision of Financial Conglomerates issued by the Joint Forum (Joint Forum on Financial Conglomerates, [JFFC] 2013) summarized financial groups into three modes. The first mode is that financial groups can directly carry out financial business and provide financial services. The second mode is that the financial group invests and holds two or more financial institutions, and the financial institutions engage in financial business. The third mode is a pure holding group. Wan Wei summarizes the main types of existing financial holding groups from the perspective of international practice, including three types, namely pure financial holding groups, universal banking financial holding groups and public financial holding groups. These three types of financial holding groups are introduced next (Wan 2018).

#### 2.2.1.1 Universal Banking Financial Holding Groups Represented by Germany

Universal banking financial holding groups take commercial banks as their parent companies, and the units engaged in financial business include two types. Functional departments engaged in banking business, securities business and other financial business are set up at the level of commercial banks in the parent group. Additionally, at the subsidiary level, it initiated the establishment of insurance companies and other financial businesses. Both parent companies and subsidiaries of universal banking financial holding groups can carry out financial business. Broadly speaking, the business scope of universal banking includes commercial banking, investment banking, insurance and investment holding non-financial enterprise business (Fan and Yin 2019).

In 1993, the European Union issued the No. 2 Banking Directive which pointed out that commercial banks can directly engage in 13 types of business such as securities underwriting and trading (Liu 2017). The European Union's universal banking mode has been established and recognized by all member States. The universal banking mode has the following advantages. (1) Adopting the universal banking mode can provide customers with securities, insurance, investment, and other services based on traditional commercial banking business, and different types of businesses can complement each other's advantages and achieve scope economic benefits. (2) The universal banking mode can comprehensively utilize various types of assets, liabilities, and collateral products for portfolio risk management by virtue of the advantages of wide business scope, thus improving the stability of financial holding groups. (3) The universal banking mode can share internal resources, improve the mobility of information, reduce the cost of information acquisition, and achieve economies of scale. The main shortcomings of the universal banking mode are as follows. The business mode is easy to cause conflicts of interests among departments, and it is difficult to coordinate. Then, there is no "risk isolation wall" between different financial industries, which is not conducive to the effective implementation of risk isolation measures, which increases the difficulty of internal risk management and external supervision departments (Shao et al. 2019). The typical structure of itis shown in Fig. 2.1.

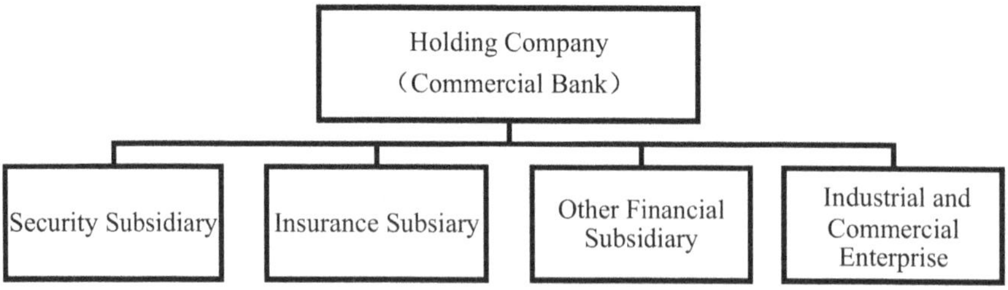


**Fig. 2.1** Structure diagram of a universal banking financial holding group. *Source* China financial stability report in 2018 (PBOC 2019)

German financial groups adopt the universal banking mode (Han and Dong 2019). The typical representatives of German financial groups are Deutsche Bank and Dresden Bank. German financial groups can serve as an entity to provide customers with integrated financial services, including commercial banking, securities, insurance and so forth. German financial groups can also hold the equity of industrial and commercial enterprises, attend the shareholders' meeting of industrial and commercial enterprises, and participate in the management of industrial and commercial enterprises. Germany's universal banking mode can promote the connection between financial and industrial and commercial enterprises and establish closer and lasting cooperative relations with customers (Han 2019).

#### 2.2.1.2 Business-Type Financial Holding Groups Represented by the United Kingdom

A public financial holding group is a professional financial institution where the parent group of the group not only engages in traditional commercial banking business, but also invests and controls securities companies, life insurance companies, fund companies and other financial businesses, and is responsible for the management of the group and its financial institutions. Through this model, a "risk barrier" has been established between the parent group and its financial subsidiaries. In addition to carrying out financial business, the parent group is also responsible for the overall strategic planning and design of the group, overall financial and capital management, effective integration of resources, risk management and control.

The mode of a public financial holding group is represented by Britain (Hao et al. 2018). The business-oriented financial holding group mode in Britain takes commercial banks as the parent group of the group and professional financial institutions of non-commercial banks as subsidiaries. This mode can isolate the business between parent group and subsidiary group, and set up a set of risk firewall, which is beneficial to the overall risk control of the group. However, in this mode, there may be conflicts between the parent group and its subsidiaries due to inconsistent interests and objectives. Its professional financial institutions should not only accept the leadership of the parent group, but also accept the supervision of the financial industry supervision department. When some business objectives of the parent group and its specialized financial institutions are inconsistent, the parent group may cross the limit of the risk barrier. Financial holding groups in Britain and European countries mainly adopt the mode of public financial holding groups. According to the different business of the parent group, financial holding groups can be divided into commercial bank-oriented, securities group-oriented, insurance group-oriented and other types of financial holding groups (Fan and Yin 2019). The typical structure of a business financial holding group is shown in Fig. 2.2.

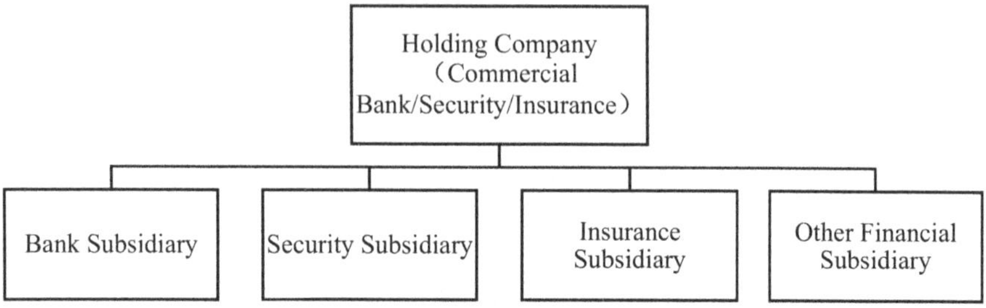


**Fig. 2.2** Structure diagram of a public financial holding group. *Source* China financial stability report in 2018 (PBOC 2019)

### 2.2.2 Characteristics of a Financial Holding Group

Each country has defined financial holding according to its actual situation. Because there are differences in the definitions of financial holding groups, the types of operations adopted by financial holding groups are different, and the corresponding characteristics are also different. In this book, the definition of China's financial holding group is implemented in accordance with the Trial Measures for the Supervision and Administration of Financial holding groups (PBOC 2020) promulgated by the People's Bank of China, that is, a group that has invested in and controlled two or more different types of financial institutions, such as banks, securities and insurance, and only invests and manages its own equity, and does not directly engage in specific business activities. According to this definition, China's financial holding groups are pure financial holding groups with the following main characteristics.

#### 2.2.2.1 Group Holding and Integrated Operation

The financial holding group is based on the group's equity control of the financial subsidiary, and the relationship between the group and the subsidiary is controlling and being controlled. In essence, financial holding groups control two or more different types of financial institutions, including 11 kinds of commercial banks, trust companies, securities companies and fund companies recognized by the People's Bank of China. Actual control mainly refers to holding more than 50% of voting rights of financial subsidiaries. From the perspective of group attributes, a group can be a simple investment institution, or a financial institution such as a commercial bank and a securities group. A financial holding group has a standardized corporate governance mechanism, and in accordance with legal requirements, it holds senior management positions for financial subsidiaries, and carries out business collaboration, consolidated management, risk monitoring and control (PBOC 2020).

#### 2.2.2.2 Implementing Separate Operation in Subsidiaries to Reduce Risks

A financial holding group may set up financial subsidiaries such as commercial banks, financial asset management companies, fund management companies, life insurance companies, property insurance companies, and its financial subsidiaries are independent enterprise legal persons, and carry out banking, fund, insurance, and other businesses respectively. The financial group and its financial subsidiaries face different financial risks. The financial holding group needs to establish a risk firewall between the group and its financial subsidiaries and needs to isolate the risks of legal person institutions, financial accounting, personnel, information technology systems, operating outlets, so as to prevent financial assets management companies, fund management companies and other financial subsidiaries from transferring their own business risks to other financial subsidiaries, or spreading the business and management risks of subsidiaries to the whole group, bringing overall risks. It is strictly prohibited to carry out internal transactions that do not meet the requirements of relevant laws and regulations of financial holding groups, to ensure that the legitimate rights and interests of financial consumers are protected (Qian 2016).

#### 2.2.2.3 Tax Combination and Self-financing

As an enterprise legal person, a financial holding group should combine the financial statements of its financial subsidiaries according to the accounting standards for enterprises and the accrual basis to form a combined balance sheet and income statement. Financial consolidation management can play the following roles. It can reflect the overall financial situation of financial holding groups, avoid repeated measurement of capital, operating income, and net profit of financial subsidiaries, and hide financial leverage and whitewash financial statements through internal transactions. Based on paying taxes in accordance with the tax law, the tax base can be considered, tax management processes can be optimized, tax planning can be carried out to prevent double tax calculations, multiple tax payments, and reasonable tax avoidance. The financial holding group is a limited liability group or a joint stock limited group, which is responsible for the debts of its financial institutions based on the amount of shareholders' investment. Its financial institutions are enterprise legal persons and are responsible for the profits and losses of their own enterprises. Its investment banks and investment companies are relatively high-risk financial subsidiaries. Such financial institutions may suffer serious losses in the face of financial crises or poor management. Taking limited liability by financial holding groups can reduce the risk of bankruptcy of the whole group due to insolvency of such financial institutions, maintain overall stability and prevent financial risks (Liu 2010).

#### 2.2.2.4 Capital Holding and Information Leakage

The financial holding group takes capital as the link and adopts the way of equity investment, establishes the group as the main body, and controls the subsidiaries at different levels. With the increasing level of holding subsidiaries, financial holding groups can gain control of their subsidiaries with less capital contribution, and gradually enlarge the capital effect. Although the relationship of holding at different levels expands financial leverage and increases financial risks, large financial holding groups have higher credit and can increase credit spillover effect. If the financial holding group has a clear strategy, large asset scale, and strong profitability, it can obtain a higher internationally recognized credit rating, improve its reputation among the public, and reduce financing costs. Financial holding groups with high reputation can acquire the equity of other financial institutions at a lower price, carry out mergers and acquisitions and expansion at a lower cost, and realize the spillover of reputation. When the financial institutions under the financial holding group provide customers with a high-quality service or financial products, the overall reputation of the financial holding group is enhanced, and the products or services of this financial institution or other financial institutions can be recommended to customers to enhance the brand effect (Liu 2010).

## 2.3 Economic Analysis of a Financial Holding Group's Operating Performance

Based on summarizing the types and characteristics of financial holding groups in the previous section, this section focuses on the scale economy effect, scope economy effect, synergy effect, risk decentralization effect and promotion of business performance of financial holding groups. The research on financial holding groups at home and abroad is summarized as follows.

### *2.3.1 Scale Economy Effect of Financial Holding Groups*

#### 2.3.1.1 Overview of the Theory on Economies of Scale

Economies of scale means that under the premise that other conditions such as production technology will not change, manufacturers can increase their economic benefits by continuously expanding their production scale. In the process of daily operations, after the manufacturers have invested different factors of production such as capital and technology, with the increasing scale of investment, the benefits brought by the increased factors of production outweigh the increased costs, and then the manufacturers are in the stage of economies of scale. If manufacturers continue to increase the input of production factors, they will reach an optimal input scale. Currently, the marginal cost is equal to the marginal benefit, thus realizing economies of scale. The scale economy curve is an inverted U-shaped curve. When the factors of production invested by manufacturers reach the optimal scale, if they continue to increase the input factors of production, the cost brought by increasing the input factors of production will outweigh the benefits, which may lead to diseconomies of scale (Gao 2021).

Compared with the non-financial industry, the financial industry has the characteristics of low asset specificity, increasing returns to scale and high comprehensive service level, which makes it easier to realize economics of scale than ordinary enterprises. Pursuing economies of scale is also the main motivation of financial holding groups to manage their financial institutions (PBOC 2019). The advantages of economies of scale are mainly reflected in the following aspects.

1. The financial industry has low asset specificity. Asset specificity (Yue 2005) is the degree of difficulty for an enterprise to allocate different types of assets for production factors that have been put into daily operating activities. Because different industries have different demands on the input factors of production, the difficulty of re-allocation of assets is different. The lower the asset specificity of the industry in which the enterprise is located, the lower the monopoly degree of the industry will be. The lower the asset specificity of the industry, the stronger the comprehensive service capability for customers, and the higher the possibility of implementation. At present, the financial industry includes banking, securities, insurance, trust and so forth, and its main production factors include three kinds, namely, capital, information, and entrepreneurial ability. Compared with the non-financial industry, the main production factors of the financial industry are applied to specific purposes to a very low difficulty. In banking, securities, insurance, and other financial sub-sectors, it exists wide adaptability, and financial institutions in different financial industries can easily enter each other to provide customers with cross-over financial services, thus realizing economies of scale.
2. Financial institutions have the effect of increasing returns to scale. Because of the strong substitutability among banking, securities, insurance and other financial industries, financial holding groups carry out integrated operations through their financial subsidiaries, and with the continuous expansion of scale, the gains are increasing. Financial industry is a typical industry with increasing returns to scale. Compared with ordinary enterprises, financial institutions have the following two distinct characteristics. Newly established financial institutions need to invest higher fixed costs. Commercial banks, securities companies, life insurance companies and other professional financial institutions in different financial industries have very strong universality of production factors and have more homogeneous assets, which can reduce the operating costs of each unit by increasing the scale of investment. Therefore, financial enterprises have more obvious advantages of economies of scale than ordinary enterprises, and the trend of increasing returns to scale has more potential. If the business scope of financial institutions remains unchanged, with the continuous expansion of the scale of

investment, the average cost of capital can be reduced, and then economies of scale can be obtained (Fan et al. 2019).

3. Diversification can reduce operating costs. In the process of diversified operation, financial institutions can reduce costs and produce economies of scale on the financial service supply side and the customer demand service side (PBOC 2019). By integrating resources, fixed costs can be reduced. Financial holding groups can integrate and optimize the assets, liabilities and business structure of their financial subsidiaries, expand the business scope and scale of portfolio management, and reduce marginal costs, thus reducing fixed costs. By improving the competitiveness of products, research and other costs can be reduced. Financial holding groups provide customers with a one-stop and life-cycle financial services through portfolio management of financial products and services, which greatly improves the market competitiveness of financial products and promotes the improvement of yield. Reducing the research cost and time cost of customers can promote the efficiency of serving customers. Additionally, information sharing between customers can reduce operating costs. Financial subsidiaries of financial holding groups can establish an information sharing platform to share customers' basic information, product, and service needs, thus reducing the repeated market research and due diligence of multiple financial institutions on the same customer, reducing time costs and daily expenses (Xu 2008).
4. There is a certain optimal scale in economies of scale. Financial institutions can expand the scale of assets and generate economies of scale by conducting business operations in various financial industries through mergers and acquisitions or newly established professional financial institutions. However, only in a certain range of asset scale, there is a positive correlation between asset scale and economies of scale. The scale effect of financial industry is usually expressed by a cost curve, and it is U-shaped. It is not the case that the larger the business scale, the more obvious the scale effect is. In addition, compared with the non-financial industry, the cost curve of the financial industry has a lower radian and changes more smoothly (Liu 2017).

#### 2.3.1.2 Foreign Research on Economies of Scale of Financial Holding Group

The research on the existence of economies of scale in diversified operations of financial institutions in foreign countries started in 1980s. Some scholars thought that there were economies of scale in financial holding groups through various research methods, while other scholars put forward inconsistent opinions.

Some scholars have analyzed the existence of economies of scale in financial holding groups through literature review, empirical research, and other research methods. Berger et al. (1999) investigated the economies of scale of many large banks in Europe and Japan by literature review and field investigation. Through research, it was pointed out that the financial industry has economies of scale, and the effect is very outstanding. Weston (1990) found that commercial banks have achieved economies of scale in two ways. After the commercial banks carry out diversified operations, different financial subsidiaries can learn from each other's strengths and make full assistance. Commercial banks provide customers with rich financial products and expand the number of product categories. Chronopoulos et al. (2011) from the perspective of risk simulation, made an in-depth study and found that there is an incomplete correlation between cash flows among financial businesses. After diversified operations, financial institutions can maintain the stability of profits by strengthening portfolio management. Kanter (2003) thinks that financial holding groups are larger than professional financial institutions, and their risks are more complex. By adopting a combination of strengthening supervision by external supervision departments and strengthening internal management and control by the group itself, risks can be prevented and managed, and resource allocation efficiency can be improved.

Some scholars conclude that financial holding groups have economies of scale through business performance evaluation and so forth. Wang (2017) used the method of business performance evaluation to study the diversification of American banking industry and reached the following conclusions. Financial institutions can significantly improve economic efficiency and effectively play the economies of scale and scope through diversification. Carrying out integrated financial business or providing diversified financial products to customers can complement each other's advantages, reduce costs, and improve efficiency. Through the comparative analysis of the returns from the sales of single financial product and diversified financial product portfolio, it is found that the average return rate of the latter is higher than that of the former, which provides strong evidence for the existence of scope economy. Yue (2005) made a comparative study on financial holding groups in Europe and America. Europe mainly adopts the all-round banking mode, while the United States adopts the pure financial holding group mode. The efficiency of its operating income and net profit is analyzed, and the research shows that the former is more efficient.

Some scholars believe that financial institutions have economies of scale within a certain business scale, and that economies of scale may not exist even if the business scale is too large or too small. Han (2019) made a special study on the economies of scale after the merger of commercial banks of different sizes. Through in-depth study, it was found that commercial banks with smaller assets can acquire the equity of other banks through mergers and acquisitions, to expand their business scale and generate potential economies of scale. If commercial banks with large assets acquire the shares of other banks by means of mergers and acquisitions, they will only increase the assets, but they will not get economies of scale. Levine et al. (2000) conducted an in-depth analysis of the stock price changes before and after the merger of large and small commercial banks and life insurance companies through empirical research. Through analysis, it was found that the stock price of large commercial banks increased significantly after the merger of life insurance companies, indicating that they have better economies of scale. However, after small commercial banks acquired life insurance companies, their share prices remained basically unchanged. Barth et al. (2000) also analyzed the economies of scale of financial institutions through empirical research and concluded that there is a close relationship between the business scale and economies of scale of financial institutions. With the gradual expansion of business scale, the marginal cost decreases. But it does not show a linear decreasing trend, the marginal cost decreases gradually. When the optimal marginal cost is reached, the marginal cost gradually rises, showing a relatively gentle U-shaped graph change.

Several studies (Qi and Wang 2017; Timme 1993) took bank holding companies in the United States as the research object, adopted the empirical research method, and took the rate of return as the index to evaluate the scale effect, and derived the following main conclusions by studying the relationship between business scale and rate of return. The economies of scale of bank holding companies are closely related to the scale of assets. With the expansion of the scale of assets, the economies of scale gradually increase, and then gradually decrease after reaching a maximum inflection point. Meanwhile, the optimal asset scale to play the role of economies of scale is discussed. When the asset scale of a bank holding group reaches about 10 billion US dollars, the rate of return brought by the growth of scale will obviously increase, resulting in the positive effect of economies of scale. Additionally, it discusses whether scale growth has always brought economies of scale. Researches show that the bigger the assets of a bank holding group, the better the economies of scale. When the assets reach a very large scale, the rate of return will show a downward trend, resulting in the negative effect of economies of scale. Hao and Wang (2018) also proved that the asset scale and economies of scale of bank holding companies showed a trend of rising first and then falling and put forward that when the asset scale of bank holding companies reached more than 50 billion US dollars, the optimal economies of scale could be brought into play, but there were some differences between the optimal asset scale and the research results of Qi and Wang (2007).

#### 2.3.1.3 Research on Economies of Scale of Financial Holding Groups in China

There is not much research on scale economy of financial holding groups in China. Among them, Yang et al. (2004) thinks through research and analysis that financial institutions can achieve the best economies of scale only when they reach a certain business scale value and cannot achieve the best below or above this business scale value. However, in practice, it is difficult to predict the business scale value of a financial institution when it reaches the optimal economies of scale. Wu (2017) also points out that the subsidiaries of financial holding groups with different financial licenses have different business fields, which can provide customers with complementary financial services, forming the effect of aggregation and convergence, and realizing economies of scale. Wan (2018) believes that financial holding groups have professional financial institutions. Different professional financial institutions can provide differentiated financial industry services for enterprises. For example, commercial banks can provide loan financing services for enterprises, securities companies can provide investment banking services for enterprises, and insurance companies can provide comprehensive insurance services such as property insurance, life insurance and pension insurance. Financial business among financial subsidiaries can complement each other and realize economies of scale. Fan and Yin (2019) also think that by expanding the business scale, large financial holding groups will bring more benefits than costs, and their financial subsidiaries can generate economies of scale in research and development of financial products, development of information management systems, and creation of customer marketing and product sales channels.

## 2.3.2 *Economies of Scope Effect of Financial Holding Groups*

### 2.3.2.1 Theoretical Overview of Economies of Scope

As early as 1975, American scholars Panzer and Willing clearly summarized the concept of scope economy. Economies of scope refers to the phenomenon that the production cost is lower than the total cost of producing each product by expanding the scope of operation and service and producing two or more products at the same time on the premise of keeping the production technology and equipment unchanged. Economies of scope and economies of scale are interrelated. When an enterprise provides a certain product, with the popularization of the product, the scale of the product becomes larger and larger, which leads to the decline of the average cost, resulting in economies of scale. When enterprises provide different kinds of financial products at the same time, the cost paid is lower than the total cost of providing products separately, which produces the economies of scope effect (Gao 2021).

In the daily operation and management of financial institutions, if the marginal cost decreases or the marginal benefit increases by increasing the types of business or products, it means that there is scope economy, otherwise, it means that scope is uneconomical. Economies of scope generally serves as an important theoretical basis for studying the diversified operation of financial institutions. Compared with other non-financial industries, the financial industry has lower asset specificity and stronger correlation. Financial holding groups have obvious comparative advantages, and it is easier to reduce marginal costs, increase marginal benefits and realize scope economy (Liu 2017). According to the theory of scope economy, combined with the financial holding group mode, scope economy can be divided into three categories: production scope economy, consumption scope economy and reputation scope economy.

1. Production scope economy. If the cost of joint production of multiple commodities is lower than the total cost of producing each commodity separately, then there is scope economy of production. Financial products are special commodities. Different financial products have low asset specificity and strong correlation. In the process of product research and development, the information of R&D

experts, capital channels, and customer demand can be shared and used to form a synthetic effect. Therefore, multiple financial products share R&D expenses and marketing costs, thus reducing the operating costs of each unit and realizing scope economy (Fan and Yin 2019).

2. Consumption scope economy. If a variety of commodities produced by an enterprise can complement each other, through product integration, the purchase cost of customers can be reduced, the marginal benefit of the enterprise can be improved, and the scope economy of consumption can be realized. Financial products are highly complementary, and financial holding groups can provide customers with "package" products and services such as banking, securities, and insurance, and provide customers with convenient and fast services, thus reducing the time cost, information cost and transaction cost of customers looking for financial products. Financial holding groups can integrate products and service resources, and provide loans, financial management, funds, insurance, and other cross-selling for the same customer, which can reduce the sales cost and information cost of enterprises, thus realizing the scope economy of consumption. If there is such consumption scope economy, customers may be willing to pay a higher price to purchase such convenient and fast integrated financial products and services (Wan 2018).
3. Reputation scope economy. Good reputation of the group's products can enhance the overall reputation and generate reputation scope economy. Financial holding groups have commercial banks, trust companies, life insurance companies and other subsidiaries. If commercial banks have good reputation and obvious brand advantages, they will promote the reputation of securities companies and insurance companies and help to enhance the overall reputation of financial holding groups (Liu 2017).

#### 2.3.2.2 Foreign Research on Economies of Scope of Financial Holding Groups

Since 1980s, foreign scholars have studied the economies of scope effect of financial holding groups, and through empirical research, analyzed universal banks and financial holding groups in the United States and Europe, and reached the following main conclusions.

Some scholars support that financial holding groups have scope economy. Financial holding groups can match the products of different financial industries according to the needs of customers through their diversified financial institutions, provide comprehensive financial services for customers, reduce marginal costs, increase marginal benefits, and obtain economies of scope.

Some scholars through empirical research and other methods, find that financial holding groups can achieve the scope of economic effects. Liu (2017) conducted an empirical study on the universal banks in the United States, and the results showed that through the combination management of some diversified financial businesses and financial products, the overall cost can be effectively reduced, and the overall yield of the created products is also significantly higher than that of individual products, thus realizing the scope economy effect. Financial institutions under the universal bank can share customer resources, sales channels, brand value and good reputation with the group and other financial institutions, to enhance market competitiveness and generate scope economy. Then, Zhou and Wang (2003) pointed out that universal banks have diversified financial products, which can reduce marginal costs and realize scope economy by allocating fixed costs to various financial products.

Liu (2009) thought that if financial institutions jointly provide integrated financial services to customers, scope economy can be obtained. Rajan (1996) also showed that the adoption of the financial holding group model can enhance the competitiveness of financial institutions and produce scope economy effect. Later, Guo (2005) made an empirical study on universal banks and thought that they have the effect of network economy, which can form a network pattern between financial institutions and customers, keep close contact, reduce information costs, enhance customer value, and realize scope economy effect. Vennet (1999) thinks that with the development of financial industry, the sources of capital demand of enterprises have changed greatly, from indirect financing such as credit and mortgage loans from commercial banks to direct financing such as issuing stocks and bonds by relying on capital markets. By carrying out diversified operations, financial holding groups can meet different types of financing needs of corporate customers at various stages, improve their financing efficiency, help maintain long-term and lasting customer relations, and produce scope economy. Financial institutions under holding companies can also obtain and share customer information from various angles, keep the symmetry of information and effectively guard against business risks. Therefore, realizing the potential scope economy and giving full play to the advantages of information sharing are the main motives for commercial banks to engage in securities business.

Some scholars have concluded that financial holding groups have scope economy effect by comparing and analyzing the operational efficiency and cost of all-round banks and professional financial institutions. Jia (2014) made a comparative analysis of the operational efficiency of universal banks and professional financial institutions and concluded that the operational efficiency of all-round banks is higher than that of professional financial institutions, and it can obtain economies of scale and economies of scope more than professional financial institutions. At the same time, it was also found that the organizational model does not necessarily have a decisive influence, and some professional financial institutions have formed their own competitive advantages in the competition with all-round banks, which are not completely inferior to universal banks. Xie (2004) studied financial holding groups from the perspective of comparative analysis of cost and concluded that financial holding groups can use the existing marketing channels of their commercial banks to sell various financial products and reduce unit costs, that is, there is scope economy effect. Through comparing European financial groups with professional financial institutions, it is found that the former can obtain the effects of scope economy, and its income efficiency is significantly higher than that of the latter, and it has stronger profitability (Yue 2005). Kanatas and Qi (2003) made a comparative study on the business development of financial institutions before and after the merger of banking business and securities underwriting business and found that after the merger of the two types of business, the success rate of financial institutions in undertaking the securities issuance business of enterprises increased, which broadened the profit sources and provided strong evidence to support the scope economy.

Some scholars do not support the existence of scope economy. Financial holding groups are limited by regulatory requirements and operating environment, so it is not easy to obtain potential scope economy. Xie (2004) made a dynamic analysis of the 20-year operation of financial institutions in four developed geographical areas, namely Europe, the United States, Japan, and Australia, and concluded that there is no sufficient evidence to show that financial institutions have scope economic effects. Wang (2009) think that the industry has not established an evaluation index system which is generally accepted and can accurately measure the scale economy effect and scope economy effect of financial holding groups. In addition, because financial holding groups are affected and constrained by domestic and international macroeconomic situation, regulatory requirements, mergers and acquisitions of financial institutions, it is impossible to simply analyze and evaluate the economies of scale and scope of a certain financial holding group.

#### 2.3.2.3 Research on Economies of Scope of Financial Holding Groups in China

Most domestic scholars believe that all financial subsidiaries of financial holding groups belong to the financial industry, which can share and use resources in terms of customers, sales channels, and information, and have economies of scope.

As early as 2001, Xia (2001) analyzed that financial holding groups integrated the resources of their subsidiaries, such as banks, securities, and insurance. By sharing customer information, subsidiaries could recommend customers to each other and implement cross-selling of financial products, which could increase the sales volume and market share of financial products and realize the scope economy effect. Huo et al. (2006) pointed out that although banking, securities, insurance, and other financial institutions all belong to the financial industry, they belong to different types of professional financial institutions, which have their own unique advantages and can complement each other in providing financing services, information sharing and risk management for enterprises, which support their economies of scale. Jin (2017) pointed out through research that financial institutions can complement each other in terms of sales channels by means of mergers and acquisitions. For example, banks, securities companies, insurance companies, trust companies and fund companies can give full play to the advantages of sales channels in their respective industries and share product sales resources.

As Wang (2017) said, commercial banks and insurance companies can sign strategic cooperation agreements to share customer information and provide integrated financial services for customers. Wu (2017) and Li (2018) made a comparative analysis of the benefits of financial services provided by financial holding groups and professional financial institutions. Financial holding groups can realize cross-selling by establishing a unified financial service platform and provide customers with a one-stop financial products and services in different financial industries. However, customers can only buy specific financial products in one professional financial institution or buy them in different professional financial institutions many times. The financial holding group mode reduces the time cost of customers purchasing financial products, shortens the purchase process and improves customer satisfaction. By sharing marketing channels, professional financial institutions under financial holding groups can reduce the cost of sales channels and share the cost of maintaining customers. In addition, the study found that some customers think that buying a variety of financial products from different financial institutions in the same financial holding group will reduce the risk dispersion effect and may reduce the purchase of products in the financial holding group.

## 2.3.3 *The Synergy Effect in a Financial Holding Group*

### 2.3.3.1 Overview of the Synergy Effect Theory

American strategist Igor Ansoff introduced collaborative strategy into management (Liu et al. 2018) Haken Hermann summarized and refined the concept of synergy (Liu et al. 2018). Then, Haken Hermann systematically expounded the synergy theory. According to synergetic, there is a connection between the systems in the whole environment, and the systems can influence each other and cooperate with each other. Synergy effect is one of the three important aspects of synergetic. The synergy effect refers to the overall effect produced by the interaction between the system and the system because of the cooperation between the carrying out of the business (Liu et al. 2018).

Enterprises can promote cost reduction and income growth in marketing, production, management, and other aspects by sharing resources, and produce overall synergy. In the book *Corporate Strategy* (Liu et al. 2018) regards synergy as one of the four main contents of strategic management and proposes that synergy is the joint exertion of advantages between the acquiring group and the acquired group to enhance the overall benefits. He believes that an enterprise itself can be used as a collaborative system, and managers can take advantage of existing advantages to effectively bring into play the benefits of enterprise resources through the synergy among independent components in sales, operation and investment, and achieve the effect of one plus one is greater than two, that is, the benefits created by the enterprise as a whole are greater than those created by the sum of the various individual departments (Chen 2020). Chen (2020) pointed out that synergy is like a free rider. When the resources of a certain department of a group can be used by other departments at zero cost, they will work together to broaden the scope of business, promote the maximization of overall interests, and achieve increasing marginal benefits, resulting in synergistic effects. Then, based on summarizing the previous research results, Wu (2017) proposed that enterprises can carry out diversified operations and strengthen the coordination and management between departments and subsidiaries by sharing resources, information, and framework integration, to reduce operating costs, expand business scope and enhance the competitiveness of enterprises.

A financial holding group has the characteristics of low asset specificity, which not only has the synergy effect of general enterprises, but also has more prominent advantages than non-financial enterprises. Financial institutions can communicate and cooperate closely with each unit's financial business, increase the depth of sharing and cooperation of resources, and promote the most effective use of synergy advantages (Li 2018). In the process of establishing a financial holding group, diversified operation can integrate various resources of the group and its subsidiaries, broaden its business scope, expand its business scale, and achieve synergy (PBOC 2019). Professional financial institutions under financial holding groups can achieve business complementarity, business regional complementarity, risk diversification, reduce operating costs, promote the overall value of the group, and gain potential excess benefits and synergy through close communication, deep sharing of common resources and corporate culture integration (Fan and Yin 2019).

According to the role played by synergy, synergy effect can be divided into business, management and financial. Business synergy means that financial holding groups can rely on the group to integrate the resources and information between the group and its professional financial institutions and between professional financial institutions, jointly develop financial products, share the customer service platform, realize the complementarity of financial products, financing services and customer structure of different professional financial institutions, and create the overall brand effect and enhance the competitiveness of the group. Management synergy means that after the financial holding group merges professional financial institutions with poor operating performance, it can improve the operating performance of professional financial institutions after the merger and achieve the goal of "$1 + 1 > 2$" through advanced strategic management thinking, leading management ideas and reshaping efficient organizations. Financial synergy means that the financial holding group can integrate the financial resources of the group and its professional financial institutions and transform the former professional financial institutions to manage their own finances, balancing the cash flow, financing channels and financing costs of different professional financial institutions, to reduce financing costs, broaden financing channels and improve the efficiency of capital use (Chen 2020).

There are many ways to achieve synergy, among which product research and development, financial services, daily marketing, and scientific and technological development have unique effects (Wan 2018). In terms of product research and development, financial holding groups can integrate the R&D forces of the group and its professional financial institutions, including R&D personnel, capital allocation, R&D equipment, and give full play to the advantages of synergy effect of R&D. Also, financial holding groups adhere to the "top-down" and "bottom-up" R&D mode. "Top-down" mode means that commercial banks, securities companies, insurance companies and so forth, which are in the front line of business, feedback product information and customer needs, and then the group organizes superior resources of product research and development to develop. It can also promote the application of financial products researched and developed centrally and improve the efficiency. In terms of financial services, financial holding groups can complement each other's advantages at the level of group and professional financial institutions. The group can establish a unified financial product and service platform to enhance the overall service capability for customers. Banks, securities companies, and insurance companies can share financial products and services from different industries and can also jointly develop and provide financial products at the intersection between two professional financial institutions to enhance the competitiveness of financial products and services.

In terms of daily marketing, the professional financial institutions under the financial holding group have their own business outlets and fixed customers. The group can integrate marketing channels and cross-sell to existing customers. For example, the business outlets of commercial banks can represent products such as financing trusts, family trusts and charitable trusts of trust companies, and can also represent fund products of fund companies. It can also dig deep into existing customer resources, provide insurance companies with property insurance, life insurance and other services, and enhance the overall sales ability of the group (Qian 2016). In terms of scientific and technological development, due to the rapid development of financial technology in recent years, information technology plays an important supporting role in business development. Financial holding groups can integrate the information technology strength of their professional financial institutions, jointly apply information technology infrastructure such as computer rooms and shared clouds, complement each other's advantages, and jointly develop customer marketing, daily management, and other information systems to reduce operating and maintenance costs (Liu 2017).

#### 2.3.3.2 Foreign Research on the Synergy Effects of Financial Holding Groups

Some scholars have studied financial holding groups in Europe and other countries through empirical research. By implementing strategic management, optimizing corporate governance, and promoting resource integration, they can give full play to operational synergy, management synergy and financial synergy. However, some scholars also put forward the opposite opinion.

Financial holding groups can bring into play the business synergy. Rupert and Sherman (2006) show that financial holding groups can promote their financial subsidiaries to adopt mutually beneficial ways to integrate their internal resources and realize joint sharing and intensive management among subsidiaries. Fei (2014) believe that the key to achieve synergy of financial holding groups is to fully integrate diversified businesses and give full play to the advantages of its banks, securities companies, insurance companies and fund companies, to effectively allocate resources and maximize the overall interests of financial holding groups. Selecting the data of financial holding groups in nine countries from 1996 to 2008, Holzhauser et al. (2010) studied the synergistic effect by means of overall analysis and comparative study. The research results show that the financial holding groups with banks as the main body can exert synergy effects, enhance profitability, and enhance market value through diversified operation. Berry (2013) conducted an empirical study on insurance companies in developing countries. The results showed that insurance companies can carry out business collaboration by implementing diversified operations and providing comprehensive financial services, which provided strong evidence for promoting the development of insurance companies.

Financial holding groups can give play to the management synergy. Kanter (2003) believes that financial holding groups can achieve synergy by strengthening management, which is the main reason for diversified operations. The financial holding group mainly carries out corporate governance, optimizes the organizational structure, and integrates customer resources, shares sales channels, and builds a trading platform among financial subsidiaries to achieve synergy. Xie (2004) believes that financial holding groups mainly integrate diversified operations into the business philosophy of holding groups and financial subsidiaries, and take it as a strategic planning arrangement, to promote efficient business collaboration between the group and its subsidiaries.

Financial holding groups can exert financial synergy. Through the analysis of the fixed cost expenditures of financial holding groups and professional financial institutions, Li (2018) found that financial holding groups can allocate the fixed costs of their professional financial institutions to more financial products and reduce the marginal costs by carrying out diversified operations. Vennet (1999) collated the financial data of financial holding groups in some European countries from 1992 to 1996. By comparing and analyzing the profitability of financial holding groups covering banking and insurance business with professional banks and professional insurance companies, it is concluded that financial holding groups can share internal resources together, actively exert financial synergy, and the return on capital is higher than that of professional financial institutions. Selecting the financial data from 2001 to 2009, Liu and Hsu (2014) conducted a study on the cash flow and profitability of financial holding groups. The result shows that financial holding groups can increase cash flow, maintain reasonable liquidity, improve the contribution of net profit per unit capital, and support the financial synergy of financial holding groups.

Some scholars believe that financial holding groups will force customers to cross-sell and have conflicts of interest when they cooperate with each other. Li (2016) pointed out that commercial banks will force their securities, insurance, trusts, funds, and other subsidiaries to carry out cross-selling, and forcibly recommend and sell bank loans, wealth management and other products to customers. It will also force the bank's customers to repay the loans through securities companies issuing bonds and listing financing. Robert (1997) made an in-depth study on the conflicts of interest in commercial banks after diversified operations. The research shows that commercial banks can share the customer information of other financial subsidiaries through diversified operations, and different financial subsidiaries may have conflicts of interest to obtain customers. For example, commercial banks and their securities companies can provide wealth management products distribution business and purchasing wealth management products is the main way for customers to invest, but the wealth management products provided by the two financial subsidiaries are homogeneous and mutually substitutive. To complete the sales performance of wealth management products, the customer managers of commercial banks may seize the customers of securities companies, resulting in unnecessary conflicts of interest between the two financial subsidiaries.

#### 2.3.3.3 Research on Synergy Effects of Financial Holding Groups in China

Domestic scholars have mainly studied the definition of synergy, the ways to realize synergy and the impact of mergers and acquisitions on synergy, and generally believe that financial holding groups have synergy effects.

Some scholars have analyzed the definition of synergy On the basis of summarizing and combing the research results of previous scholars, combined with the development status of financial holding groups, Zhang and Zhang (2010) think that synergy is that under the premise of competition and cooperation, different financial subsidiaries of financial holding groups can accelerate the optimal allocation of group resources and promote the overall value of the group through cooperation and resource sharing in the daily operation management and business handling process.

Some scholars have studied the ways to achieve synergy. Chen (2014) pointed out that financial holding groups have many ways to achieve synergy, mainly by adjusting organizational structure and optimizing business structure. Among them, adjusting the organizational structure can be achieved by adjusting the service structure externally and adjusting the management structure internally. Optimizing the business structure can be realized by changing from single operation to diversified operation and from unilateral investment to diversified portfolio investment management. Yan (2008) focused on the research and analysis of the synergy effect formed in the process of financial holding groups investing in projects and held that there are different synergy effects in four links in the process of project management, namely, realizing the financing of funds, selecting projects for investment, managing the invested projects, and realizing profits.

Dong (2008) believes that the financial holding group adopts the mode that the group invests and controls its subsidiaries, and the subsidiaries carry out separate operations, which is different and unique from professional financial institutions in terms of management methods. Financial subsidiaries are set up according to business categories, and resources can be shared among subsidiaries, to play a synergistic effect and improve the level of return on assets of financial holding groups. Chen et al. (2013) summarized that financial holding groups can achieve synergy through four aspects: one is to achieve synergy through economy, the other is to achieve synergy through strategic management, the third is to achieve synergy through financial management and the fourth is to achieve synergy through operational management.

Some scholars have studied the impact of mergers and acquisitions on synergy. According to Zhang (2012), the synergy effect of financial holding groups can be realized in many ways. One is that synergy effects can be achieved through mergers and acquisitions of other financial institutions, and the other is that by strengthening the daily operation and management of the group and diversified subsidiaries, synergies can be exerted in various aspects, of which the latter is the main aspect of synergy. At the same time, he also studies and puts forward the process and methods of evaluating the synergy effect. The first step is evaluating the strategic management, system control and resource integration capabilities of the group and its subsidiaries in exerting synergy. The second is analyzing the actual effect of synergy after the integration of the above resources. The last is evaluating synergy through the changes of financial indicators before and after the resource integration of the group and its subsidiaries.

Zhang et al. (2012) thinks that financial institutions can achieve synergy by acquiring other financial institutions themselves. Gao and Zhang (2012) have studied the synergy effect of financial enterprises after mergers and acquisitions. Through research, they believe that the synergy effect is reflected in two aspects. One is the cash flow of financial enterprises after mergers and acquisitions has improved, and the cash flow of financial institutions after mergers and acquisitions is higher than the sum of the two financial institutions before mergers and acquisitions. After the merger, the overall value of the merged financial institutions is higher than the sum of the two financial institutions before the merger.

## 2.3.4 *Decentralized Risk Effects of a Financial Holding Group*

### 2.3.4.1 Theoretical Overview of Decentralized Risk Effects

In 1952, Markowitz put forward the theory of securities portfolio, which indicates that to maximize the benefits and minimize the risks, diversified investment should be implemented (Huang 2021). Modern portfolio risk theory holds that by carrying out portfolio management, we can achieve the purpose of dispersing and reducing risks and stabilizing returns. The effect of risk diversification mainly lies in the appropriate portfolio and the correlation of each asset (China Banking Association, [CBA] 2021).

Portfolio management of assets can spread risks. Diversification of financial business by financial institutions is the application of risk diversification theory in financial industry, and the purpose of risk diversification can be achieved by implementing diversification. Taking the financial holding group as an example, the financial holding group has a wide business scope, and generally invests in commercial banks, securities companies, insurance companies, trust companies, and equity investments. Under the uncertain business environment, it is easier to obtain stable profits than a single professional financial institution, which plays a role in hedging and reducing risks (Wan 2018). Financial institutions that carry out diversified operations can quickly adapt to changes in the market environment and maintain the stability of customers. There are many profit channels, which can reduce the fluctuation of income. Listed financial holding groups with less volatility in return rate can gain more attention and recognition from investors such as shareholders and creditors, which are conducive to enhance the brand awareness of the group and facilitate financing and business expansion of subsidiaries in the later period (Ma 2002). American scholars have made a comparative analysis of commercial banks before and after the financial crisis in the United States in 2007. Through research, it is found that after the financial crisis, 80% of the failed banks have relatively simple business scope, and most of the banks that have not closed down have relatively diversified business scope, including securities trading business. It is concluded that the capital adequacy ratio of commercial banks with single business scope is very low, and the risk compensation ability is relatively poor and banks with diversified operations have more profit channels and stronger risk resistance (Chen 2008).

Weakly correlated portfolio of assets can diversify risks. According to modern investment portfolio theory, various assets in an asset portfolio may be correlated, and a portfolio of assets with lower correlations can achieve a better risk diversification effect. Although there are related transaction risks among the group and subsidiaries, the business among subsidiaries is relatively independent, and the risk transmission is isolated by establishing a firewall system. By developing low correlation portfolio, we can achieve the goal of dispersing the overall risk of financial holding groups (Wan 2018). Some scholars have made an empirical study on the bank holding group in the United States and found that the financial holding group's business with low correlation of operating income and business combination can spread risks and reduce the volatility of earnings. Although the risk of securities business is higher than that of banking business, the correlation between banking business income and securities business income is relatively low. The financing method of customers has changed from bank credit to securities financing in the capital market. Although the banking profits of financial holding groups declined, they increased their profits through securities business. In addition, the bank holding group can share the customer information and operating conditions obtained when handling banking and securities business and reduce the risks of non-performing loans in banking business and underwriting of securities business (Li 2018).

#### 2.3.4.2 Foreign Research on Risks of a Financial Holding Group

In the academic field, there is a lot of research on the risks of financial holding groups. Up to now, at the academic and practical levels, there is no unified conclusion on whether the integrated operation of financial holding groups will increase or reduce risks. Most scholars have shown through research that the diversification of financial holding groups is conducive to reducing the risks of financial institutions in many aspects, while some scholars think that the integrated operation of financial holding groups increases the risks of supervision.

1. Research on supportive views of decentralized risk effects of a financial holding group

Foreign scholars have studied the relationship between diversified operation and risk diversification from four aspects: diversified operation of financial institutions, integrated operation of commercial banks, merger of financial institutions in different financial industries and strict restriction of diversified operation.

Diversification of financial institutions can reduce risks. Taking 123 bank holding companies and 62 professional financial institutions as research objects, Santomero and Chung (1992) studied the change of return on assets before and after the merger by simulating the merger of specialized financial institutions by bank holding companies and proved that diversification of financial institutions can reduce risks. Bensen (1989) believes that financial institutions can manage different types of asset business, debt business and mortgage guarantee business in a combined way, and through the combined management of business and risk, the risk of financial institutions' bankruptcy can be reduced. But at the same time, it is believed that if diversified financial institutions do not carry out portfolio management such as asset business, the parent group cannot improve the safety of operation. Wall et al. (1993) have studied the bank holding companies in the United States. The research shows that the bank holding companies in the United States, after carrying out diversified operations, have stronger ability in risk control and higher income return level than specialized commercial banks, thus proving that the diversification of financial institutions can reduce operational risks and improve the level of remuneration. Saunders and Walter (1994) studied the financial holding group by adopting the method of risk simulation. The research shows that the diversification of the financial holding group can reduce the risk of expansion for two reasons. It can stabilize the income source, among which, developing three core main businesses can form a stable profit source. It can stabilize cash flow. More than two business departments can have different cash flows, and the correlation between different business departments is relatively low.

Integrated operation of commercial banks can reduce risks. Kahn and Winton (2004) pointed out that commercial banks can isolate risks by means of financial subsidiaries. For example, commercial banks and equity investment companies operate low-risk corporate and personal loans, high-risk equity investment and financing, which can reduce regulatory arbitrage and guard against moral hazard through isolated operations. Li (2018) believes that commercial banks can respond to changes in the external business environment in a timely manner, enhance their competitiveness, and diversify their business risks by carrying out integrated operations. Lin (2012) used regression analysis method to study the diversification degree and related risk fluctuation of commercial banks. The research shows that commercial banks can reduce operational risks by implementing integrated management.

Mergers between financial institutions in different financial industries can diversify risks. Wall and Eisenbeis (1984) studied the operating data of financial holding groups from 1970 to 1980 and showed that there was a negative correlation between the income from the main business of commercial banks and the brokerage commission income of securities companies. Diversification of financial institutions can reduce the fluctuation of operating income and help reduce operating risks. Benston (1989) thinks that if financial institutions can handle commercial banking and investment banking for customers at the same time, then financial institutions can improve the level of reward and return without increasing the overall risk. Then, three scholars respectively conducted simulated mergers and acquisitions research. Boyd et al. (1993) simulated the merger of American bank holding companies with life insurance companies. Graham et al. (1993) simulated the merger of bank holding companies with property insurance companies. Hewitt et al. (1993) simulated the merger of bank holding companies and securities companies. They found that if American bank holding companies merge life insurance companies and property insurance companies, they can reduce risks. If securities companies are merged, the operational risks will be increased. Herring and Litan (1995) studied and established the risk evaluation index after the merger of financial institutions between different financial industries, that is, the coefficient of change of asset return. The research shows that after the merger of banking and insurance financial institutions, the risks are negatively correlated, and the development of insurance business by banking financial institutions can reduce the risks. Kwan (1997) studied the related risks between bank holding companies and affiliated securities companies in the United States. The research shows that the income correlation between bank holding companies and affiliated securities companies is very low, and the securities business of bank holding companies can spread the risks.

Strictly restricting the business of commercial banks has a higher probability of crisis than allowing commercial banks to carry out diversified operations. Barth et al. (2001) respectively made a comparative study and analysis on the probability of crisis in countries where commercial banks are allowed and strictly restricted to carry out non-banking business. The results show that strictly restricting commercial banks to provide customers with services such as commercial insurance and securities business restricts commercial banks from improving the quality and effectiveness of their operations, increases the probability of banking crisis, and affects financial stability. Barth et al. (2000) conducted an empirical study by setting up a financial market intertemporal measurement model, which showed that restricting commercial banks from carrying out securities business and other non-bank business has a higher probability of crisis than allowing commercial banks to carry out non-bank business.

2. Some scholars believe financial holding groups will increase risks.

Some foreign scholars believe that financial holding groups have multi-dimensional regulatory risks from the perspectives of risk supervision and mergers and acquisitions of financial institutions. Compared with a single financial institution, it has increased risks, especially after the merger of commercial banks and securities companies.

Financial holding groups have multi-dimensional risks and need to strengthen supervision. The EU Financial Group Supervision Guidelines (Liu 2017) pointed out that financial groups have risks such as low capital adequacy, more intra-group transactions, high risk concentration and so forth, and need to strengthen supervision. Iman et al. (2003) think that because the financial group is different from the single financial institution in scale, it may be faced with risk management problems. The financial institution supervision department should improve the supervision ability and level of the financial group. Santamero and Eckles (2000) found that financial groups are closely connected and have many financial subsidiaries, and the risks among financial subsidiaries can infect each other. If a financial subsidiary has a crisis, a chain reaction effect will be formed, and the risks will be transmitted to other financial subsidiaries or groups, so the risks of financial groups are more contagious. Arthur (2002) thinks that the supervision and management department of financial institutions should strengthen the risk management of financial holding groups from three aspects, such as strengthening supervision and management, isolating deposit insurance funds, and strengthening bankruptcy risk prevention. Arthur (2001) focuses on the potential risks of American financial groups. He believes that compared with a single financial institution, financial groups have centralized management of capital allocation and risks, which has improved the concentration of credit risks and market risks. Although risk isolation measures such as setting up firewalls have been taken, it is difficult to play the role of risk prevention and control; At present, the regulatory authorities cannot control the supervision of financial group concentration and other risks, which further aggravates systemic risks.

Some scholars adopt empirical research methods such as comparative analysis and think that financial holding groups increase risks. Demsetz and Strahan (1997) conducted empirical research and made a comparative analysis of the risk situation of large and small bank holding companies in the United States. They found that although large-scale bank holding companies have a higher degree of diversification than small-scale ones, the degree of diversification is not inversely proportional to the degree of risk. In comparison, large-scale bank holding companies have higher risks. Bhargava and Frase (1998) believe that the development of integrated financial services by commercial banks may increase risks and increase the difficulty of supervision. For example, through integrated operation, commercial banks underwrite corporate bonds with preferential loans, and cross-subsidize the business of different financial industries. Although the competitiveness is improved and the market share is increased, the risks of commercial banks are increased, and it is more difficult for the banking supervision and management departments to manage risks. Ellul and Yerra (2013) constructed an index to measure the internal governance level of financial holding groups and proposed that financial holding groups should establish strong risk management departments, strengthen the risk management of inter-subsidiary business, and effectively prevent risks.

There are differences in risk changes after mergers and acquisitions among different financial industries. Mergers and acquisitions of securities companies and real estate companies by bank holding companies will increase operational risks. With the method of scenario analysis, Boyd (1993) studied the risk changes before and after the bank holding group acquired financial institutions in the insurance industry and the securities industry and found that bank holding group's merger with the life insurance group or with the property insurance group will reduce the risk of operation. However, bank holding companies would acquire non-financial companies such as securities companies or real estate companies, which would increase the operational risks. With the method of empirical analysis, Boyd et al. (1993) studied the operating data of bank holding companies from 1971 to 1987. It indicated that after the bank holding group acquires the life insurance group or the property insurance group, the business risk will be reduced. However, after the bank holding group merges with the securities group, it may increase the risk of operation. Saundersa (1994) pointed out that the securities business of commercial banks will increase the risk of bankruptcy and the risk probability of securities business failure of commercial banks in developing countries is much higher than that in developed countries. Allen and Jagtian (2000) found that commercial banks may bring benefits after merging securities companies or insurance companies, but the risks brought by the merger also increase, and the degree of increase in risks is greater than the degree of improvement in benefits. Commercial banks carry out securities business and other non-banking business, which provides high systemic risk.

#### 2.3.4.3 Research on Financial Holding Groups in China

Domestic scholars have studied the risk management of financial holding groups mainly from the dimensions of cross-risk contagion and strengthening risk supervision.

Some scholars believe that diversification can spread risks. Xia (2001) proposed that financial holding groups can integrate financial institutions, make up for the restrictions of separate operations, and diversify risks. By establishing a mathematical model, Li (2006) made a quantitative analysis of the risks of traditional commercial banks and commercial banks carrying out investment banking business. The research indicated that commercial banks carrying out investment banking business moderately have the function of dispersing risks compared with traditional commercial banks. Xie (2004) analyzed that when financial institutions carry out mixed operations, they can prevent the risk transmission and effectively isolate the risk transmission by establishing a risk prevention wall between the group and its subordinate financial institutions and between financial institutions. Some scholars believe that carrying out diversified management may face risks, but it can effectively manage risks. Jiang and Ye (2014) pointed out through research that financial holding groups can effectively prevent risks by strengthening the construction of an internal control management mechanism. Zhang et al. (2013) pointed out from the perspective of control rights that financial holding groups can strengthen the management and control of financial risks by adopting centralized or decentralized methods and improve operating efficiency.

Some scholars believe that mixed operation increases risks. Zhang and Zhang (2010) believe that financial groups are more likely to transmit risks than general professional financial institutions. If a financial group has problems, it will affect the overall image, reputation, and credit of the group. Han and Liu (2019) proposed that a financial holding group, as a financial institution, will encounter some special risks based on credit risk, market risk and operational risk faced by the original general financial institutions. For example, the risk transmission between the group and subsidiaries is relatively fast, there are many related businesses among subsidiaries, and the financial holding group is relatively large in scale and has a strong monopoly on business. Zheng (2020) adopted the method of regression analysis and found that the investment banking business of commercial banks increased the volatility of operating income, which may not achieve the effect of risk dispersion.

Some scholars believe that the supervision of financial holding groups should be strengthened. Han (2019) pointed out that compared with general financial institutions, financial holding groups have lower information transparency, which easily leads to greater moral hazard, and the risks they face are more diverse and complex. The regulatory authorities should strengthen the inspection of major asset transactions within financial holding groups, transactions between affiliated companies, and the establishment of risk firewalls. Wang and Yin (2019) pointed out through research that financial holding groups hold financial institutions in the form of holding equity and they can hide the actual structure of the group, make false or circular capital injection to its subordinate financial subsidiaries, evade the supervision of the regulatory authorities, and carry out regulatory arbitrage. In view of this, it is suggested that the regulatory authorities should strengthen the supervision of the shareholders of financial holding groups and adopt differentiated regulatory measures.

### *2.3.5 The Operating Performance Improved by a Financial Holding Group*

Business performance evaluation is a comprehensive evaluation of business performance such as profitability by using statistics and operational research methods. The performance evaluation of financial holding groups is developed based on the performance evaluation of ordinary enterprises. The concept and main methods of business performance evaluation will be mainly introduced in Chapter Four, and this section mainly summarizes the relevant literature on business performance research of financial holding groups.

#### 2.3.5.1 Foreign Research on the Operating Performance of Financial Holding Groups

Foreign scholars have explored the operating performance of financial holding groups since 1990s, and the main research objects are financial groups in Europe, America, and Japan. Foreign scholars mainly use the methods of comparative analysis and regression analysis to study the operating performance of financial holding groups in Europe and America. Most scholars support that the financial holding group mode can promote the operating performance through empirical analysis, and some scholars have put forward different opinions.

Some scholars adopt the method of classification and comparative study and think that the performance of diversified financial institutions is better than that of single financial institutions. Barth et al. (2000) selected 142 commercial banks from 19 European Union countries and the Group of Ten (G10) as research samples, and the scale of the samples all ranked among the top 10 in the country. They made a comparative analysis of the business performance of commercial banks in carrying out and not carrying out non-banking business. The research results indicated that the business performance of commercial banks carrying out securities and insurance business is better than that of commercial banks with restrictions. Yamori (2003) studied Japanese financial holding groups and compared professional commercial banks with commercial banks under a financial holding group and concluded that commercial banks under a financial holding group had higher operating performance. Barth et al. (2000) made an empirical study on restricting banks from carrying out diversified operations. Through analysis, it is considered that the possibility of crisis in commercial banks that restrict securities, insurance and investment business is not lower than that of commercial banks that allow mixed operations.

Guo (2015) inspects some typical banks in Europe, and studies them by means of comparative analysis and regression analysis. According to the difference of business scope, commercial banks are divided into three categories—professional financial institutions, financial holding groups and universal banks. The research shows that the income efficiency of a financial holding group is higher than that of professional financial institutions, and the cost efficiency of all-round banks is better than that of professional financial institutions. Taking financial institutions in the Netherlands and Belgium as research objects, Vennet (1999) studied financial groups, specialized banks and specialized insurance companies in Holland and Belgium, among which the selected financial groups provided both banking services and insurance services. Methods Comparative analysis of business performance was used in the study. The results showed that the return on net assets of financial groups was higher than that of other financial institutions. Chronopoulos and Girardone (2011) used the method of comparative analysis to study the operating efficiency of financial holding groups and specialized banks in ten EU countries. The data come from their financial reports from 2001 to 2007. The research also proves that the operating efficiency of financial holding groups was better than that of specialized banks.

Some scholars have conducted empirical research by using data envelopment analysis, and support that the financial holding group mode can improve business performance. Berger, Hancock and Humphrey (1993) use the parameter boundary method to study the profit of universal banks in the United States. Through analysis, it shows that the main reason for the enhancement of profitability of all-round banks is the increase of operating income, not the decrease of operating cost, which drives the increase of net profit. Fei (2014) divided financial institutions into three groups: financial groups, specialized banks, and specialized insurance companies, and selected the data of financial statements from 1992 to 1996, and constructed an evaluation index system with four indicators, such as the return on net assets. By studying the four-year average of the three groups of financial institutions, it was shown that the financial group's operating performance and return on net assets were the highest among the three groups of financial institution.

Stiroh (2004) investigates 661 financial holding groups in the United States and selects the financial data of the above institutions from 1991 to 1997. Some indicators such as profit are processed by the method of cost–benefit function. He finds that the operating performance of financial holding groups has been continuously improved in the past six years, of which the main reason is the improvement of production efficiency. Using data envelopment analysis, Kang et al. (2010) collects and sorts out the data of 94 financial holding groups that conducted M&A transactions in the United States from 1991 to 1996. The conclusion is that the profit efficiency of financial holding groups is higher than the average level of financial institutions, while the cost efficiency is lower than the average level of financial institutions.

Some scholars have studied on the theoretical level and think that developing diversified management is beneficial to improve business performance. Schaeck (2008) believes that financial institutions can provide customers with a "package" of integrated financial services through diversified operations and promote the improvement of financial institutions' operating performance. Chen (2012) inspects the financial holding groups in Croatia and finds that the financial holding groups can promote the improvement of business performance by carrying out diversified operations. Conducting an empirical study on Bank Holding Group of America from 1997 to 2002, Stiroh and Rumble (2006) that bank holding group could obtain higher profitability by carrying out diversified operations. Although the non-interest income brought by diversification has certain volatility, the increase in operating income made up for the volatility of non-interest income.

Some empirical research results do not support that the financial holding mode plays a positive role in improving performance. Taking 661 financial holding groups with assets ranging from 38 million yuan to 366 billion yuan in the United States as research samples, Stiroh (2010) processed the data from 1991 to 1997 according to the distribution free method (DFA) and found that there was little difference in cost efficiency between large and small financial holding groups, and the operating performance of large financial holding groups was not necessarily high. Yeager and Harshman (2004) conduct a dynamic analysis of financial holding groups listed in the United States and select two financial statements such as balance sheet and income statement for comparative analysis. They take the three years from 1996 to 1999 as the first-time stage and the three years from 2000 to 2003 as the second time stage. Through comparative analysis, the following conclusions are drawn. The stock returns in the second stage are lower than those in the first stage, which also shows that the diversification of financial institutions in a relatively short period of time cannot promote the improvement of business performance.

#### 2.3.5.2 Research on Performance Evaluation of Financial Holding Groups in China

In November 2020, the Trial Measures for the Supervision and Administration of Financial holding groups was promulgated, which defined it for the first time in China. As financial holding groups are in the preliminary stage of development in the country, domestic research on financial holding groups is later than abroad (Guo et al. 2019). There are relatively few studies on China's financial holding groups, and there are fewer studies on financial holding groups' empirical research and business performance evaluation methods.

Some scholars use factor analysis and regression analysis to explore the performance evaluation of domestic financial holding groups. Most of them think that the financial holding group mode promotes the improvement of business performance, while some scholars do not support this view. Feng et al. (2015) conduct a study on six financial holding groups led by the Industrial and Commercial Bank of China and Bank of China, use capital adequacy ratio and loan-to-deposit ratio as evaluation indicators, and select financial data from 2007 to 2013 to conduct regression analysis. The results show that the return on total assets of financial holding groups is higher than that of professional commercial banks. Xia (2007) takes listed commercial banks as the research object and selects indicators such as profitability and risk management ability. The research thinks that the factor analysis method can objectively evaluate the operating performance of listed banks. Lu (2015) studies the relationship between diversified development and business performance of China's large state-owned commercial banks and joint-stock commercial banks from 2009 to 2013 by empirical means and factor analysis. The research shows that the diversified development of large state-owned commercial banks is faster than that of joint-stock commercial banks. The relationship between diversified development degree and business performance is not always positive, among which joint-stock commercial banks are positive, while large state-owned commercial banks are rising first and then falling. Taking some commercial banks in China as research samples, Tang et al. (2010) select the three-year operation from 2005 to 2007 to study and divide commercial banks into two categories. One is the commercial bank under the financial holding group (referred to as the financial control bank), and the other is the commercial bank with the background of non-financial holding group. The factor analysis method is used to evaluate the operating performance. The research shows that the operating performance of commercial banks under financial holding groups is better than that of commercial banks without financial holding group background.

Some scholars have studied the operating performance of financial holding groups in Taiwan by comparative analysis. In June 2001, the Financial Holding Group Law was issued and implemented in Taiwan Province, China. After more than 10 years of development, the financial holding group has formed a certain scale, and it is generally believed that the financial holding group mode has improved the operating performance. Taking 13 commercial banks owned by financial holding groups and 22 traditional commercial banks as research samples and selecting the financial reports from 2002 to 2005 as data sources, Yao (2007) calculates the profit efficiency value by the least square method through the multiple output beyond logarithmic profit function model. The research shows that the operating performance of commercial banks with financial holding group background is better than that of professional commercial banks and after the financial holding group acquires the commercial bank, it can improve the operating profit of the commercial bank. Ji (2003) uses empirical research to analyze 12 listed financial holding groups in Taiwan. The financial reports from 2001 to 2002 are used as data, and the operating performance of the financial holding groups is studied by the method of stochastic boundary cost function. The conclusion is that the larger financial holding groups were more efficient. After Financial Holding Group Law is promulgated, Jiang and Zheng (2018) inspect 33 commercial banks, among which, 12 are commercial banks under financial holding groups. Through comparative analysis, it is concluded that the business performance of commercial banks under the financial holding group is better than that of banks with non-financial holding group background.

## 2.4 Summary of This Chapter

Financial holding groups are still in the initial stage of development in mainland China, and their operation and management are not regulated in the early stage in terms of laws and regulatory systems. Domestic and foreign literatures on the theory, evaluation methods and empirical analysis of China's financial holding groups and related business performance evaluation are rare. At present, most of them mainly focus on exploring the necessity of China's financial industry management system reform and the choice of regulatory mode.

This chapter discusses the connotation of financial holding group, combs its concept, studies its main types and characteristics, discusses the research status of domestic and foreign scholars, and studies its supporting theory. The supporting theories of financial holding groups include economies of scale, economies of scope, synergies, risk dispersion and so forth, which are studied from different angles and provide the theoretical foundation for this study. Based on reviewing the theoretical research on scale economy, scope economy, synergy effect and risk dispersion of financial holding groups, this chapter also introduces the recent research on operating performance, which will be used for empirical research and analysis of operating performance of financial holding groups in China.

# Chapter 3
# The Development of China's Financial Holding Groups

## 3.1 Environment for the Development of Financial Holding Groups

In recent years, the world economic growth has slowed down, China's economic growth has changed from high-speed growth to medium–high growth, financial reforms such as interest rate marketization and capital marketization have been further promoted, the proportion of direct financing has gradually increased, finance and technology have been deeply integrated, financial management and investment of enterprises and residents have diversified, and the profit growth rate of traditional banks has declined. According to the development experience of financial institutions in Europe and America, integrated operation of financial institutions is an important way to cope with macroeconomic changes, diversify customer needs, and enhance profitability and risk resistance. Some domestic financial institutions have held various financial licenses through establishment, merger and acquisition, and transformed into financial holding groups.

### *3.1.1 Macroeconomic Situation*

Growth in the global economy is slowing. Since 2007, with the subprime mortgage crisis in the United States, the international market competition has become fiercer, the conflicts of commercial trade between countries have been increasing, and the global economic growth rate has gradually decreased. According to the data released by the World Bank (World Bank. (2020), the global Gross Domestic Product (GDP) is 85.79 trillion US dollars. The growth rate dropped from 12.63% in 2007 to 6.06% in 2018, a decrease of 6.57% points. In Annex A shows the details of global gross value generated from 2007 to 2018, and the overall weak recovery has not changed significantly. See Annex A for details.

 
X. Ning, *Performance Evaluation of Financial Holding Companies*,
https://doi.org/10.1007/978-981-97-8128-7_3

China's economy has entered a new normal. In the past few decades, China's economy has been developing at a high speed. According to the National Bureau of Statistics (National Bureau of Statistics 2019), the growth rate of the GDP has been maintained above 10% for many years, and the GDP exceeded 10 trillion yuan in 2000. From 1998 to 2008, China's economy has changed from high-speed growth to medium-speed growth, and the growth rate of GDP has dropped to single digits. See Annex B for details.

### 3.1.2 Interest Rate Marketization Reform

In recent years, the People's Bank of China has further accelerated the reform of interest rate marketization and achieved positive results. After the reform of interest rate marketization, the customer demand for traditional commercial banks has changed, the interest rate difference between deposits and loans has narrowed, the competitiveness between markets has increased, and the profitability has weakened day by day.

Customer's demand for financial services has changed. With the acceleration of interest rate marketization and the upgrading of financial services' demand of enterprises and residents, commercial banks urgently need to promote comprehensive management, shifting from a simple deposit and loan model to a management system that pays equal attention to the deposit and loan model, to the transaction and investment model and to the value management model. Additionally, commercial banks also need innovative development of fund, securities, leasing, insurance, and other license-based emerging businesses to establish a diversified and sustainable pattern of profit growth.

Market competitiveness has increased. Before the interest rate marketization reform, the deposit interest rates and loan interest rates of commercial banks with different maturities were implemented according to the regulated interest rates promulgated by the PBOC. After the reform of interest rate marketization, commercial banks set their own deposit interest rates and loan interest rates according to customers' risk situation and income situation.

To attract customers, commercial banks will increase the competition of deposit and loan interest rates, and the pressure of market competition among commercial banks will increase. At the same time, securities companies, asset management companies, and consumer finance companies can provide financing services for enterprises and individual customers through various channels and other ways. Commercial banks are facing increasing pressure of market competition, which needs to change from the traditional mode of making profits by relying solely on deposit and loan spreads, to the mode of providing trading investment and wealth management for customers. In 2018, the proportion of non-interest income was 22.11%, an increase of 2.81% points over 2011 (China Banking and Insurance Regulatory Commission [CBIRC] 2019). From 2011 to 2018, the proportion of non-interest income in China's banking industry has shown an upward trend, as shown in Annex C.

The profit growth shows a downward trend. After implementing interest rate marketization, the deposit and loan interest rates will be determined by the supply and demand relationship in the capital market, with frequent changes and more unpredictable trends. At present, the profit of commercial banks mainly comes from the difference between the interest rates brought by absorbing deposits and issuing loans, and the income brought by it is constantly decreasing and the fluctuation range is gradually expanding, which will lead to the increase of uncertainty of its profit and the slowdown of its growth. In recent years, the capital profit rate, asset profit rate and net interest margin of China's banking industry have shown a downward trend. Among them, the net interest margin of China's banking industry in 2018 was 2.18%, down 0.52% points from 2011. In 2018, the asset profit rate was 0.90%, which was 0.4% points lower than that in 2011 (CBRC 2019). These trends are shown in Annex D.

### *3.1.3 Capital Market Reform*

With the intensification of capital market reform and the diversification of financing structure, the development of financing structure is constantly diversified, enterprises and residents have various investment needs, the proportion of direct financing increases, and the pace of financial disintermediation accelerates.

There are many ways for enterprises and individuals to deal with their money. Before the reform of interest rate marketization, the deposits of enterprises and individuals were mainly deposited in commercial banks, and the interest rates of all commercial banks were subject to the requirements of the People's Bank of China. With the marketization of interest rates and the reform of capital market, enterprises and residents can directly invest their deposits in private funds with higher yields, equity investments, and the purchase of shares of listed companies. Due to the strict management of the scope of investment targets of commercial banks, the deposit interest rate and financial management yield of commercial banks will be relatively low. This has caused many deposits of enterprises and residents to be transferred out of commercial banks and invested in high-yield products, thus increasing the liquidity risk of commercial banks.

The proportion of direct financing has gradually increased. With the reform of capital market, especially the full implementation of the registration system of stock listing, enterprises have diversified financing channels, and can choose direct financing methods such as listing, issuing additional shares, issuing credit bonds and equity investment. The financing cost of the former is higher than that of the latter. In recent years, the proportion of direct financing in China's social financing scale has increased significantly. At the end of 2018, China's direct financing accounted for 13.52%, an increase of 8.29% points over the end of 2013 (PBOC 2019). The

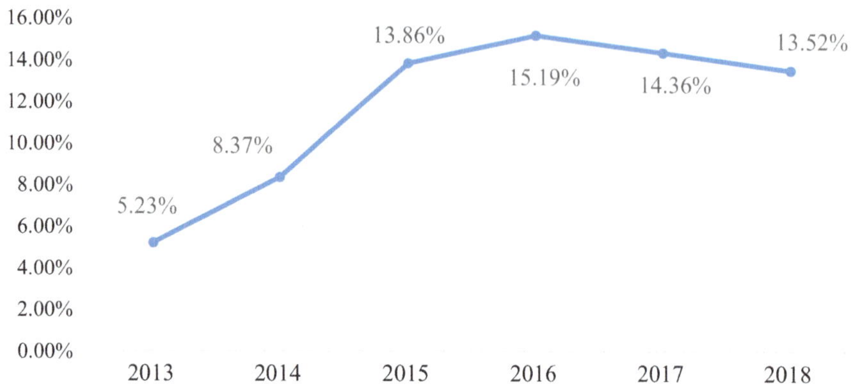


**Fig. 3.1** The proportion of direct financing in China from 2013 to 2018. *Source* Website of the People's Bank of China

proportion of direct financing from 2013 to 2018 in China in recent years is shown in Fig. 3.1

### 3.1.4 Financial Technology Development

The new generation of information technology and financial industry are deeply integrated and developed, forming a strong competitiveness for commercial banks. On the one hand, the third-party mobile payment has attracted the vast number of users through fast, convenient, and free technical services, making them separate from the bank and greatly reducing the bank's income in handling fees and commissions for related businesses. On the other hand, emerging technologies, such as big data statistics and application, distributed shared accounting technology, network cloud computing and storage, and artificial intelligence, are constantly emerging, accelerating the pace of reform and innovation in China's financial industry, and promoting the emergence of new formats such as Internet and mobile payment and settlement, Internet loans, intelligent investment, and financial consultants.

Large Internet companies have entered the financial industry one after another, increasing their competitiveness with commercial banks. Internet companies rely on the advantages of the Internet to apply for the establishment of financial institutions. In 2015, Alibaba Group and Tencent Group applied for the establishment of Zhejiang Online Commercial Bank and Qianhai Weizhong Bank, respectively, using the capital accumulated in the early stage of e-commerce. By virtue of the customer base and technological advantages of the Internet platform, online services were used instead of offline outlets to provide customers with 24-h and full-space banking services. Internet companies rely on Internet technology to improve the quality of financial services. Relying on many existing online customer resources, Internet enterprises actively explore banking services based on providing Internet services, and provide personalized services such as mobile payment, big data credit reporting, intelligent risk management and control, customized financial management to meet the diversified needs of customers. Ant Financial Service was established in October 2014. Ant Financial has created a "3–1–0" online lending model through big data algorithm. The number "3" means that the loan application process takes 3 min, "1" means that the system only needs 1 s to process the loan application, and "0" means that no manual operation is required. From 2014 to 2017, 4 million small enterprises obtained convenient and fast loans through Ant Financial Services. By the end of 2018, Alipay, a subsidiary of Ant Financial Services, and its subsidiaries had 1 billion active users (WB 2020).

## 3.2 Development History of China's Financial Holding Groups

From 1995 to 1998, the Chinese government promulgated the Commercial Bank Law of the People's Republic of China (National People's Congress, [NPC] 1995), the Insurance Law of the People's Republic of China (NPC 1995) and the Securities Law of the People's Republic of China (NPC 1998), which clarified that commercial banks, securities companies, insurance companies have basically formed a pattern of separate operation and separate supervision according to the principle of separate operation and supervision and management by industry.

Since 2000, the globalization of financial industry has accelerated, and the innovation of financial market has developed rapidly. Based on separate operation, China's financial industry gradually develops integrated operation. In 2002, the State Council approved CITIC Group, Everbright Group and Ping An Group, to become the pilot of the comprehensive financial holding group, which marks that China's financial industry has gradually entered the stage of integrated operation from the early stage of separate operation and supervision. Since February 2005, the State Council of China has allowed commercial banks to set up fund management companies, and commercial banks such as the Industrial and Commercial Bank of China, the Bank of China, and the China Construction Bank, have successively applied to the regulatory authorities and approved the establishment of fund management companies, and the pace of integrated operation of financial institutions has accelerated.

In February 2008, the 11th Five-Year Plan for the Development and Reform of the Financial Industry (PBOC 2009) clearly stated for the first time that financial institutions would be encouraged to promote cooperation among businesses in different financial industries by gradually promoting the pilot work of integrated operation of the financial industry, so as to improve the speed and quality of resource allocation in the financial market. In 2012, the National Financial Work Conference, held every three years, also clearly stated that it would gradually promote the pilot work of integrated operation in the financial industry. The 12th Five-Year Plan for the Development and Reform of the Financial Industry (PBOC 2012) also proposes that financial institutions can expand, set up or hold different types of financial institution service platforms and carry out pilot work of integrated operation on the premise of taking the implementation of integrated operation as the strategic development planning direction and effectively preventing and managing financial risks. Service functions are extended to improve diversified financial service capabilities and provide customers with integrated financial service solutions. In 2013, an inter-ministerial joint meeting system for financial supervision and coordination is established (SC 2013). Led and organized by the PBOC, which laid a good foundation for promoting the comprehensive operation and development of the financial industry and the smooth communication between regulatory authorities.

After more than a decade of development, some integrated financial holding groups have been established in China's financial industry. Three financial holding groups, including CITIC Group, China Everbright Group and Ping An Group, which have been approved by the State Council to carry out integrated operation pilot, have covered banking, securities, insurance, trust, and other businesses, forming a business pattern of relatively complete financial licenses. The Industrial and Commercial Bank of China, the Bank of China, the China Construction Bank, and other bank holding groups represented by banks, have covered banking, securities, insurance, and other businesses. State-owned local financial holding groups led by some local governments, such as Shanghai International Group and Beijing Financial Holding Group, were gradually established. Some private enterprises hold financial institutions such as banks, securities, insurance, and trusts, forming private financial holding groups.

## 3.3 Classification of China's Financial Holding Groups

With the slowdown of China's economic growth, the deepening of interest rate marketization and capital market reform, the disintermediation of the financial industry is accelerated, and the level of information technology is improved, financial innovation is intensified and regulatory control over the separate operation of the financial industry is gradually loosened. In recent years, China's financial enterprises have set up several financial subsidiaries through establishment and acquisition. Some enterprises that do not engage in financial business have controlled a number of financial institutions in different financial industries by applying for establishment and acquiring shares of other companies, and initially set up holding groups with the nature of financial holding groups.

China Financial Stability Report points out that China's financial holding groups can be divided into five categories: financial institutions, central enterprises, financial holding groups established by local governments, financial holding groups established by private enterprises and the Internet financial holding group (PBC 2020), as shown in Annex E.

Financial holding group mainly takes commercial banks, insurance companies, asset management companies as its parent companies. The parent companies not only provide the business and services of their own financial institutions, but also hold other types of financial institutions such as trusts, financial leases, funds through establishment, investment or mergers and acquisitions, and manage them as financial subsidiaries, thus establishing a financial holding group that provides integrated financial services to customers.

According to different types of holding financial institutions, financial holding groups can be divided into banking financial holding groups, insurance financial holding groups and asset management companies. Among them, banking financial holding groups take banks as the core holding platform and hold other types of non-banking financial institutions. For example, large commercial banks such as the Industrial and Commercial Bank of China, the China Construction Bank, and the Bank of Communications, have adopted the methods of establishment or mergers and acquisitions to hold fund companies, financial leasing companies, insurance companies, forming a financial holding group subsidiary based on commercial banks (Liu 2017). Insurance financial holding groups take insurance companies as the core holding platform. Asset management financial holding groups take asset management companies as the core holding platform. Annex F shows the classification of major financial holding groups.

At present, the domestic financial holding groups are mainly banking financial holding groups. At the end of 2018, the total assets of banking financial institutions were 290 trillion, accounting for 98.8% of the total assets of financial institutions (PBOC 2019). According to the annual disclosure reports issued by listed banking financial holding groups from 2014 to 2018, the financial licenses held by some banking financial holding groups are sorted out. See Annex G for details.

## 3.4 Introduction to Typical Financial Holding Groups

### *3.4.1 I Bank*

#### 3.4.1.1 Brief Introduction

I Bank was established in 1987 with the approval of the People's Bank of China and initiated by China I Group. It is the first joint-stock commercial bank founded by an enterprise in China, and its shareholders are enterprises, and its business scope is nationwide. Since its establishment more than 30 years ago, I Bank has been a pioneer in China's banking industry, leading the pace and direction of reform of China's banking industry.

It is the first to introduce the All-in-One Card in China, which can link the assets, liabilities and business handled by customers in I Bank to the same customer account and realize the unified function of inquiring and managing assets. It is the first to launch One Netcom, through which customers can handle loans, time deposits, purchase wealth management, funds, and other businesses in one stop. They can handle business directly through the Internet. It is the first one to introduce a dual-currency credit card, which is made according to international standards. Customers with credit cards can use it abroad and exchange RMB with foreign currencies. Among domestic commercial banks, Bank I was the first to put forward and build an exclusive brand of financial services, providing financial consulting and services for customers with personal assets exceeding 500,000 yuan, and constructing a management system for high-end customers' financial services. It is the first to launch an intelligent investment consulting product, relying on financial technology means such as artificial intelligence and big data analysis to provide customers with intelligent investment consulting services.

In the ranking of global business income published by Fortune magazine, I Bank has been in the top 500 for eight consecutive years since 2010, and its business income ranks 188th among the top 500 in the world in 2018. In 2019, the Tier 1 capital of I Bank ranked 19th among the top 1000 global banks, and the brand value of I Bank ranked 9th among the top 500 global banks (I Bank [IB] 2019).

#### 3.4.1.2 Development Course and Structure of Comprehensive Financing

I Bank established I International Financial Holdings Limited in Hong Kong in 1993 and I Bank Fund Management Limited in 2002 and began to seek to build an integrated operation platform.

The integrated management structure of I Bank has basically taken shape and the integrated management pattern is becoming more and more complete. From 2002 to 2015, I Bank successively established I Bank Life Insurance Group, Financial Leasing Group and Consumer Finance Group, and acquired P Bank overseas. Among them, I Bank Fund was established in December 2002 with a registered capital of 1.31 billion yuan. I Bank Life Insurance, established in August 2003, is the first life insurance group jointly funded by domestic and foreign enterprises after China became a member of the World Trade Organization, with a registered capital of 2.8 billion yuan. I Bank Leasing was established in March 2008 with a registered capital of 6 billion yuan. In 2009, the equity of overseas P Bank was acquired by I Bank, and P Bank became a subsidiary of I Bank. In March 2015, I Bank applied for and established a consumer finance group with a registered capital of 3.8 billion yuan. In addition, to expand its international business, I Bank has set up six branches and three representative offices overseas. Annex H. shows details of integrated financial development of I Bank. By the end of 2018, I Bank had formed an international commercial banking group with commercial banks as the main body and financial leasing companies, insurance companies, consumer finance companies and overseas banks as its subsidiaries. Annex I shows the organizational structure of the integrated financial development of I Bank.

#### 3.4.1.3 The Promoting of Comprehensive Financial Services

In recent years, I Bank has set its strategic transformation goal as developing a "light bank", by constantly optimizing its business structure, implementing digital construction, promoting the development of integrated operation and international operation, and achieving quality improvement, efficiency improvement and scale expansion. The main operating indicators are as follows (I Bank [IB] 2019).

Core profitability continues to increase. In 2018, the annual operating income was 248,555 million yuan and net profit reached 8081.9 million yuan, up 12.52% and 14.41% respectively, year on year. Non-interest income increased to 35.47%, up 1.04% points over the previous year.

Return on equity remains high. Return on equity was 16.57%, a 0.03% point increase over that of last year, the total asset return rate was 1.24%, up 0.09% points from the previous year and provisions coverage rate was 358.18%, an increase of 96.07% points over the previous year. Five indicators, including return on equity, return on total assets, and provision coverage rate, ranked first among the 16 listed national banks.

Thirdly, asset quality remains excellent. Both the balance of non-performing loans and the non-performing ratio have reduced, of which the non-performing loans account for 1.36%, down 0.25% points from the end of the previous year, the lowest among the 13 listed national banks, while the asset quality is stable and good. By the end of June 2019, the total market value of I Bank reached 899.5 billion yuan, ranking the top 10 in the global banking market value. For many years, the indicators such as the price-to-book ratio, the price-to-earnings ratio and other indicators have ranked first among domestic listed banks for many years. Major operating indicators of I Bank from 2014 to 2018 are shown in Annex J.

I Bank has promoted integrated operations at both the group and subsidiary levels and has achieved some results.

1. The group level

The group continues to promote value management. I Bank has built a refined capital management system with value management as the core and based on the indicators of capital return rate and net profit in the early stage, the risk cost and capital cost are considered. The application of value evaluation indicators such as Risk Adjusted Return on Capital (RAROC) and Economic Value Added (EVA), which take risk and cost into consideration, in the business target assessment, customer manager performance evaluation and business approval of branches and sub-branches, are promoted. The group closely tracks the latest achievements in the reform of Basel Accord, promotes the application of internal capital adequacy assessment procedure (ICAAP), dynamically manages the supply side and demand side of capital, and improves the efficiency of capital allocation.

The establishment of a comprehensive in-depth customer management model has been sped up. Through the combination of "financing" and "intelligence integration", we design and provide comprehensive service solutions for customers. Based on financial services of a traditional bank, financial intelligence services such as capital operation, financial restructuring, and high-end wealth management are carried out, which provides customers with a series of diversified financial service solutions. In the aspect of serving corporate customers, it comprehensively uses a variety of business models, such as on-balance-sheet financial products and off-balance-sheet financial products, commercial banks and investment banks, capital financing and consulting, and changes from providing traditional credit financing services to integrated financial services, and from traditional commercial banks providing loans to investment banks, trading banks and wealth management banks.

In 2018, I Bank realized a net non-interest income of 88,171 million yuan, up 15.95% year-on-year, including 73,046 million yuan in commission charges, up 4.49% year-on-year.

As for fee categories, the total fee income from custody, agency and other comprehensive financial services accounted for 49.39%, nearly half of the total. Refer Annex K for details.

As for agency sales, the sales of personal wealth management products reached 10.71 trillion yuan, a year-on-year increase of 16.73% points. The total amount of open-end funds of sales agents reached 767,858 million yuan, an increase of 8.8 pp over the same period of the previous year, and the total amount of trust products of sales agents reached 322,306 million yuan, an increase of 43.35 pp over the same period of the previous year. Through insurance sales agency, the premium income was 70,453 million yuan.

2. Subsidiary level

In the aspect of securities, I Bank International Financial Holding Co., Ltd has total international assets of HK$ 23,571 million and net assets of HK$ 7805 million in 2018. At the same year, its share of the IPO market in Hong Kong was about 5.9%, ranking first.

In terms of fund business, I Bank Fund Management Co., Ltd has total assets of 6612 million yuan, net assets of 4872 million yuan and total asset management business of 944,414 million yuan. Net profit reached 894 million yuan in 2018.

As for insurance business, I Bank Life Insurance Co., Ltd. has total assets of 45,332 million yuan and net assets of 5783 million yuan. In 2018, the income from insurance business reached 15,062 million yuan and the net profit was 1045 million yuan.

The proportion of net profits of major subsidiaries of I Bank in 2018 is shown in Annex l.

### 3.4.2 E Bank

#### 3.4.2.1 Brief Introduction

E Bank was founded in 1908. After being re-established in 1987, E Bank officially opened its business and became China's first national state-owned joint-stock commercial bank. It was listed on the Hong Kong and Shanghai Stock Exchanges in 2005 and 2007, respectively. The Bank follows the development strategy of taking the path of internationalization and integration and building the best wealth management bank, thus "186" strategic construction drawing is formulated. The number "1" means a strategic goal that highlights building the best wealth management bank with the essence of creating common values and offering first-class services. The number "8" refers to the implementation strategy of the eight strategic plans.

Putting customers first is a priority. Then, taking the road of internationalization and comprehensive development. The third is to adopt the "two-wheel" drive management strategy of combining business division system reform and enhancing branch management. The fourth is to carry out the combination of online business and offline business, and the "two lines" will develop together and cooperate with each other. The fifth is to increase the development of financial technology and improve operational efficiency. The sixth is to improve the management ability of talents and improve the enthusiasm of employees. Seventh, strengthen risk prevention and control to ensure business development needs. Eighth, strengthen the construction of corporate culture, focusing on building a happy home and gathering the spiritual strength of employees. The number "6" refers to the business strategy of "three growth and three decline" in business development, that is, to promote the steady growth of effective customers, drive the steady growth of core liabilities, promote the increase of operating income in the direction of bank transformation, reduce the cost of risk occupation, reduce the cost of capital consumption and reduce the cost of daily operation (E Bank [EB] 2019).

#### 3.4.2.2 Development Course and Structure of Comprehensive Financing

E Bank has been operating in a comprehensive way earlier than other domestic banks. In 2000, E Bank Insurance was established, which indicated that it took the first step towards comprehensive management. The business scope of E Bank includes deposit and loan business, payment and settlement, fund raising and sales, asset management, financial leasing, life insurance, housing loans, securities investment. E Bank group owns several non-banking companies including E Bank Financial Leasing Group, E Bank Insurance Group, E Bank Financial Asset Investment Group, and holds share of some companies including E Bank Fund Management Group and so forth. Also, E Bank invested in S Rural Commercial Bank, becoming the largest shareholder of S Rural Commercial Bank and the joint largest shareholder of R Bank. As a strategic investor, it invested in Hainan Bank and became the controlling shareholder of four village banks. Its development course and structure are shown in Annex M and Annex N.

#### 3.4.2.3 The Promoting of Comprehensive Financial Services

As early as 2008, E Bank took integrated operation as an important transformation direction, and through the implementation of integrated operation and business strategy of exploring the global market, it made great efforts to turn E Bank into an excellent commercial bank group with wealth management as its business characteristics. E Bank Group has set up subsidiaries such as commercial banks, securities, funds and so forth, but its operating performance, especially profitability, is weak.

The rate of return on total assets is relatively low. By the end of 2018, the total assets of E Bank Group reached 9,531,171 million yuan, 2.79 trillion yuan more than that of I bank while net profit reached 74,165 million yuan, 6654 million yuan less than that of I Bank. The total asset return rate was 0.80%, 0.44% points lower than that of I Bank, ranking 12th among the 13 listed national banks.

The rate of return on net assets shows a continuous slowdown. In 2018, E Bank Group's return on equity was 11.17%, 5.4% points lower than that of I Bank, the lowest among the 13 listed national banks for 6 consecutive years.

The proportion of non-interest income is not ranked high. Although E Bank Group holds more non-bank financial institutions, its non-interest income accounted for 38.44%, ranking 5th among the 13 listed national banks.

The cost-to-income ratio accounts for a relatively high proportion. In 2018, the cost-to-income ratio of E Bank Group was 31.50%, which was only 1.08% points lower than that of M Bank with the highest cost-to-income ratio among the 13 listed national banks, ranking the second highest. The details of major operating indicators of E Bank in recent years can be seen in Annex O.

1. The group level

E Bank is committed to developing into a comprehensive financial service group with commercial banks as the main body and trust companies, insurance companies, investment companies and fund companies as the support. E Bank has set up several branches overseas to provide cross-regional financial services for customers. It insists on deepening reform, improving top-level design, continuously strengthening comprehensive financial services, improving comprehensive operating efficiency, and providing customers with domestic and overseas financial services, direct and indirect financing, money market and capital market.

Although E Bank adheres to the strategy of integrated financial services, from the composition of fee income, the proportion of bank card settlement fee income to fee income of E Bank Group is still the highest, and it is the main increase point, which is consistent with the situation of traditional commercial banks. In 2018, E Bank Group achieved fee income of 41,237 million yuan, an increase of 686 million yuan or 1.69% year-on-year. Among them, the bank card fee income was 20,114 million yuan, an increase of 3847 million yuan or 23.65%, which was 5.6 times of the total fee income. However, service fee income of agency (agency insurance, trust, and other business), investment bank service fee income, guarantee commitment service fee income and other comprehensive financial service charge are relatively low. The proportion of E Bank's service charge sources is shown in Annex P.

2. The subsidiary level

In 2018, E Bank Financial Leasing Limited Group achieved a net profit of 2737 million yuan with total assets of 231,743 million yuan, net assets of 21,756 billion yuan and a balance of leasing assets of 220,407 million yuan. It further expanded business in aircraft leasing and ship leasing. The relevant assets amounted to 128,267 million yuan, accounting for 58.20% of the total leased assets.

In terms of trust business, E Bank International Trust Co., Ltd. realized a net profit of 1057 million yuan in 2018 and managed assets of 883,047 million yuan, of which the total inherent assets of 12,526 million yuan and trust assets of 870,522 million yuan.

As for fund business, E Bank Fund Management Co., Ltd. realized net profits of 478 million yuan, total assets of 375 million yuan and net assets of 3041 million yuan in 2018. At the end of 2018, the amount of assets under management reached 438,876 million yuan.

The proportion of net profits of major subsidiaries of E Bank in 2018 is shown in Annex Q.

## *3.4.3 M Bank*

### 3.4.3.1 Brief Introduction

Established in October 1992, M Bank has become the fifth listed bank in China since its IPO in 2003. In July 2019, M Bank ranked 56th in terms of tier-one capital and 67th in terms of asset size in the word (Banker 2019). In accordance with the list of the world top 2000 listed companies, M Bank was in 265th place (M Bank [MB] 2019).

In the annual report disclosed by listed companies in 2018 (MB 2019), M Bank proposed that it will uphold the "five development concepts", adhere to the "four strategic directions", "six development directions" and "two major values", and build a "big, strong, stable and excellent" financial holding group. Adhering to the "five development concepts" includes adhering to the concept of innovation, green, coordinated, open and shared. Adhering to the "four strategic directions", includes relying on deposits as the foundation of banks, relying on technology to make banks prosperous, relying on talents to make banks strong, and relying on risk management and control to ensure bank safety. "Six development directions" includes the development direction of characteristics, digitalization, lightness, specialization, integration, and internationalization. "Two values" includes creating value for customers and creating value for shareholders. At the end of 2018, the total assets reached 2,680,580 million yuan, up 6.84% from the beginning of the year and operating income reached 72,227 million yuan, up 8.80% (MB 2019). The main operating indicators of M Bank from 2014 to 2018 are shown in Annex R.

Furthermore, the operating performance of M Bank in recent years shows the following characteristics, which require urgent transformation and development.

The non-performing loan ratio continues to increase. At the end of 2018, the non-performing loan ratio of M Bank was 1.85%, ranking second among the 13 listed national banks. It has increased for 7 consecutive years, rising by 0.97% points at the end of 2018 compared with the end of 2012.

The provision coverage rate continues to drop. The provision coverage rate is 158.59%, showing a decreasing trend in the past eight years. The provision coverage rate at the end of 2018 decreases 149.62% points from the end of 2011.

The net interest margin continues to decline. The net interest margin is 1.95%, showing a decreasing trend in the past eight years. The net interest margin in 2018 is 0.86% points lower than that in 2011. The net interest margin of M Bank in the past eight years is shown in Annex S.

The cost-income ratio is in the forefront. The cost-income ratio is 32.58%, the highest among the 13 listed national commercial banks.

#### 3.4.3.2 Comprehensive Financial Organizational Structure

Currently, only M Financial Leasing Group is under administration of M Bank and it opened in May 2013 with a registered capital of 6 billion yuan and M Bank holds 82% of the shares. At the end of 2018, M Financial Leasing Group had total assets of 75,602 million yuan, total liabilities of 67,304 million yuan, net assets of 8298 million yuan, and net profit of 705 million yuan.

#### 3.4.3.3 The Promoting of Comprehensive Financial Services

By adhering to the "six development goals", M Bank will strengthen the reform of its system and mechanism, continuously optimize asset quality, promote the improvement of operating efficiency, and promote the business transformation and development of the bank.

M Bank and its subordinate financial leasing companies jointly carry out banking and leasing business, and actively promotes the establishment of branch in Hong Kong. It strengthens FinTech development to deepen the implementation of finance technology strategies. It adheres to the market-oriented orientation and provides customers with a series of integrated financial service solutions and financial service solutions around the changes in customer needs. At the same time, it strengthens cooperation with other financial institutions such as trust companies, securities companies, and insurance companies, adheres to customer-centered and market-oriented, continuously strengthens customer comprehensive operations, deepens cooperation with trust, funds, securities, insurance, futures, and other business organizations, and enriches and improves wealth management means and methods.

## 3.5 Research Questions About Financial Holding Groups

According to the above macro-economic background, the development process and trend of China's integrated financial management, typical enterprises of China's financial holding groups, and in combination with the previous literature review, the following research questions are put forward (please see Fig. 3.2).

### *3.5.1 Before Transition: How to Promote Business Performance Through Transition?*

Under the background that China's economic growth is slowing down and facing structural adjustment, the interest rate marketization reform of loans and deposits is further deepened, the trend of "financial disintermediation" is accelerating, the pace of integrated operation is accelerating, and the new generation of information technology and financial industry are deeply integrated, bank interest margin space is narrowing, homogeneous management is becoming increasingly serious, profitability is declining, and the impact on traditional banks is rising. Referring to the development process of China's integrated financial management and the transformation experience of benchmark financial enterprises, how to transform and reform to increase business performance of commercial bank has become an urgent problem to study (shown in Fig. 3.3).

There is an example. At present, M Bank has only set up a subsidiary, the Financial Leasing Group (E Bank [EB] 2019) (MB 2019). Its core operating indicators, such

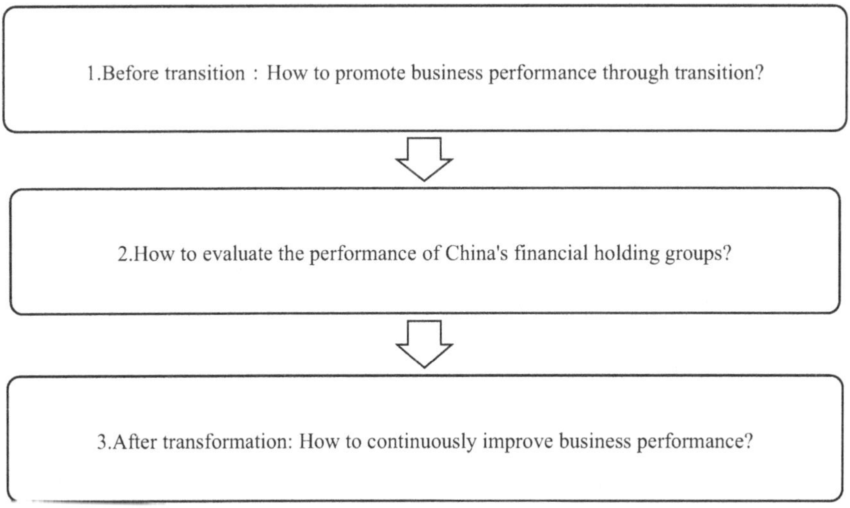


**Fig. 3.2** Main research questions

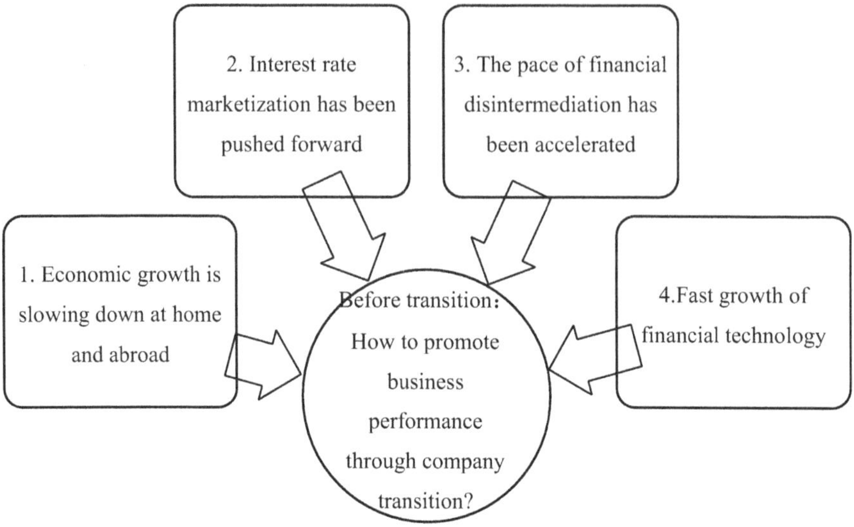


**Fig. 3.3** The first research question

as the non-performing loan ratio and the non-interest income ratio, have been ranked low for a long time, so its transformation and development are relatively urgent. First, the non-performing loan rate has been high for a long time. By the end of 2018, the bank's non-performing loan ratio was 1.85%, the second highest among the 13 listed national commercial banks. From 2008 to 2018, it ranked among the top 13 listed national commercial banks. Second, non-interest income is relatively low. At the end of 2018, the bank's non-interest income accounted for 28.64%, which was the lowest among the 8 listed national joint-stock banks of the same type, about 7% points below the average non-interest income. From 2008 to 2018, it ranked last among 8 listed national joint-stock commercial banks. Third, the cost-income ratio is the highest. In 2018, M Bank's cost-to-income ratio was 32.58%. From 2008 to 2018, it ranked the highest among 13 listed national commercial banks.

### *3.5.2 How to Evaluate the Performance of China's Financial Holding Groups?*

Performance evaluation is an important management tool for shareholders, regulatory authorities, and internal managers of financial institutions to understand the current operation and development status of financial institutions and judge the future development trend of financial institutions. They will make decisions and judgments based on that tool to take corresponding measures. Some foreign scholars (Bergor 1999; Levine 2000; Qi 2003; Kanter 2003) believe that there are economies of scale,

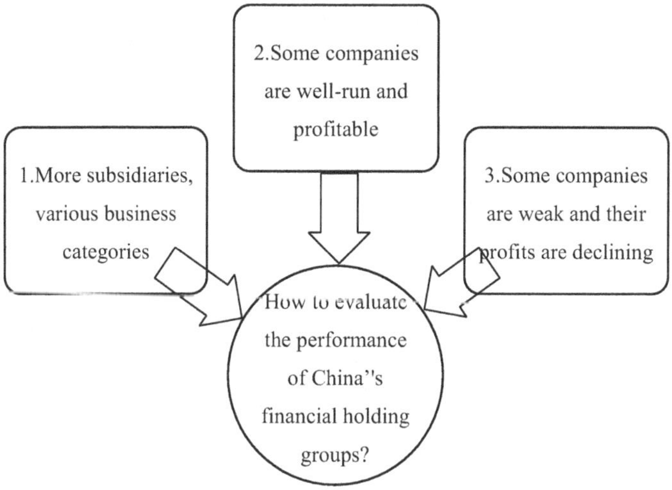


**Fig. 3.4** The second research question

economies of scope, synergy effects and diminishing risks in comprehensive management. They have also used empirical methods to study financial holding groups in Europe and in the United States and concluded that financial holding groups in relevant countries indeed have economy of scale and economy of scope and the business performance is improved significantly.

Based on actual situation of China's banking financial holding groups, how to establish an evaluation index system and evaluation model for the operating performance of China's banking financial holding groups, and whether diversification has a positive effect on improving the operating performance of China's banking financial holding groups, as well as improving the ability of risk compensation, profitability and cost control, have become important research issues (as shown in Fig. 3.4).

### *3.5.3 After Transformation: How to Continuously Improve Business Performance?*

As matters stand, after some financial institutions are transformed into financial holding groups, their overall profitability is relatively weak, and their inherent advantages have not yet been brought into play. As for a large part of financial holding groups, their subsidiaries still do business on their own and have not formed an integrated operation and service mode. At the financial holding groups' level, there are problems such as unrealized economies of scale and scope, unobvious efficiency improvement effect, unobtrusive financial synergy value, unapparent innovation synergy effect and risk dispersion effect, and unobtrusive brand effect. The basic advantages of financial holding groups such as real resource sharing, customer

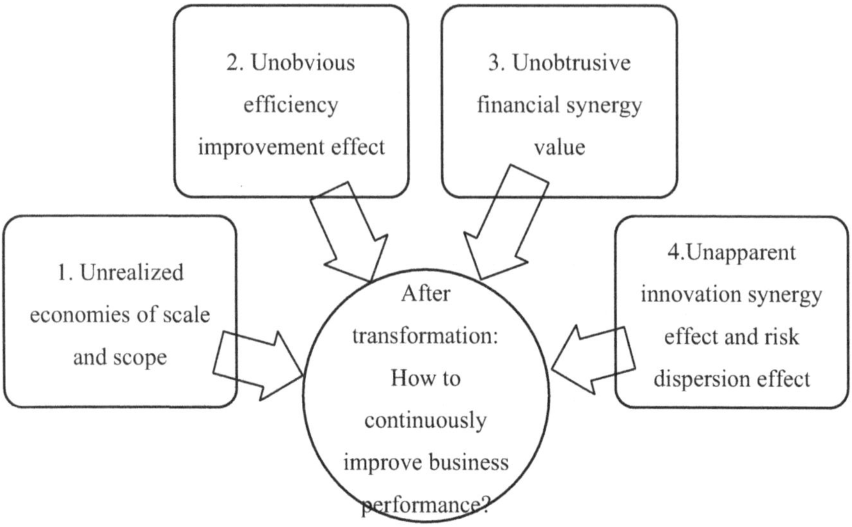


**Fig. 3.5** The third research question

sharing, business complementarity and risk diversification have not been realized. The overall business performance of the whole group is relatively weak. Figure 3.5 makes a summing up and analysis of which aspects have a significant impact on the promotion of business performance by China's financial holding groups.

For example, E Bank has an earlier comprehensive operation among domestic banks, and its subsidiaries include commercial banks, trusts, funds, financial leasing, insurance, and other professional financial institutions (EB 2019), but its comprehensive operation capability and advantages are relatively weak and unobvious. In 2018, the return on net assets of E Bank was 11.17%, and the return on net assets has been showing a downward trend from 2010 to 2018. In 2018, the return on equity decreased by 8.91% points from 20.08% in 2010, and it ranked last among 13 listed national commercial banks from 2013 to 2018. Second, the intermediate business income is still dominated by bank card handling fees, and the comprehensive operation advantage is relatively weak. In 2018, E Bank Group realized a net fee and commission income of 41,237 million yuan, of which bank card fee accounted for the majority (49%), while agency (including insurance, trust) fee income accounted for 7%, investment bank fee income accounted for 11%, and guarantee commitment fee income accounted for 6%. Third, the cost-income ratio is relatively high. In 2018, the cost-income ratio of E bank Group was 32.58%, ranking second among the 13 listed national commercial banks, only lower than M Bank.

After transformation, some financial institutions have continuously enhanced their profitability and value creation capabilities by means of in-depth promotion of value management. Based on the traditional banking business, financial holding groups carry out comprehensive financial service, focusing on developing the business of non-traditional banking financial institutions. Combing macroeconomic development and financial industry reform, financial holding groups optimize business development strategies, expand the width of profit sources, and realize the transformation from relying only on the interest rate difference between loan and deposit business as the income source in the past to increasing the revenue of various businesses. Through providing comprehensive management and service to customers, financial holding groups have improved service efficiency and quality and reduced operating costs, while effectively realizing the decentralization of economies of scale and scope, reducing operating risks and enhancing profitability. Looking at these typical cases will help us propose management and control suggestions to enhance the business performance of China's financial holding groups.

Taking I Bank as an example, it deepens value management and increases profitability (I B 2019). First, I Bank invested and controlled diversified financial institutions. I Bank owns domestic and overseas commercial banks, fund companies, financial leasing companies and other financial subsidiaries through establishing a new group or mergers and acquisitions and accelerates the integration of diversified financial subsidiaries to provide integrated financial services to customers. By providing integrated financial services, I Bank will change from providing financing services for customers to providing financing services plus financial intelligence services, optimize the business service mode, and provide integrated service solutions for customers. Second, the core profitability has been continuously enhanced. ROAA, ROAE and other indicators of capital and assets' ability to create benefits have maintained a high level and improved continuously for many years, while risk management indicators such as non-performing loan balance and non-performing loan ratio showed a downward trend, and asset quality remained at a relatively high level.

In 2018, the rate of return on net assets was 16.57%, ranking fourth among the 13 listed national commercial banks, and now it ranks first. Third, the total market value ranks among the best. By the end of June 2019, I Bank had a total market value of 899.5 billion yuan, ranking among the top 10 banks in the world. Its price-to-book ratio and price-to-earnings ratio continued to rank first among the major listed banks in China.

## 3.6 Summary of This Chapter

Based on the literature review in the previous chapter, this chapter first introduces the macroeconomic background of China's financial holding groups. Because the domestic macro-economy has changed, the profit growth rate of traditional banks has declined, and some financial institutions have transformed into financial holding groups. Then it expounds the course and trend of China's financial integrated management, and the pace of China's financial institutions' integrated management. Thirdly, it describes the classification of China's financial holding groups. The People's Bank of China divides China's financial holding groups into three categories, among which financial institutions can be divided into banking financial holding groups, insurance financial holding groups, and asset management companies according to different holding entities. Among them, banking financial holding groups take banks as the core holding platform. Finally, this book analyzes three typical cases of China's financial holding groups, including I Bank, E Bank and M Bank, and puts forward three problems in promoting the operating performance of China's financial holding groups. The next chapter will discuss the research methods and design.

# Chapter 4
# Innovative Methods for Evaluating Operational Performance of Financial Holding Groups

## 4.1 Main Methods for Evaluating the Operating Performance of Financial Holding Groups

Performance evaluation of financial enterprises based on the operating characteristics of the financial industry is a part of comprehensive evaluation. DuPont Analysis, Wole Scoring Method, Factor Analysis Method, CAMELSS and GYROSCOPE are used in the performance evaluation process. At present, domestic scholars mainly conduct performance evaluation research on domestic commercial banks through factor analysis method and other methods but have not conducted evaluation on other financial institutions such as financial holding groups.

### *4.1.1 The Concept of Performance Evaluation*

Serving as an important part of financial analysis, performance evaluation takes the financial statements of one or more companies and other relevant financial information as its foundation and focuses on comprehensive evaluation of the group's financial analysis indicators to further summarize and evaluate the financial and operating conditions of the relevant companies.

#### 4.1.1.1 Comprehensive Performance Evaluation

Comprehensive performance evaluation (Ministry of Finance [MF] 2021) is usually a kind of business performance evaluation from the perspective of business owners or investors. There are three main aspects to carry out comprehensive performance evaluation. One is to establish a comprehensive evaluation index system for related

 
X. Ning, *Performance Evaluation of Financial Holding Companies*,
https://doi.org/10.1007/978-981-97-8128-7_4

enterprises and formulate evaluation criteria for related indexes. Secondly, the performance evaluation lays stress on business performance and efforts of the enterprise in a certain period of operation, including profitability, asset quality, debt risk and other indicators. Thirdly, in the evaluation process, quantitative evaluation and qualitative analysis are mainly carried out through the application of mathematical statistics, operations research, and other methods. Many research methods are used to carry out comprehensive performance evaluation, such as the Wole Scoring Method, the DuPont Analysis Method, and the Factor Analysis Method.

#### 4.1.1.2 Performance Evaluation of Financial Enterprises

Financial enterprise performance evaluation (MF 2016) refers to the process that the financial enterprise management department selects the range of financial indicators to evaluate financial enterprises, then determines differentiated scoring standards according to the operating rules of different financial industries and evaluates the operating performance of financial enterprises according to the time span of a fiscal year. The scope of evaluation indicators mainly covers the debt repayment situation of enterprises, the ability to earn profits, the quality of assets under control, and the improvement level of performance on the original basis. In view of the background that domestic financial industry is still dominated by commercial banks, at present, domestic scholars' research on performance evaluation of financial enterprises mainly focuses on commercial banks. In the selection of evaluation methods, Factor Analysis Method, Wall score method and DuPont Analysis Method are frequently used. Internationally, the CAMELSS rating method is mainly used for credit evaluation of commercial banks and other financial institutions, while in recent years, the GYROSCOPE evaluation system has been used to comprehensively evaluate the steady development ability of commercial banks in China. However, there are few evaluations on other financial institutions such as financial holding groups at home.

### *4.1.2 Introduction to the Main Performance Evaluation Methods*

There are two kinds of methods to evaluate the operating performance of financial enterprises, namely traditional performance evaluation methods and industry supervision rating or evaluation methods. The former includes DuPont Analysis method, Wole Scoring Method and Factor Analysis Method. In recent years, financial supervision departments or financial industry associations have increasing number of evaluation methods such as CAMELSS in the United States and GYROSCOPE in China. In the following subchapters, the above methods will be mainly introduced based on the situation of financial enterprises.

#### 4.1.2.1 The DuPont Analysis Method

DuPont Analysis (MF 2021) is a method that can be used to evaluate the ability of financial institutions to make profits through operation and management and to obtain returns for shareholders' investment. This method mainly analyzes the financial situation of financial institutions comprehensively and evaluates the operating results according to the relationship between the ratios of core financial indicators. The DuPont Analysis Method is not only widely used in the analysis of financial statements of listed companies, but also applied in commercial banks for the intra comparative analysis of financial statements for several years.

DuPont Analysis can explain the reasons and trends of the changes in the main evaluation indicators of financial institutions and point out the direction for taking management and control measures (Wang 2016). In the analysis of financial statements of commercial banks, it analyzes the change trend of the data of the return on equity ratio, asset return rate and equity multiplier in the past five years, especially conduct the vertical analysis of financial statements to figure out the existing problems affecting the return on equity ratio of financial enterprises and puts forward the solutions to the problems.

#### 4.1.2.2 The Wole Scoring Method

The Wole Scoring Method (MF 2021) was proposed by Alexander Wole, one of the pioneers of studying enterprise financial comprehensive analysis. This evaluation method evaluates the credit level of financial enterprises by selecting some financial proportion indexes of financial enterprises and linking them together by using a linear relationship. With the application of the Wall scoring method in the practical work of financial enterprises, relevant personnel have improved and constantly perfected the Wole scoring method. It is generally believed that the content of evaluating the financial situation of financial enterprises can be divided into three parts, namely profitability, solvency, and growth ability, which can be distributed according to the proportion of 50%, 30% and 20%, respectively. Also, it is mainly applied to the performance analysis of commercial banks and other financial institutions.

In the performance analysis and application of the Wole scoring method in commercial banks (Wang 2016), in the selection of indicators, the indicators for evaluating the profit-making level include three financial indicators such as the rate of return on net assets, the indicators for evaluating the debt repayment ability include five regulatory indicators such as capital adequacy ratio, and the indicators that reflect the growth of financial enterprises include three year-on-year growth indicators such as the growth rate of net profit, as shown in Annex T.

The standard value is obtained by referring to the industry average level, or competitor level. The weight of the evaluation index system is mainly determined according to other relevant literature research results, and the total value of the weight ratio is 100%.

#### 4.1.2.3 The CAMELSS Method

CAMELSS credit rating index system is implemented by American financial supervision and management agencies for financial institutions.

At present, the financial management agencies mainly include the Federal Reserve Bank, the Federal Deposit Insurance Corporation and the U.S. Securities and Exchange Commission, and the implementation object is mainly a method adopted by the financial management authorities to assess the credit rating of commercial banks and other financial institutions (Xiao 1990). Some scholars believe that financial holding groups, as other financial institutions, are included in the scope of credit rating.

The evaluation of the CAMELSS method (Luo and Pan 2013) mainly covers five parts: capital adequacy, asset quality, management, earnings, and liquidity. In 1991, The Federal Reserve System improved and perfected the camel credit rating index system and increased the Sensitivity of Market Risk based on evaluating the five parts in the early stage. Because the marketization degree of interest rate and exchange rate in China is relatively low, and it is still in the state of supervision and control, and domestic financial institutions do not disclose this part in the financial statements, the five parts of the Camel Credit Rating Index System, excluding market risk sensitivity, is adopted (Zhou 2016).

Based on the evaluation of financial institutions' risk management ability, the CAMELSS method includes indicators such as the complexity of operation and management and the classification of risk levels into the evaluation category and establishes an evaluation model focusing on evaluating the stable operation of financial institutions. In the scoring rules, individual scoring and overall scoring are selected, and each scoring standard is divided into five grades, among which the first-grade scoring standard is the healthier and the fifth grade scoring standard is the unhealthier. The main indicators and evaluation criteria are shown in Annex U.

#### 4.1.2.4 GYROSCOPE

GYROSCOPE evaluation system (China Banking Association [CBA] 2016) was put forward by the China Banking Association from 2013 to evaluate the stability of the operation and management of major commercial banks in China from multiple dimensions. The target entities of the evaluation system are commercial banks in China.

The GYROSCOPE Evaluation System consists of nine parts which are: corporate governance, yield sustainability, risk control, operational management, service quality, competitiveness, organization intelligence, personnel competence, and equity funding. This evaluation system evaluates and analyzes the steady development ability of commercial banks from the above nine aspects.

The index selection of the GYROSCOPE Evaluation System selects business indicators according to the following main principles: multi-dimensional and relatively complete evaluation, evaluation plays a leading role, based on the availability of data, maintaining the independence of evaluation, and keeping the evaluation process transparent. The data source of the evaluation index mainly includes two parts. One part of quantitative data comes from the published annual reports of commercial banks, mainly balance sheet, income statement, cash flow statement and other financial report data. The other part is not disclosed in the annual report of commercial banks, and its quantitative data and indicators are derived from the "Questionnaire on the Steady Development Ability of Commercial Banks". This part is organized by the China Banking Association, and all participating commercial banks are required to fill in and report to the China Banking Association according to the actual situation of the Bank. The Evaluation Committee of China Banking Association scored the qualitative indicators in the Questionnaire on the Steady Development Ability of Commercial Banks submitted by various commercial banks according to the relevant scoring standards. Combined with the scores of quantitative indicators and qualitative indicators of commercial banks, the scores of steady development ability are comprehensively determined and graded.

## 4.2 Selection of Operating Performance Methods for Financial Holding Groups

### *4.2.1 Introduction to the Factor Analysis Method*

Factor Analysis Method (Chen and Li 2011) was proposed by British psychologist C.E. Spearman. It is a multivariate statistical analysis method, starting from the study of internal dependence of variables, and integrating and simplifying some variables with complex relationships into several representative comprehensive factors.

The basic idea of Factor Analysis is to classify the original variables to simplify and analyze multidimensional data. When classifying them, the original variables with higher correlation are classified into one class. Among them, in the same category, the correlation between each original variable is relatively high. Among different types, the correlation between each one is relatively low. Each type of primitive variable symbolizes a common element, also known as a common factor. Factor Analysis is an attempt to explain more original variables by studying and analyzing a relatively small number of "common factors" and "special factors".

### *4.2.2 Comparative Analysis of Main Management Performance Evaluation Methods*

At present, the domestic research on the evaluation method of financial holding group's operating performance is relatively few, and it is in the initial stage of exploration. There is no special evaluation method for financial holding group's operating performance. There are mainly five methods to evaluate the operating performance of financial enterprises, including the DuPont Analysis Method, the Wole Scoring Method, the Factor Analysis Method, the CAMELSS and GYROSCOPE evaluation systems. The above five evaluation methods have their respective advantages and disadvantages. Their comparative analysis is as follows.

#### 4.2.2.1 Advantages and Disadvantages of the DuPont Analysis Method

The advantages the of DuPont Analysis Method are as follows (Huang 2013). A whole set of evaluation index system has been established. DuPont Analysis decomposes return on equity into the product of three key business indicators, and on this basis, it can be further decomposed in detail to form a relatively complete combination of financial evaluation indicators. Additionally, the relationship between evaluation indicators is logically clear. The evaluation index is obtained by decomposing the return on equity step by step, with clear hierarchy and organization, which is convenient for comparative analysis of the operation and management effects of financial enterprises. Thirdly, it is widely used. The DuPont Analysis Method has been widely used in business performance evaluation and has also been applied to a certain extent in business performance evaluation of financial institutions such as commercial banks.

However, it also has disadvantages. From the perspective of comprehensive evaluation, the DuPont Analysis Method only cover financial indicators, which cannot fully reflect the operation and management of financial enterprises, so this method cannot comprehensively and objectively evaluate the operating performance of financial institutions. From the perspective of sustainable development, this method mainly focuses on short-term financial evaluation indicators such as return on equity and profit rate of assets, which will prompt the management of enterprises, especially financial institutions, to pay too much attention to short-term operating results, ignoring the risk status, long-term development, and value realization of enterprises. From the perspective of the time stage of evaluation, this method mainly evaluates the operating performance of financial institutions already generated and lacks the influence and prediction of the existing operating performance on the future operating performance. In addition, financial institutions are operating at risk, which is significantly different from ordinary enterprises. The DuPont Analysis Method lacks the evaluation of financial institutions' risk management and other management capabilities.

#### 4.2.2.2 Advantages and Disadvantages of the Wole Scoring Method

The Wole Scoring Method has some strengths (MF 2021). It breaks the phenomenon of traditional performance evaluation method that only pays attention to financial indicators. Through the combination of financial indicators and non-financial indicators, it focuses on evaluating the business performance of enterprises from four aspects, ranging from customers, finance, internal operation to learning and growth, which provides strong support for the strategic management of enterprises. This method pays more attention to team cooperation and has a better incentive effect on employees and management. However, it also has shortcomings. In terms of practical operation, indicators such as learning and growth and internal operation are subjective and cannot be determined objectively when evaluating financial institutions. The operation cost is high, so it takes more time and cost to discuss the value and importance of performance evaluation index, and it is difficult to determine the performance evaluation index objectively and reasonably. The cost of post-adjustment is relatively high. If the strategic objectives and business structure of financial institutions change, the relevant evaluation indicators in the Wole scoring method need to be redesigned, which will cost more manpower and material resources.

#### 4.2.2.3 Advantages and Disadvantages of CAMELSS and GYROSCOPE

CAMELSS and GYROSCOPE that are mainly used to evaluate commercial banks have the following advantages (Liu 2018). This kind of evaluation method involves many indicators and has a wide range of evaluation aspects. It can show the performance of commercial banks comprehensively and objectively. However, every coin has two sides. CAMELS and GYROSCOPE have their own drawbacks. The weight of the index is artificially set, so these evaluation methods and results are of a certain subjectivity. The performance of commercial banks in the same category is not well differentiated, so it is not convenient to distinguish the performance evaluation among such commercial banks.

### *4.2.3 Reasons for Selecting the Factor Analysis Method*

Through the comparative analysis in the previous section, it can be concluded that the evaluation methods such as the DuPont Analysis Method, the Wole Scoring Method, CAMELSS and GYROSCOPE evaluation systems have disadvantages, such as traditional selection of evaluation indexes, subjective design of evaluation weights, numerous evaluation indexes and small degree of differentiation, so it is difficult to reflect the real situation of financial holding groups objectively and accurately. Especially since the research on the operating performance of China's financial holding groups is at the initial stage of exploration, using Factor Analysis to evaluate the operating performance of China's financial holding groups has more advantages (Ding and Qiu 2010). Comparative analysis of the advantages and disadvantages of main management performance evaluation methods is shown in Annex R.

#### 4.2.3.1 Advantages of the Factor Analysis Method

Combining statistic software such as Statistical Package for the Social Sciences and the Factor Analysis Method data can be analyzed. The advantages of Factor Analysis are as follows.

Common factors can be extracted from many original variables. By using the Factor Analysis Method and statistical analysis software, a limited number of public factors can be extracted from many original variables that affect the operating performance of Chinese financial holding groups, and the public factors are representative, thus determining the main factors affecting the performance evaluation of China's financial holding groups and analyzing the influence of the main factors.

The number of original variables can be reduced. By using Factor Analysis Method and statistical analysis software, common factors can be extracted from original variables with high correlation degree, and then the number of original variables used for statistical analysis can be reduced. In addition, the relationship between different original variables can be tested by the linear relationship of common factors.

The weight of common factors is determined objectively and reasonably. Common factors are selected from many original variables and the weight of common factors is determined. Common factors and corresponding weights are not determined by subjective will, but calculated by statistical analysis software, which is objective. In particular, the weight of common factors is determined by calculating the corresponding variance contribution degree by statistical analysis software, which is unique, thus avoiding the arbitrariness of determining the weight of common factors subjectively. Statistical software calculates that the greater the variance contribution of the corresponding variables, the more important the original variables are and the greater the corresponding weights are.

The calculation process can be implemented by software. If the Factor Analysis Method is adopted, the whole calculation process can be completed by statistical analysis software. IBM SPSS® software is a professional statistical analysis tool developed and applied earlier, which is very convenient and fast, easy to operate and has strong operability. In this research, IBM SPSS® statistical analysis software, which is commonly used in China, is used for the analysis.

Therefore, compared with other methods, at present, using the Factor Analysis Method to evaluate the operating performance of China's financial holding groups is a more scientific, objective, practical and simple comprehensive evaluation method.

#### 4.2.3.2 The Features of the Factor Analysis Method

The features of the Factor Analysis Method are as follows (Liu 2017).

1. It has characteristics of comprehension. In the empirical process, an infinite number of variables can be selected if indicators, data, and other conditions are available. Statistical analysis software extracts the relevant indicators in the index system reflecting the performance evaluation of China's financial holding groups

by dimension reduction from many original variables. Through Factor Analysis Method, the evaluation results are more comprehensive.

2. It is of good interpretability. Common factors extracted by the Factor Analysis Method can be rotated, and the values in the factor load matrix after rotation processing will show polarization, to highlight the correlation between variables, and further ensure the close relationship between the common factors and the variables with larger load and ensure that the finally extracted factors have more accurate economic meaning and can give reasonable explanation.
3. And it is objective. In the empirical process of Factor Analysis Method, the weight of the factor is not artificially determined. It is the contribution degree after factor rotation processing, which can ensure the objectivity of factor weight calculation, to make the evaluation results of business performance more convincing.

Five business performance evaluation methods such as the DuPont Analysis Method are compared and analyzed. After summarizing and sorting out, the advantages and disadvantages of the main business performance evaluation methods are shown in Annex V. To sum up, in view of the above advantages and characteristics of the Factor Analysis Method, it is very suitable to apply this method to the management performance evaluation of China's financial holding group.

The choice of management performance evaluation method is very important. Using reasonable and objective evaluation methods to evaluate financial enterprises' operating performance has many benefits. It is conducive to truly reflecting the business performance and management level of financial enterprises and provides a basis for objectively and reasonably evaluating the actual management level of business managers. It contributes to discovering the problems existing in operation management and asset financial operation and promoting the improvement of the operation and management level of financial enterprises. It makes for promoting the implementation of strategic management objectives of financial enterprises and maintaining healthy development. Through the comparative analysis of the advantages and disadvantages of the main operating performance evaluation methods in the early stage, this research adopts the Factor Analysis Method as an empirical study on the operating performance evaluation method of China's financial holding groups and implements it according to the following flow chart (Fig. 4.1).

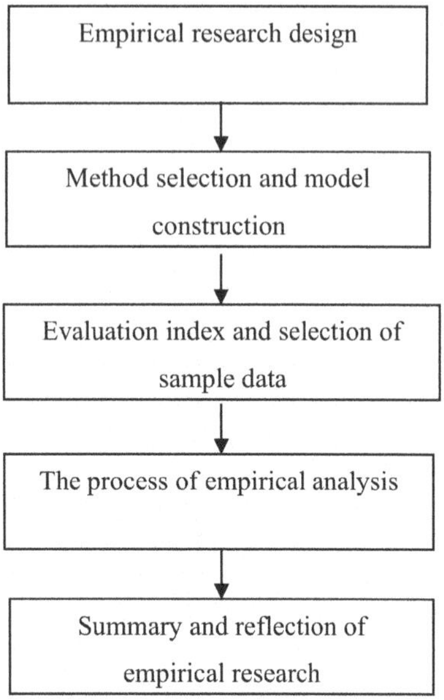


**Fig. 4.1** Flow chart of empirical research

## 4.3 Selection of Performance Evaluation Indicators for Financial Holding Groups

### *4.3.1 Sample Selection of Financial Holding Groups*

#### 4.3.1.1 Sample Selection

In recent years, with the continuous improvement of China's financial marketization, a group with the characteristics of financial holding groups has formed (PBC 2019). This research intends to select the financial holding banks which are listed and have branches nationwide. The main reasons are as follows.

China's financial holding groups are in their early stages of development. At present, most financial holding groups in China only make financial investments in more than two financial subsidiaries in the form of equity to obtain their share of dividend income. Although some enterprises have formed the rudiments of financial holding groups, they have simply combined the financial subsidiaries and initially set up the organization and management structure of financial holding groups, without unified management of the financial subsidiaries they hold.

China's financial holding groups are mainly banking financial holding groups. At present, domestic financing still gives priority to indirect financing, with banking financial holding groups occupying a prominent position in the financial system. From 2016 to 2018, the domestic indirect financing accounted for about 86%, and in

2018, the domestic indirect financing accounted for 86.48% ([PBOC] 2018). Bank-controlled financial holding groups have been established for a long time in China's financial holding groups, and their development is standardized. Bank subsidiaries are the most important financial holding groups, and they are still in a basic position in China.

There are many listed bank-controlled financial holding groups with sufficient information disclosure. There are many listed companies in banking financial holding groups, which have been listed for many years, with sound corporate governance, regular information disclosure and accumulated business data. Other types of domestic financial holding groups are also actively seeking listing to raise funds and enhance brand influence. By studying the listed banking financial holding groups, we can learn from the development of other types of China's financial holding groups.

It is planned to select 13 national bank financial holding groups currently listed in Chinese mainland as the research objects, namely Bank A, Bank B, Bank C, Bank D, Bank E, Bank F, G Development Bank, Bank H, Bank I, Bank J, Bank K, Bank L and Bank M.

It is for two reasons. (1) The above-mentioned 13 banking financial holding groups all hold two or more financial licenses, belong to financial holding groups, and have a nationwide scope of business. They have been established for a long time and are standardized in development. Therefore, their performance evaluation results can generally reflect the development status and trend of China's financial holding groups.

(2) In financial institutions, these 13 enterprises have a large share of business scale. Now, relevant data on the scale of China's financial holding groups are not available. Judging from the total assets, total liabilities, and net profits of these 13 banking financial holding groups in the country's banking and financial institutions, the scale is relatively large, and the proportion is relatively high. In 2018, the total assets of the above 13 banking financial holding groups reached 146.60 trillion yuan, accounting for 69.82% of the total assets of the national banking industry and 49.95% of the total assets of China's financial institutions. The total liabilities of the above-mentioned 13 banking financial holding groups reached 133.99 trillion yuan, accounting for 54.34% of the total liabilities of the national banking industry and 50.05% of the total liabilities of China's financial institutions while net profit reached 1.40 trillion yuan, accounting for 76.50% of the national banking net profit (China Banking and Insurance Regulatory Commission [CBIRC] 2019). The above-mentioned 13 banking financial holding groups are taken as samples for research and have strong representativeness.

#### 4.3.1.2 Data Collection of Samples

At present, scholars generally use the annual data of financial institutions for research. To avoid the errors brought by sampling, this book chooses 13 bank financial holding groups' annual financial and accounting reports from 2014 to 2018 as the research objects.

1. Resources of sample data

The sample data comes from the annual financial accounting reports of listed companies from 2014 to 2018 disclosed by 13 sample banks such as A Bank, audit reports issued by accounting firms and annual disclosure reports, among which the annual disclosure reports cover the main information of the group, the analysis and discussion of the annual operating conditions, the report of the group's management mechanism. In addition, the data source of the sample also includes the main operating indicators and information published by the official websites of all sample banks, the website of the People's Bank of China, the website of the China Banking Regulatory Commission.

2. The period of sample data selected

Taking following factors into consideration, we mainly select data from 2014 to 2018.

One is to consider the integrity of the data. In recent years, the regulatory policy has become stricter, the information disclosure management of listed companies and their subsidiaries has become more standardized, the information in financial statements is more comprehensive and abundant, and the annual financial data are more stable and of higher quality.

The second is the comparability of data. As China's interest rate liberalization and other financial reforms have deepened in recent years, the operating mode of financial institutions has undergone profound changes. If the time span is long, the comparability is weak.

The third is to consider the consistency of data. Since 2006, the domestic financial industry has started to promote the pilot of integrated operation of the financial industry based on separate operation of banking, securities, and insurance (PBOC 2012). In 2013, the People's Bank of China, together with the China Securities Regulatory Commission, the China Banking Regulatory Commission, the Foreign Exchange Bureau, and the China Insurance Regulatory Commission, established an inter-ministerial joint meeting system for coordination of financial supervision (CSC 2013), laying a foundation for promoting the development of comprehensive operation of the financial industry. Financial institutions have obtained financial licenses, accelerated the pace of integrated operation, and gradually formed a financial holding group structure. From 2019 to 2021, a new coronavirus epidemic occurred in China, which had a great impact on the economy and on financial holding groups. To keep the comparability and consistency of data, the data from 2014 to 2018 are selected for analysis.

## *4.3.2 Principles for Selecting Performance Evaluation Indicators*

### 4.3.2.1 Principles of Commercial Bank Management

The operating principles of a commercial bank are embodied in security, profitability, and mobility (Huang 2021).

The principle of profitability means that commercial banks strive to obtain maximum profits at the lowest cost in their business activities. It occupies a core position in the management of commercial banks. The principle of security refers to the fact that commercial banks operate and manage risks themselves. It is necessary to avoid all kinds of uncertain factors affecting their daily operations and ensure the stable operation of commercial banks. And the principle of mobility means that commercial banks provide daily deposit withdrawal and loan service for customers and need to ensure that the payment and return of funds are at a reasonable level. The "three characteristics" of commercial banks complement each other and are indispensable. Based on the safety of capital operation, companies should do a good job in asset liquidity management and strive to achieve maximum profit.

### 4.3.2.2 The Principle of Combining Financial Information and Non-Financial Information Evaluation

Financial statement serves as the main body of management evaluation system of traditional financial holding groups, and it indicates the operation results and management level of financial holding groups in the past while lacks the impact on future value reflected by non-financial information.

The financial statement is the basic summary of the business situation. The financial statements of financial holding groups can not only be used to review the financial operation of a certain stage in the past, but also to sort out and analyze the defects existing in the financial operation and management, to provide decision-making reference and basis for the next improvement of operation and management. The financial statements only reflect the performance level of financial holding groups in financial operations, but they cannot objectively reflect their overall operating performance level in multiple dimensions.

Non-financial information is also an important part of business evaluation. The financial information in the financial statements can only reflect the quantitative business information calculated by monetary measurement, but not the qualitative business information of non-monetary nature. The financial statement information is the embodiment of the final financial operation results, and it can't reflect the process management that has great influence on the financial holding group, which is of great significance to the management and future development of the financial holding group. Therefore, it is quite limited to evaluate the performance of financial holding groups only through financial statements (MF 2021). Analyzing financial holding groups through non-financial statements is also a very important part of business performance evaluation.

The evaluation method adopts the combination of ratio analysis and ratio analysis. The commonly used evaluation methods for financial information and non-financial information include ratio analysis and ratio analysis (MF 2021). Proportional analysis is based on the logical relationship between the cause and the result, and forecasts and analyzes the business situation. Ratio analysis method is to calculate, analyze and predict the future business trend through the ratio between business indicators. When evaluating the performance of financial holding groups, the combination of proportional analysis and ratio analysis can make a more comprehensive analysis, find out the business development trend and provide important support for business decisions.

#### 4.3.2.3 The Principle of Evaluating a Financial Holding Group

The selection of indicators is the basis and key to evaluate the operating performance of financial holding groups and has a very important impact on the results. Therefore, the selected indicator system should not only comprehensively reflect the operating performance of financial holding groups, but also grasp the key points. The selection of indicators should follow the following principles (MF 2016).

Principle of comprehensiveness. The selected evaluation index of financial holding groups can not only reflect the "three principles" commonly used in evaluating financial institutions, such as liquidity, security, and profitability, but also cover financial information and non-financial information, and can comprehensively evaluate the operation and management of financial holding groups. The evaluation index selected in this study covers the "three principles", considering financial information and non-financial information, and embodies the principle of comprehensiveness.

Principle of importance. There are many indicators to analyze financial holding groups, and it is impossible to include every analysis indicator in the operating performance evaluation system. According to the degree of importance, select the indicators that have great influence on the performance evaluation results of financial holding groups, and give play to the leading role of performance evaluation of key indicators. Based on sorting out the previous research results, according to the development stage of China's financial holding groups, this study focuses on selecting 15 business indicators for business performance evaluation.

Principle of hierarchy. According to the nature and characteristics of the evaluation indexes of financial holding groups, the evaluation indexes of multiple dimensions are classified, and the evaluation indexes with similar properties are classified into one index category. Combined with the previous research, this study divides the evaluation index into five levels.

Principle of operability. The data of each index should be easily obtained so that the model is practical.

### 4.3.3 *Selection of Performance Evaluation Indicators*

According to the principle of index selection, CAMELS credit rating index system (Wang 2016), GYROSCOPE evaluation system (Luo and Pan 2013), and domestic and foreign scholars' performance evaluation of financial holding groups and commercial banks, the performance evaluation index of financial holding groups (as shown in Annex R) in this book specifically includes the following aspects.

#### 4.3.3.1 Indicators of Profitability

Indicators of profitability include the return on equity, return on total assets, net profit, and non-interest income. The return on equity and total return on assets mainly reflects the production capacity and effect of resources that was input by financial holding groups in a certain period of operation. In addition, net profit and non-interest income mainly reflect the financial holding group's profitability in a certain period of operation.

#### 4.3.3.2 Indicators of Business Growth

The indicators of business growth include the rate of return on economic added value, the growth rate of operating income and the growth rate of net profit. Those indicators mainly reflect the financial holding group's operating growth level, capital appreciation status and development potential within a certain operating period.

#### 4.3.3.3 Indicators of Solvency

The indicators of solvency include the capital adequacy rate, tier-one leverage capital and asset-liability ratio, which mainly reflect the financial holding group's debt level, ability to repay debts and ability to resist financial risks during a certain period of operation.

#### 4.3.3.4 Indicators of Asset Quality

Indicators of asset quality include the non-performing loan ratio, the provision coverage ratio, and the core capital adequacy ratio, which mainly reflect the efficiency of using existing resources, the management level of assets and the risk management ability of assets of financial holding groups in a certain operating period.

#### 4.3.3.5 Indicators of Business Management

The indicators of business management include the cost-to-income ratio and earnings per share, which mainly reflect the management results achieved by financial holding groups in a certain period of operation after taking management measures, including management costs and after-tax profits per share.

### *4.3.4 Performance Evaluation Indicator Analysis*

The determination of performance evaluation of financial holding groups is based on three principles of modern commercial bank, combination of financial information and non-financial information as well as three principles of index selection.

#### 4.3.4.1 Indicators of Profitability

The profitability of financial institutions is the concentrated embodiment of benefits, and it is also the fundamental guarantee for them to maintain their competitive position in the financial industry. Deriving from the balance sheet, income statement and cash flow statement that reflect the actual value of the profitability evaluation index where higher is better.

1. Return on equity

Return on equity (MF 2021) is calculated by the ratio of the net profit created by the financial holding group within one year to the net assets at the end of the year. This index shows the ability of each shareholder's equity to obtain net profit, and it is an important index to measure the benefit created by the capital invested by shareholders. The larger the ROE index value, the higher the net profit of each equity invested by shareholders.

2. Return on total assets

The total asset return rate (MF 2021) refers to the ratio of the net profits realized by financial holding groups in a certain operating period to the average balance of assets in the corresponding operating period. It reflects the financial holding group's ability to use all assets to obtain profit, which is the net profit generated per 1 yuan asset. The larger the value of this index, the higher the net profit created by the financial holding group per unit asset, and the more economic benefits it has achieved. If the value of this index is smaller, it means that the financial holding group's operating results are contrary, and it needs to be improved in terms of generating income, reducing costs, and improving the efficiency of capital use. This index can urge the management of financial institutions to pay attention to the efficiency-creating ability of each unit of assets, optimize the refined management of increasing income and reducing costs, and promote the efficiency improvement.

3. Net profit

Net profit (MF 2021), also called after-tax profit, refers to the total profit realized by a financial holding group within a certain operating period after deducting income tax. Income tax refers to the tax paid by financial holding groups to relevant tax authorities in accordance with the standards for calculating tax rates stipulated in the national tax law.

4. Non-interest income

It is presented in Sect. 4.3.5.

#### 4.3.4.2 Indicators of Business Growth

The indicators mainly include the rate of return on economic added value, growth rate of business income, growth rate of net profit, which come from the income statement in the financial statements.

1. The rate of return on economic added value

The rate of return on economic added value is an important indicator in the performance evaluation system of financial holding groups, and it is explained in Sect. 4.4.

2. Growth rate of business income

Growth rate of business income (MF 2021) reflects the ratio of the increase in operating income realized by the financial holding group this year to that of the previous year. It is also an important indicator to evaluate the operation and development of financial holding groups, market share and the future development trend of financial holding groups.

3. Growth rate of net profit

Growth rate of net profit (MF 2021) is the ratio of net profit increase realized by the financial holding group this year to net profit of the previous year and is an important indicator to evaluate the profitability of the financial holding group within a certain operating period.

#### 4.3.4.3 Indicators of Solvency

The indicators of solvency include the capital adequacy ratio, the core capital adequacy ratio, and the asset-liability ratio, which mainly originate from non-financial statements.

1. Capital adequacy ratio

The capital adequacy ratio (CBRC 2005) is the percentage ratio between the total net capital and the total risk-weighted assets of financial institutions within a certain operating period and is the specific value of the ratio that must be achieved to ensure the normal operation and development of financial institutions of commercial banks. This ratio shows that if a financial institution loses money due to market risk and credit risk, operational risk and so forth, then this financial institution can use its own capital to absorb the losses. The financial supervision departments of various countries usually attach great importance to the capital management of financial institutions, and clearly stipulate the capital adequacy requirements of different types of financial institutions and the punishment measures for non-compliance. According to the regulatory requirements of the China Banking Regulatory Commission, the capital adequacy ratio of commercial banks should not be less than 8%.

Besides, the definitions and calculation methods of core capital, deduction of core capital, risk-weighted assets and market risk capital shall be implemented in accordance with the "Measures for the Administration of Capital Adequacy Ratio of Commercial Banks" (China Banking Regulatory Commission Decree No.2 of 2004) and relevant laws and regulations.

2. Core capital adequacy ratio

The core capital adequacy ratio (CBRC 2005) is the ratio between the core capital of financial institutions and the total value of weighted risk assets at the end of the year. According to the regulatory requirements of the China Banking Regulatory Commission, core capital adequacy ratio of commercial banks should not be less than 4%.

The Measures for the Administration of Capital Adequacy Ratio of Commercial Banks formulated by the financial supervision and management department clearly stipulates the specific definitions and calculation formulas of risk-weighted assets, market risk capital and other indicators used in calculating capital adequacy ratio (CBRC 2005).

3. Asset-liability ratio

The Asset-liability ratio (MF 2021) refers to refers to the ratio between the total liabilities and the total assets held by a financial holding group in the balance sheet through accounting. This index can reflect the level of the financial holding group's daily operation and effective use of funds by using the creditor's funds and can also be used to check whether the financial operation and management of the financial holding group can remain stable.

#### 4.3.4.4 Indicators of Asset Quality

The asset quality index of a financial holding group reflects the security degree of the assets held by a financial holding group and can reflect the ability to manage and dispose of the risky loans and other assets held by a financial holding group, to recover the economic losses as much as possible. The asset quality evaluation index mainly comes from the information of balance sheet and non-financial statements in financial statements. This kind of index is mainly evaluated by indicators such as non-performing loan ratio.

1. Non-performing loan ratio

The Non-performing loan ratio (CBRC 2005) refers to the percentage ratio of non-performing loan balance and various loan balances in a certain period of operation of a financial holding group, which is mainly derived from non-financial statement information.

According to the classification standards in the "Notice on Promoting and Perfecting the Classification of Loan Risks" issued by the China Banking Regulatory Commission, non-performing loans are classified into five categories, ranging from normal loans, noteworthy loans, secondary loans, doubtful loans, and loans brought about losses. Among them, the latter three categories of loans can be classified as non-performing loans. At present, the main profit source of commercial banks is still the interest income of loans, and its risk management directly determines the profit level and the sustainable development ability of commercial banks in the future. The higher the non-performing loan ratio, the larger the loan number of financial institutions classified into the last three categories according to the five-level classification. It is expected that the greater the percentage ratio between the loans that cannot be repaid in the future and the total loans, the stronger the risk management ability of loans. The lower the non-performing loan ratio, the stronger the risk management ability of loans.

2. Provision coverage ratio

Provision coverage ratio (CBRC 2005) is the percentage ratio of loan loss provision and non-performing loans withdrawn by a financial holding group during a period of operation. The provision coverage ratio is an important indicator to evaluate the adequacy of loan loss provisions withdrawn by financial institutions. If the provision coverage ratio of financial holding groups is sufficient, then the financial situation is relatively stable and the risks are under control, which shows that it has the capability of risk defense.

3. The adequacy ratio provisions for loan losses

The adequacy ratio provisions for loan losses (CBRC 2005) is the ratio of the actual provision and the provision to be made for loans of financial holding groups. Loan loss provision refers to the difference between the book amount of a loan issued by a financial institution and the present value of the estimated repayment amount of the loan in the future. According to the requirements of the regulatory system, financial institutions need to accrue loan loss reserve according to the risk classification results of each loan. When judging the risk classification results, they need to comprehensively consider the loan repayment ability and collateral of loan enterprises or individuals, and comprehensively judge the risk status of the business.

#### 4.3.4.5 Indicators of Business Management

The business management indicators can reflect the results achieved by financial holding groups through the adoption of management measures. These indicators can help investors to know more about the operation and management of a financial institution within a certain period of operation to estimate the future development trend of the financial holding group's operation performance and make reasonable business choices according to the current situation and predictions. Indicators of business management status mainly come from the income statement and non-financial statement information in financial statements.

1. Cost-to-income ratio

The Cost-to-income ratio (MF 2021) is the proportion of operating expenses that a financial holding group spends relative to the operating income that it obtains during a certain operating period. It reflects the amount of operating expenses that a financial holding group needs to spend for each yuan of operating income. The higher the cost-to-income ratio index is, the weaker the financial holding group's ability to obtain operating income will be and the higher the operating expenses it needs to spend to obtain operating income each yuan. On the contrary, it shows that the financial holding group has a strong ability to obtain operating income. Therefore, the cost-to-income ratio is the main reference index to evaluate the profitability of a financial holding group.

2. Earnings per share

Earnings per share (MF 2021) is an indicator specially used to analyze the financial situation of listed enterprises and can be used to evaluate the management performance and management effect of financial holding groups. Earnings per share includes basic earnings per share and diluted earnings per share. This research adopts the commonly used basic earnings per share. Investors often use basic earnings per share to assess the profitability of common shares of financial holding groups and the risk level corresponding to investments during a certain period of operation.

### *4.3.5 Differences from Traditional Commercial Bank Evaluation*

Non-interest income index is added in the process of evaluating financial holding groups, which is the main difference from the main evaluation indexes of traditional commercial banks.

Non-interest income (Xu 2012) refers to the part of the operating income obtained by a financial holding group within a certain operating period and this income excludes the margin income of loan and deposit. The main sources of non-interest income are intermediate business income, such as financial management fees, and income obtained from engaging in financial market business, investment business, and enterprise consulting.

For a long time, interest rates in China have been controlled by the government. For instance, interest rates for deposits and loans are determined and promulgated by the People's Bank of China, and commercial banks carry out the policy. Therefore, most of the operating income and profits of China's financial institutions, especially commercial banks, are derived from the income generated by the spread between deposits and loans, and the non-interest income. The non-interest income, such as intermediate business income and investment business income, accounts for a very low proportion of operating income. Compared with non-interest income, deposit and loan interest income has greater volatility and it is mainly affected by two aspects. The adjustment of deposit and loan interest rates has a greater impact on the deposit and loan interest income. Additionally, the fluctuation of the economic cycle, particularly during downturns, can quickly expose the risk of credit business, leading to an increase in the non-performing loan rate and a reduction in profits. Non-interest income is less affected by the shock of business cycle, and its source will not be obtained by consuming the bank's risky assets and capital, so this index can reflect the ability of a commercial bank to implement light capitalization operation and management. Light capitalization operation is to strengthen the management of capital-saving mode, reduce the proportion of businesses with more capital occupation, and improve the return level of capital. Therefore, in recent years, China's commercial banks have gradually increased the distribution and expansion of non-interest income business, which has become an important strategic choice for the transformation and development of commercial banks.

In recent years, the People's Bank of China and CSRC have accelerated the marketization reform of interest rates and capital, and the spread between deposits and loans has declined, which has a great impact on the traditional commercial banks that obtain the main sources of income and profits through the deposit-loan spreads. This traditional business model of commercial banks has been greatly challenged, and the situation of creating non-interest income has become an important symbol to measure commercial banks' ability to enhance business innovation and promote business transformation and development (Wei 2012). At the same time, increasing non-interest income of commercial banks can also promote the development of business diversification, reduce the impact on the fluctuation of interest rate difference between deposits and loans, and help consolidate and enhance the overall ability to earn net profits (Su and Wang 2014). Therefore, non-interest income is included in the evaluation index as an important indicator reflecting the degree and level of diversified development of bank financial holding groups.

## 4.4 Performance Evaluation Introducing the Economic Value Added EVA Model

### *4.4.1 Economic Value Added*

Economic value added (Cheng and Zhou 2012), also called EVA for short, is a tool to analyze and evaluate the business operation.

Economic added value refers to the remaining part of the after-tax net profit realized by financial holding groups after deducting the opportunity cost occupied by investors' investment capital in a certain operating period. EVA is the core index of the EVA model evaluation system. The most outstanding characteristic of the EVA index is to redefine the net profit of financial holding group from the perspective of investors and the profit is not traditional accounting profit, but economic profit. Because capital investment of investors will create opportunity cost, when the net profit created by financial holding groups is lower than the capital cost of investors, it cannot create value for shareholders. The economic value-added index can comprehensively measure the level of value created for shareholders by the management supervisors using the existing capital invested by investors in the financial holding group. In addition, the EVA index can effectively prevent the managers of financial enterprises from making management decisions for short-term benefits, which is more conducive to the long-term and sustainable development of financial holding groups. It can be expressed as follows.

$$\mathbf{EVA = netoperatingprofitaftertax(NOPAT) - costofcapital(COC)} \tag{4.1}$$

$$\mathbf{Costofcapital = totalcapital(TC) \times weightedaveragecostofcapital(C\%)} \tag{4.2}$$

Based on the income statement disclosed by the financial holding group, net operating profit after tax can be calculated.

Total capital (TC) is the capital invested in financial holding groups, including debt capital and equity capital.

The weighted average cost of capital (C%) represents the overall cost of capital invested in the financial holding group. The cost of capital includes two types. One is the cost of debt capital, that is, the interest rate corresponding to debt capital such as bonds undertaken by financial holding groups; The other is the cost of equity capital, that is, the expected level of return on capital put forward by shareholders investing in financial holding groups. The calculation formula is as follows.

$$\begin{aligned}&\mathbf{Weightedaveragecostofcapital(C)\%}\\&\mathbf{= theproportionofequitycapital \times costratioofequitycapital}\\&\mathbf{+costratioofdebtcapital \times (1 - incometaxrate)}\\&\mathbf{\times theproportionofdebtcapital}\end{aligned} \tag{4.3}$$

According to previous literature research (MF 2021), there are usually three methods to determine the weighted average cost of capital, the current one-year deposit interest rate of commercial banks, the current five-year treasury bond interest rate and the one-year liquidity loan interest rate. The "Measures for the Performance Evaluation of Financial Enterprises" (MF 2016) calculates the cost of capital according to the one-year liquidity loan interest rate published by the People's Bank of China in the year. If the interest rate has been adjusted once or several times within one year, the average implementation interest rate will be weighted according to the actual interest rates implemented at different time intervals within that year. This method is used in this book.

### *4.4.2 Return on Economic Value Added*

The return on economic value added (Cheng and Zhou 2012) refers to the ratio of economic value added, and economic capital realized by financial holding groups within a certain period, reflecting the financial holding groups' ability to create value by using capital, that means the value created by total capital per 1 yuan. The higher the ratio, the better the financial holding group's ability to create value, and vice versa.

### *4.4.3 Comparison of the Economic Value Added Model and Traditional Performance Evaluation Indicators*

The traditional performance evaluation is mainly an evaluation index system centered on profit or return on net assets. On this basis, the economic added value model considers all costs, long-term goals. The two evaluation methods are compared as follows.

1. The shortcomings of traditional performance evaluation

There are two types of traditional indicators used in performance appraisal and evaluation of financial institutions. One type focuses on the evaluation of profit, with specific indicators including net profit, cost and expense profit rate, return on assets, and other indicators closely related to the creation of net profit. The other type centers on the evaluation of the ROE index, where the main approach is to conduct reasoning and deduction based on the calculation formula logic of financial institutions' ROE, decomposing it into various business indicators to compare the business performance of enterprises.

The major shortcomings of traditional performance evaluation are as follows.

The traditional performance evaluation index is mainly focused on profit index and cannot measure the value created for shareholders. The net profit is an accounting profit which does not consider the opportunity cost of the capital invested by investors.

It cannot completely cover the cost range of financial enterprises, nor can it accurately measure whether the financial holding group creates value for shareholders and how much value it creates.

The traditional performance evaluation index is based on financial statements and has a certain distortion. The ratios of profits to cost, asset return rate, return on equity and other indicators are calculated in the light of the financial statements of the financial holding group. Compared with the operation and management indicators, the financial indicators calculated according to the financial statements that are made in accordance with the accounting standards have a certain distortion. For instance, setting the index of return on equity only takes debt capital into account, but does not take equity capital into account. The cost of debt capital is deducted, but the capital cost corresponding to equity capital is not deducted.

Managers tend to pursue short-term behavior rather than long-term development if they follow the traditional performance evaluation indexes. Net profit and other indicators are calculated according to accounting standards, which may be manipulated by managers to maximize short-term profits that is inconsistent with or quite different from the actual situation of the financial holding group. Therefore, the traditional performance evaluation index with profit as the core, may guide managers of financial holding groups to pursue the maximization of short-term interests, while ignoring the maximization of shareholders' interests, which is not conducive to the long-term development of financial holding groups and the sustainable development of financial enterprises.

2. Advantages of economic value added model evaluation

Compared with traditional performance evaluation methods, the EVA model evaluation method is a more objective and comprehensive method to reflect the real performance of financial holding groups and it reflects the value creation ability of financial holding groups (Li 2019). The main advantages of the EVA model evaluation method are as follows.

It considers all costs. Different from traditional performance evaluation indexes such as net profit, ratio of profits to cost, return on asset and return on equity, the economic value added model includes the cost of capital invested by investors in terms of cost expenditure. And the scope of the expenditure cost is more comprehensive, which reflects the interests of investors. The application of the EVA model evaluation method enables managers of financial holding groups to realize that there is an opportunity cost in using investors' capital in their daily operations. It also reminds them to use of investors' capital investment more effectively. Net income shown in the financial statement is not the final profits created by companies. The true value excludes the cost of debt capital and the cost of capital of investors.

The accounting distortion is taken into consideration. As the basic principle for accounting work, "Generally Accepted Accounting Principles" (MF 2014) accounts for interest expenses operating income and net profit of financial holding groups within a certain operating period from an accounting perspective, but do not consider the interests of shareholders. In terms of internal operating performance management, the EVA model method makes certain adjustments to the financial holding group's income statement and balance sheet. And it maximizes interests and value creation of investors. It is incorporated into the operating performance evaluation index system, which is conducive to objective evaluation of the financial holding group's performance.

It pays attention to long-term goals. Compared with the traditional performance evaluation index with net profit as the core, the EVA model evaluation method can combine the interests of investors, consider the opportunity cost of investment capital, and set more explicit and long-term operational objectives for financial holding groups. The increase in economic value added reflects the value growth of financial holding groups. The long-term increase in economic value added reflects the long-term value growth of financial enterprises, which embodies the target of value maximization and is conducive to main long-term and sustainable development of the financial holding group.

## 4.5 Steps to Implement Business Performance Evaluation

### *4.5.1 Research Hypotheis Setting*

The research object of this book is the financial holding group. Combined with previous literature, it is hypothesized that the financial holding group has a positive effect on the improvement of the overall operating performance, profitability, solvency, and cost control.

### *4.5.2 Conduct Performance Evaluation Data Analysis*

When carrying out Factor Analysis, the original variables of different indicators may have different data values because of their different dimensions, which is not conducive to comparative analysis of correlation between indicator variables. To facilitate factor analysis, it is necessary to standardize the original data. In this book, IBM SPSS® statistical analysis software is used for standardization.

### *4.5.3 Reliability and Validity of Questionnaire*

The "Dimension Reduction" function module in statistical software has the function of factor analysis. In this study, two types of model tests are carried out on 15 original variables such as capital adequacy ratio by using the analysis and test models of relevant modules in IBM SPSS statistical analysis software, one is KMO model test, the other is Bartlett sphere model test.

If the conclusions drawn from the above two models meet the requirements of factor analysis, it means that there is correlation between the 15 original variables, which is suitable for factor analysis. Through KMO model test, it is concluded that KMO measurement value is not less than or equal to 0.7. At the same time, it meets the test of Bartlett sphere model, and the measured value meets the standard of approximate chi-square and value.

### 4.5.4 *The Empirical Analysis Process of Performance Evaluation of Financial Holding Groups*

In the process of factor analysis, the key step to ensure the smooth implementation of factor analysis is to calculate the factor load matrix according to the collected sample data. There are seven methods to extract factors from original variables in statistical software, among which principal component analysis is the most used method. In this book, the principal component analysis method is used for analysis (see Fig. 4.2 for the process diagram of factor analysis).

In the process of factor extraction, eigenvalue criterion and gravel test criterion are adopted. To better analyze the results of the factor analysis solution, it is often necessary to decompose the factor load into a form that is easier to explain. The commonly used methods are the varimax procedure and the oblique rotation. The load matrix is formed by maximizing the variance of each factor. This method is helpful to obtain the arrangement and combination of factors of each original variable and further construct the factor analysis model. Evaluate and analyze the sample data by factor analysis model.

## 4.6 Summary of This Chapter

This chapterintroduces the five method of business performance evaluation and the research method adopted in this book. Based on the comparative analysis of the advantages and disadvantages of the main operating performance evaluation methods in the early stage, combined with the actual situation of China's financial holding groups, this research uses factor analysis to conduct an empirical study on operating performance. Then, the collection of data needed for research is introduced, including the selection of samples and the collection of sample data. Among them, the sample is mainly selected from 13 banking financial holding groups, and the data period of the sample is five years, Thirdly, the selection of evaluation indexes is described. This research selects 15 important evaluation indexes and regards non-interest income and other indexes as the differences between financial holding groups and traditional commercial banks' performance evaluation indexes. At the end of this chapter, the

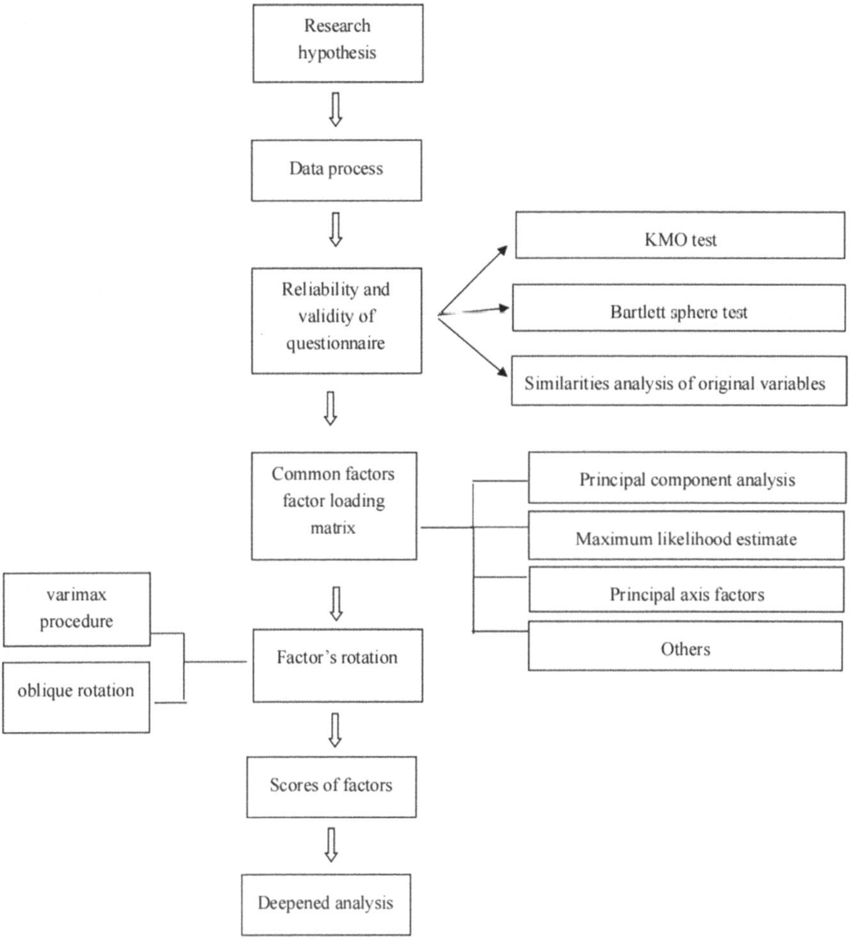


**Fig. 4.2** For the process diagram of factor analysis

EVA model is introduced in the evaluation index. The fifth chapter will introduce the research results and analysis.

# Chapter 5
# Research Results and Analysis

## 5.1 Research Hypotheses

According to the theories of scale economy, risk diversification and scope economy, hypotheses of the relationship between integrated operation and profitability, risk offset, cost control, and operation performance are put forward in this research with the combination of research documents of previous scholars.

### *5.1.1 Hypothesis of Integrated Operation and Profitability*

Scale economy theory shows that with the expansion of scale, the average cost decreases, and the return on scale increases, thus the income and competitiveness increase.

Williams (1985) thinks that the financial industry, featured by low asset specificity, has greater potential of scale economy and obvious effect of increasing returns on scale. Saunders and Walter (1994) point that because of the incomplete correlation of cash flows among financial businesses, financial institutions can maintain the stability of profits by strengthening portfolio management after diversified operations. Vander (1998) finds that the combination of banking, securities and insurance business of financial institutions can reduce the average cost and bring economies of scale. Adopting the mode of financial holding group to implement diversified operation can promote the operation speed and quality of the financial system. Vennet (1999) shows that financial groups and universal banks have stronger profitability than single banks.

Based on all above, this book puts forward research hypobook 1: the implementation of integrated management has a positive impact on the profitability of Chinese financial holding groups.

 
X. Ning, *Performance Evaluation of Financial Holding Companies*,
https://doi.org/10.1007/978-981-97-8128-7_5

### 5.1.2 Hypothesis of Integrated Operation and Solvency

According to the risk dispersion theory, financial institutions, especially financial holding groups, can provide customers with comprehensive financial services by implementing diversified operations. Under the uncertain business environment, it is easier to obtain stable profits than a single professional financial institution, which plays the role of hedging and reducing risks. By carrying out asset portfolio management and matching the businesses of different professional financial institutions, the purpose of dispersing and reducing risks and stabilizing returns can be achieved.

Bensen (1990) points that diversification of financial institutions is conducive to risk profile and risk reduction. Saunders and Walter (1994) think that diversified businesses of financial holding groups can generate relatively stable profit sources, cash flow and reduce the risk of expansion. Song (2012) shows that banks can achieve the goal of risk diversification through diversified business development after comprehensive financial management.

Therefore, the hypobook 2 is put forward: the implementation of integrated management has a positive impact on the solvency of China's financial companies.

### 5.1.3 Hypothesis of Integrated Operation and Cost Control

The theory of scope economy holds that According to the theory of scope economy, under the premise of keeping the production technology and equipment unchanged, when manufacturers provide different kinds of products by expanding the scope of production operations and services, the cost paid is lower than the sum of the costs when products are provided separately. Compared with non-financial assets, financial assets have more commonality and can be linked with each other. Financial institutions can achieve scope economy and reduce operating costs faster by expanding their business scope and implementing diversified and integrated business models.

Steinheer and Huveneers (1990) think that universal banks, compared with a single bank, have the characteristics of diversified products, and can obtain economies of scope. They can reduce costs by allocating customers' fixed costs to diversified financial products. Llewellyn (1996) points out that financial holding groups can use the existing marketing channels of their commercial banks to sell all kinds of financial products and reduce unit costs, that is, there is scope economy effect. So, hypobook 3 is put forward: the implementation of integrated management has a positive impact on the improvement of cost control capability of China's financial holding groups.

### 5.1.4 Hypothesis of Integrated Operation and Business Performance

It is known from the previous scholarly literature that most of studies support that business diversification is positively related to business performance.

Barth et al. (2000) selected 142 commercial banks from 19 EU countries and the Group of Ten as research samples, and through comparative analysis, the results showed that the commercial banks that carried out securities and insurance business performed better than those that restricted them. Reinvaded (1993) inspected some typical banks in Europe. The research showed that the income efficiency of financial holding groups was higher than that of professional financial institutions, and the cost efficiency of all-round banks was better than that of professional financial institutions. Schaeck (2008) thought that financial institutions can design and provide customers with comprehensive financial services covering deposit and loan business, securities investment and listing counseling, personal health insurance and property loss insurance and so forth, and promote the improvement of financial institutions' operating performance. Making an empirical study on Croatia's financial market, Pervan (2012) finds that financial holding groups could promote the improvement of business performance through diversified business operations.

According to the above studies, hypobook 4 is stated: the implementation of integrated management has a positive impact on the improvement of the operating performance of China's financial holding groups.

### 5.1.5 Summary of Research Hypotheses

To sum up, according to the scale economy theory, risk diversification theory, scope economy theory and other relevant documents, four research hypotheses are put forward, as shown in Table 5.1.

**Table 5.1** Summary of research hypotheses

| Serial number | Research hypotheses |
|---|---|
| 1 | The implementation of integrated management has a positive impact on the profitability of China's financial holding groups |
| 2 | The implementation of integrated management has a positive impact on the solvency of China's financial holding groups |
| 3 | The implementation of integrated management has a positive impact on the cost control of China's financial holding groups |
| 4 | The implementation of integrated management has a positive impact on the business performance of China's financial holding groups |

To verify the rationality of the research hypotheses, empirical research will be carried out. In this book, the five-year (2014–2018) listing disclosure annual reports and financial accounting reports of 13 banking financial holding groups are chosen as the foundation of the study, and they are classified into three groups based on the number of financial licenses held by the 13 banking financial holding groups. Return on economic added value, return on net assets and other 15 important indicators are chosen as performance evaluation indicators of financial holding groups. Factor analysis method will be used in this research and the chi-square test model will be used to verify the four research hypotheses.

## 5.2 Conduct Performance Evaluation Data Analysis

The factor analysis method is a statistical method that analyzes various original variables by adopting factor analysis model. It integrates some original variables with complex relationships, summarizes and simplifies them into several representative common factors, and then analyzes them.

There are many kinds of statistical analysis software to carry out factor analysis, among which the main quantitative analysis software is SPSS, Stata, SAS (Pan 2015). Based on relative literatures, we can know that the advantage of SPSS lies in carrying out factor analysis by combing and comparing the advantages and disadvantages of SPSS, Stata, SAS, and other software. Combined with the actual performance evaluation of China's financial holding business, this research uses IBM SPSS® 21st edition statistical analysis software developed by IBM to carry out factor analysis, cluster analysis and Chi-square test model verification. The main advantages and disadvantages of statistical analysis software is shown in Annex X.

The main idea of the factor analysis method is classification and refinement. Many original variables are classified. The criterion of classification is the degree of correlation between the original variables. The correlation between the original variables that are classified as different types is very low, and the correlation between the original variables of the same type is very high. Representative factors are extracted from each kind of original variables. After summarizing and extracting, the original variables of each class are representative factors, that is, common factors. Factor analysis method is used to simplify many original variables to form a few simplified representative factors and analyze them. Before factor analysis is carried out by statistical analysis software, some original variables should be processed positively, and the original data should be standardized.

### 5.2.1 Index Forward Processing of Performance Evaluation

In the process of comprehensive evaluation of multiple operating indicators of financial holding groups, according to the logical relationship between operating indicators and evaluation results, indicators can be divided into positive index, reverse index, and moderate index.

To be more specific, the greater the value of the index, the more positive the evaluation of the results. This index is called a positive index, also known as a benefit index. Conversely, the smaller the value of the index, the more positive the evaluation of the results. This operational index is called a reverse index, also known as a cost index. At last, if the value of an index is closer to a certain value and the evaluation of the result is more positive when that happens, then the index is called a moderate index.

Because the values of benefit indicators (positive indicators) and cost indicators (negative indicators) have opposite changed directions, to facilitate statistical analysis and ensure the rationality of the results, it is necessary to treat business indicators in the same direction before comprehensive evaluation. The usual method is to change the cost index into the same trend as the benefit index (Ye 2003). In practical applications, reciprocal inverse transformation method is frequently used by many scholars, that is a method of taking the reciprocal of the inverse index.

Fifteen indicators are selected in this research, and they are divided into positive index, reverse index, and moderate index. Since the numerical trends of reverse index, moderate index and positive index are quite different, it is necessary to treat the numerical values of reverse index and moderate index in the same direction, and the treatment methods are shown in Annex Y.

1. Positive indexes. They do not need to be processed. Positive indexes include ten indicators such as the capital adequacy ratio ($X_1$), tier-one leverage capital ($X_2$), the rate of return on economic added value ($X_4$), the rate of return on net assets ($X_5$), the return on equity ($X_6$), net profit ($X_7$), non-interest income ($X_8$), the provision coverage ratio ($X_{11}$) and the adequacy ratio provisions for loan losses ($X_{12}$).
2. Reverse indexes. The cost income ratio ($X_9$) and the non-performing loan ratio ($X_{10}$) belong to reverse indexes. The inverse of the reverse index is used for forward processing.
3. Moderate indexes. Only the asset-liability ratio ($X_3$) is included in the moderate index. Since the China Banking Regulatory Commission has cancelled the regulatory requirements on the asset-liability ratio and other indicators (the National People's Congress Standing Committee [NPCSC] 2015), the indicator will not be processed for the time being.

### *5.2.2 Standardization of Raw Data for Performance Evaluation*

After the forward processing, the original data needs to be standardized. Due to the different dimensions of the different index variables, there may be great differences in the numerical performance of index variables. To eliminate the influence of different index variables on factor analysis caused by dimensional differences and facilitate correlation comparison analysis between index variables, the original data need to be standardized before factor analysis is carried out. For example, the indicators such as net profit, non-interest income, provision coverage rate and loan loss reserve adequacy ratio adopted in this research have dimensional differences with other index variables, and the data values of this index are quite different from those of other index variables.

At present, the most used method to eliminate dimensions is the standardization method. With the function of standardization processing, statistical software can automatically deal with the original data.

## 5.3 Reliability Analysis and Validity Analysis

Reliability analysis and validity analysis are required before carrying out statistical analysis research work. Reliability analysis tests the credibility of the data and validity analysis tests the validity of the data. It is meaningful to carry out statistical analysis only if it is ensured that the data meets the requirements of reliability analysis and validity analysis. Factor analysis method is one of the commonly used methods for statistical analysis of data, which requires a higher degree of credibility and validity of the data.

### *5.3.1 Reliability Analysis*

Reliability analysis is a test of the reliability and veracity of the results of the selected sample answers. Statistical software can be used to implement the reliability analysis. The sample selected in this book is composed of listed financial holding groups, and the source of sample data is the annual disclosure reports of listed companies. Enterprise Accounting Standards—Basic Standards (MF 2014) issued by the Ministry of Finance and Measures for the Administration of Information Disclosure of Listed Companies issued (CSRC 2021) by the China Securities Regulatory Commission have made clear requirements on information disclosure and the quality of annual financial reports of listed companies to ensure the reliability and authenticity of the sample data, and this book will not carry out the reliability analysis of the sample data. Annex Z shows the data sources of evaluation indicators used in this book.

#### 5.3.1.1 Quality Requirements of Accounting Information of Listed Group

The 13 financial holding groups selected for this research are all enterprises. So, the financial reports issued by the 13 financial holding groups are required to comply with the basic requirements present in the Basic Accounting Standards for Enterprises—Basic Standards issued by the Ministry of Finance for accounting and quality assurance of enterprise accounting information.

The Accounting Standards for Business Enterprises—Basic Standards (MF 2014) specifies the accounting rules for businesses, which is promulgated and implemented in the form of laws. It mainly includes seven principles.

Principle of reliability. A financial holding group should recognize, account for and report transactions based on the contract and the actual financial business transactions. Accounting elements and information related with financial business transactions should be reflected completely and they must be measured accurately to ensure the reliability of accounting information.

Principle of relevance. Users of financial reports, such as investors of financial holding groups and analysts can assess the operation of financial holding groups through financial report information.

Principle of understandability. The content of financial reports should be easy-to-understood and clear, which enables investors and other users of financial reports to understand the content correctly. It is conducive to investors to use financial reports conveniently and quickly.

Principle of comparability and consists of two aspects. First, the accounting information in the financial reports of the same financial holding group for different accounting periods can be compared. Second, the accounting information in the financial reports of different financial holding groups in the same accounting period can be compared.

Principle of substance is more important than form. The sixth is the principle of importance. The seventh is the principle of prudence. The last one is time-based principle.

#### 5.3.1.2 Disclosed Requirements of Listed Companies' Information

The 13 financial holding groups selected in this book are all financial enterprises that have been listed on A shares or H shares in China for many years. As listed companies, 13 financial holding groups need to disclose their annual and quarterly financial reports regularly and irregularly according to the quality standards and format specifications specified in the Administrative Measures on Information Disclosure of Listed Companies (CSRC 2021). Based on the accounting standards for enterprises, higher requirements such as reliability, authenticity and timeliness are further put forward.

This method (CSRC 2021) further refines the responsibilities and obligations that listed companies need to perform in information disclosure, further improves the disclosure system of periodic reports, the audit of the contents of external disclosure reports, and the quality of disclosed information, and greatly increases the legal responsibilities and costs that need to be borne due to inadequate performance of duties, so as to ensure the quality of information disclosure.

In view of the laws, regulations, and China Securities Regulatory Commission's explicit provisions on the obligations of information disclosure persons, regular disclosure reporting system and annual report auditing of listed financial holding groups, the authenticity, accuracy, and completeness of the annual report are guaranteed. This book intends to use the annual reports of 13 listed financial holding groups for research and analysis.

### 5.3.2 *Validity Analysis*

Validity analysis is mainly used to judge the validity and accuracy of the designed questionnaire and to measure the rationality of the design of test questions. In this book, through the dimension reduction function of IBM SPSS® statistical software, KMO test and Bartlett sphere test are carried out on the variables in the model, and the KMO value and Sig. values are generated by the test model respectively, to determine whether the 15 original variables of the selected 13 financial holding groups are suitable for factor analysis.

#### 5.3.2.1 KMO Test

KMO test is a model for testing the suitability of 13 samples extracted from all financial holding groups (Zhang 2016). This model mainly tests the linear correlation coefficient and partial correlation coefficient between 15 original variables extracted from 13 financial holding groups.

Combined with the frequently used measurement standard of the KMO test model, there are four situations. If the value is above 0.7, it means that the original variable is suitable for factor analysis. If the value is between 0.6 and 0.7, it means that the original variable is barely suitable for factor analysis. If the value is between 0.5 and 0.6, it means that the original variable is not suitable for factor analysis. If the value is below 0.5, it means that the original variable is extremely unsuitable for factor analysis.

Through the dimension reduction function in the statistical software, the KMO test is carried out on the 15 original variables of the 13 financial holding groups in the model. Annex AA shows the KMO and Bartlett test results. As can be seen from the table above, the KMO measurement value is 0.712. According to the KMO measurement standard proposed by Kaiser, the value of KMO is greater than 0.7, which means these 15 original factors are suitable for factor analysis.

#### 5.3.2.2 Bartlett Sphere Test

The Bartlett sphere test can be used to test the correlation between the 15 original variables of the 13 financial holding groups in the corresponding matrix.

The Bartlett sphere test uses the correlation coefficient matrix between the original variables as the basis for judging the degree of independence of the related variables and considers that the correlation coefficient matrix is the identity matrix as a prerequisite. If the correlation matrix between the original variables is shown as identity matrix, it shows that there is no dependency between the original variables, and it also shows that representative common factors cannot be extracted from this group of original variables, so it is impossible to carry out factor analysis. On the contrary, factor analysis can be carried out.

If the significant level p-value is less than 0.05, it means that the original variables have statistical significance and are suitable for factor analysis; otherwise, it means that the original variables are not suitable for factor analysis. And the smaller the significance level between the original variables, the more significant the correlation is.

From the results of the Bartlett test shown in Annex AA, the approximate chi-square is 1350.517 and the Sig. value is 0.000. The approximate chi-square value is relatively large, and the Sig. value is < 0.05 (the $p$ value is < 0.05), indicating that the test results for the 15 original variables reject the null hypobook. It also shows that the significant level of the original variables is extremely small, and these variables have statistical meaning, which indicates that they are suitable for factor analysis.

### *5.3.3 Commonalities Test of the Original Variables*

The commonality of the original variable reflects the degree to which all common factors explain the variance of the original variable. It is generally believed that if the commonality of original variables is above 0.4, then such original variables have statistical significance, while if the commonality of the original variables is less than 0.4, such original variables have no statistical significance and needs to be deleted in the study.

In this study, by using statistical analysis software and principal component analysis method, the variables' commonalities table is extracted and generated (see Table 5.2 for details). It can be seen from Table 5.2 that the commonality of the selected 15 original variables is above 0.596, which is higher than 0.4, indicating statistical significance.

From Table 5.2, the section of variables communalities is sorted out and made into the communalities range table, presented in Table 5.3. It can be seen from Table 5.3 that among the 15 original variables selected in this book, 67% of them are in the range of 0.8 and 1, and 47% of them are in the range of 0.9 and 1, indicating that the extracted common factors have basically reflected more than 67% of the information of the original variables, and the commonality of the original variables

**Table 5.2** Communalities table

| Operation indicator | Original variables | Initial | After extraction |
|---|---|---|---|
| Capital adequacy rate | $X_1$ | 1 | 0.949 |
| Tier-one leverage capital | $X_2$ | 1 | 0.928 |
| Asset-liability ratio (after normalization) | $X_3$ | 1 | 0.873 |
| Net profit (after normalization) | $X_4$ | 1 | 0.911 |
| Non-interest income (after normalization) | $X_5$ | 1 | 0.914 |
| Rate of return on economic added value | $X_6$ | 1 | 0.938 |
| Return on equity | $X_7$ | 1 | 0.944 |
| Return on total assets | $X_8$ | 1 | 0.956 |
| Non-performing loan ratio (after normalization) | $X_9$ | 1 | 0.714 |
| Growth rate of total operating revenue | $X_{10}$ | 1 | 0.596 |
| Provision coverage ratio (after normalization) | $X_{11}$ | 1 | 0.848 |
| Provisions for loan losses (after normalization) | $X_{12}$ | 1 | 0.784 |
| Year-on-year growth rate of net profit | $X_{13}$ | 1 | 0.794 |
| Earnings per share | $X_{14}$ | 1 | 0.862 |
| Income-cost ratio (after normalization) | $X_{15}$ | 1 | 0.614 |

**Table 5.3** Communalities range

| Communalities range | Numbers of variables | Proportion (%) |
|---|---|---|
| 0.590–0.700 | 2 | 13.33 |
| 0.700–0.800 | 3 | 20.00 |
| 0.800–0.900 | 3 | 20.00 |
| 0.900–1 | 7 | 46.67 |
| Total | 15 | 100.00 |

is higher. The common degree of 15 original variables is high, which indicates that the original variables can be explained by common factors to a higher extent. After the 15 original variables are replaced by the common factors, the corresponding original variables are explained to a higher degree, and the effect of factor analysis using these 15 original variables is better.

## 5.4 The Empirical Analysis Process of Performance Evaluation of Financial Holding Groups

The decisive step of factor analysis method is to calculate the factor load matrix of sample data. Statistical analysis software can provide seven software calculation methods for refining common factors, among which principal component analysis is widely used. Principal Component Analysis (PCA) is a statistical analysis method, which changes and adjusts a group of variables that may have correlation, into a group of linear variables that do not have correlation through orthogonal transformation. After adjustment, the variables whose linearity is not correlated with each other are called principal components (Lin and Du 2013). This method is used in this research.

## *5.4.1 Factor Extraction*

The variance contribution of a common factor refers to the sum of squares of the load of the 15 original variables of the 13 financial holding groups, which reflects the explanatory power of the common factor to the 15 original variables. The explanation degree of the common factor to the 15 original variables can be obtained by calculating the sum of squares of the loads of the 15 original variables. The greater the variance contribution of a common factor, the greater the importance of it. There are two main methods to extract common factors, one is the eigenvalue criterion method, and the other is the gravel graph test criterion method.

### 5.4.1.1 Eigenvalue Criterion

The Eigenvalue criterion means to extract principal components from the original variables as initial factors that will be decided to extract or discard according to the eigenvalues.

To be more specific, if the eigenvalue of the principal component is greater than or equal to 1, it should be taken as the initial factor while if the eigenvalue of the principal component is less than 1, it should be discarded. The larger the variance contribution of the extracted single principal component factor is, the more important the corresponding factor is. The total value of variance contribution of the whole principal component factor should usually exceed 70%. According to the variance contribution ratio of the factors from high to low, public factors with high importance can be extracted.

In this book, the factors are extracted from the original variables by using statistical analysis software, and the eigenvalues and contribution ratios of the correlation coefficient matrix are calculated. See Table 5.4 for details. From the table, four initial eigenvalues larger than one can be obtained. The initial eigenvalues are 5.485, 4.608, 1.361 and 1.172, and the variance contribution are 36.57%, 30.72%, 9.08% and 7.82%, respectively, with a total variance contribution of 84.19%. In general, if the cumulative variance contribution reaches 80%, the extracted factors can replace the original variables well, in principle. The cumulative variance contribution of the four factors extracted in this research reaches 84.185%, exceeding 80%, which shows that the four factors can well explain the operating performance of 13 sample financial holding groups from 2014 to 2018.

It is shown in Table 5.4 that the variance contribution of the first factor with the greatest information extraction ability is 36.57%, the variance contribution of the

**Table 5.4** The total variance table

| Component | Initial eigenvalue | | | Extraction sums of squared loadings | | |
|---|---|---|---|---|---|---|
| | Total | Variance (%) | Cumulative (%) | Components | Variance (%) | Cumulative (%) |
| 1 | 5.485 | 36.57 | 36.57 | 5.485 | 36.57 | 36.57 |
| 2 | 4.608 | 30.72 | 67.29 | 4.608 | 30.72 | 67.29 |
| 3 | 1.361 | 9.08 | 76.37 | 1.361 | 9.08 | 76.37 |
| 4 | 1.172 | 7.82 | 84.19 | 1.172 | 7.82 | 84.19 |
| 5 | 0.882 | 5.88 | 90.07 | | | |
| 6 | 0.462 | 3.08 | 93.15 | | | |
| 7 | 0.351 | 2.34 | 95.49 | | | |
| 8 | 0.318 | 2.12 | 97.61 | | | |
| 9 | 0.123 | 0.82 | 98.43 | | | |
| 10 | 0.108 | 0.72 | 99.15 | | | |
| 11 | 0.052 | 0.35 | 99.50 | | | |
| 12 | 0.033 | 0.22 | 99.72 | | | |
| 13 | 0.025 | 0.16 | 99.88 | | | |
| 14 | 0.011 | 0.07 | 99.95 | | | |
| 15 | 0.008 | 0.05 | 100.00 | | | |

second factor is 30.72%, the variance contribution of the third factor is 9.08%, and the variance contribution of the fourth factor is 7.82%. Through the proportion of variance contribution, it can be concluded that the first factor represents the largest amount of information and the highest degree of explanation. After rotation, the variance contribution of the first factor up to the fourth factor is 32.34%, 24.73%, 18.14% and 8.98% respectively, and the cumulative variance contribution is 84.19%, as shown in Table 5.5.

By rotation and loading, the structure of variables is simplified, which is conducive to comparative analysis and can better evaluate the operating performance level of financial holding groups. Extracting four factor representatives from fifteen original variables can help to achieve the purpose of dimension reduction.

**Table 5.5** Total explanation of variance

| Component | Rotate sum of squares load | | |
|---|---|---|---|
| | Total | Variance (%) | Accumulation (%) |
| 1 | 4.851 | 32.34 | 32.34 |
| 2 | 3.709 | 24.73 | 57.07 |
| 3 | 2.722 | 18.14 | 75.21 |
| 4 | 1.346 | 8.98 | 84.19 |

#### 5.4.1.2 Scree Test Criterion

According to the sequence of extracting factors, the criterion of scree test shows the eigenvalue change graph corresponding to different factors.

Scree plot can directly show the eigenvalue and cumulative variance contribution rate of different components. The horizontal axis coordinate in the gravel map represents the serial number of the extracted factor, that is, the number of components. The vertical axis coordinates represent characteristic values. The importance of the factor can be demonstrated by the gradient of the line segment in the drawn graph. It can be seen from Annex AB that the first four points with eigenvalues greater than 1 form a "cliff", and the remaining 11 points with eigenvalues less than 1 are like "gravel" on the edge of the "cliff", and the cumulative variance contribution rate of the first four eigenvalues is 84.19%.

### *5.4.2 Economic Significance of Rotating Component Load Matrix and Factors*

To better analyze the results of factor analysis, it is often necessary to decompose the factor load into a form that is easy to interpret.

#### 5.4.2.1 Rotating Component Load Matrix

The factor rotation aims to facilitate the conversion into an easy-to-explain form by rotating the coordinate axis of the factor.

There are two methods of factor rotation that are frequently used. One is the Varimax procedure, the other is Oblique Rotation. Varimax procedure can simplify the factor load matrix and concentrate the data of the original variables. After the Varimax procedure, the eigenvalues of common factors change, but the common degree remains unchanged (Zhen 1995).

The rotation method can change the load amount of each original variable in each factor and make it easier to explain the factor load amount. In this research, the load matrix is rotated by the Varimax method in statistical software, so that it is easier to define common factors. Table 5.6 shows it.

#### 5.4.2.2 Economic Significance of Common Factors

Rotating load matrix by the variance-maximum method of principal component analysis in IBM SPSS® statistical software, we can obtain a rotation elements matrix table (see Table 5.6). It is shown that the 15 original variables have higher loads on 4 factors, respectively:

**Table 5.6** The rotation matrix of the different components

| Operation indicators | Variables | Components | | | |
|---|---|---|---|---|---|
| | | 1 | 2 | 3 | 4 |
| Capital adequacy rate | $X_1$ | 0.964 | – 0.082 | 0.102 | 0.046 |
| Tier-one leverage capital | $X_2$ | 0.961 | – 0.032 | – 0.011 | 0.066 |
| Asset-liability ratio (after normalization) | $X_3$ | – 0.882 | 0.298 | 0.075 | 0.037 |
| Net profit (after normalization) | $X_4$ | 0.885 | 0.297 | – 0.197 | 0.029 |
| Non-interest income (after normalization) | $X_5$ | 0.91 | 0.183 | – 0.217 | 0.07 |
| Rate of return on economic added value | $X_6$ | – 0.064 | 0.927 | 0.213 | 0.17 |
| Return on total assets | $X_7$ | 0.442 | 0.846 | 0.165 | 0.072 |
| Return on equity | $X_8$ | – 0.16 | 0.914 | 0.277 | 0.133 |
| Non-performing loan ratio (after normalization) | $X_9$ | – 0.014 | 0.575 | 0.427 | – 0.449 |
| Growth rate of total operating revenue | $X_{10}$ | – 0.358 | 0.434 | 0.407 | – 0.338 |
| Provision coverage ratio (after normalization) | $X_{11}$ | 0.088 | 0.311 | 0.86 | 0.067 |
| Provisions for loan losses (after normalization) | $X_{12}$ | 0.045 | 0.599 | 0.635 | 0.141 |
| Year-on-year growth rate of net profit | $X_{13}$ | – 0.256 | 0.219 | 0.785 | – 0.255 |
| Earnings per share | $X_{14}$ | – 0.402 | 0.093 | 0.601 | 0.575 |
| Income-cost ratio (after normalization) | $X_{15}$ | 0.137 | 0.22 | – 0.04 | 0.739 |

1. Common factor $F_1$

The five original variables, such as capital adequacy ratio $X_1$, tier-one capital adequacy ratio $X_2$, asset-liability ratio $X_3$, net profit $X_4$ and non-interest income $X_5$, have higher loads on the first common factor, which are 0.964, 0.961, – 0.882, 0.885 and 0.910, respectively.

Among them, capital adequacy ratio $X_1$ reflects the strength of a financial holding group to use its own capital to make up for the loss gap if the assets of creditors suffer losses due to poor management. $X_1$ has the highest load in $F_1$. Tier-one capital adequacy ratio $X_2$ reflects the ability of core capital to bear risk-weighted asset losses. Asset-liability ratio $X_3$ is used to check the soundness of financial status of financial holding groups, and it reflects the ability of financial holding groups to conduct business activities with the funds provided by creditors. These three original variables indicate the solvency capability of financial holding groups.

Net profit $X_4$ reflects the benefits realized in a certain operating period and non-interest income $X_5$ reflects the income of financial holding groups except for the interest spread of deposits and loans and represents the light-weight operation ability of commercial banks, which is an important strategic choice for transformation and development. To some degree, net profit and non-interest income indicate the profitability of financial holding groups. Commercial banks are mainly risk-oriented and need sufficient capital to support their business development. Risk compensation index is a quantitative standard adopted by commercial banks to judge the strength of using their own profits and capital to make up the loss gap if assets are lost due to poor management, including profitability and capital adequacy ratio (CBRC 2005). At present, in endogenous financing, domestic banks mainly rely on the cumulative way of extracting income from annual net profit to supplement core capital (Sheng 2013). Net profit, non-interest income, are closely related to solvency such as capital adequacy ratio, tier one capital adequacy ratio and asset-liability ratio.

Common factor $F_1$ can be called "solvency factor". It can reflect 36.57% information of total sample data and can explain the ability of financial holding groups to offset risk losses to a greater extent. The higher the common factor score, the stronger the financial holding group's ability to offset the risk loss, and on the contrary, the lower the common factor score, the weaker the financial holding group's ability to offset the risk loss.

2. Common factor $F_2$

The five original variables, such as the rate of return on economic value added $X_6$, the rate of return on total assets $X_7$, the rate of return on net assets $X_8$, the proportion of non-performing loans $X_9$ and the growth rate of operating income $X_{10}$, have relatively high loads on the second common factor $F_2$, which are 0.927, 0.846, 0.914, 0.575 and 0.434 respectively.

Among them, the rate of return on economic value added $X_6$ reflects the ability of financial holding groups to create value, and this variable has the highest load in common factor $F_2$. The rate of return on total assets $X_7$ reflects the ability of financial holding groups to use all assets to obtain income. The return on net assets $X_8$ shows the ability of shareholders' investment funds to obtain net profit. The growth rate of operating income $X_{10}$ reflects the development of operating income of financial holding groups and predicts the future development trend of operating income.

The ratio of non-performing loans $X_9$ shows the quality of credit assets as the main source of profit, which determines the profitability of financial holding groups. An important part of the profits of domestic commercial banks is used to make provision for asset impairment losses of non-performing loans, to make up for the losses, and to deal with the uncertainty brought by the possible increase of non-performing loans and cyclical changes of macro-economy in advance (Sheng 2013). Therefore, non-performing loans are closely related to profits.

The rate of return on economic value added, the rate of return on total assets, the rate of return on net assets, the proportion of non-performing loans and the growth rate of operating income reflect profitability of a financial holding group. So, common factor $F_2$ is named "profitability factor". This factor can reflect 30.72% of the information in all sample data. The higher the common factor score, the stronger the profitability of financial holding groups, on the contrary, the lower the common factor score, the weaker the profitability of financial holding groups.

3. Common factor $F_3$

The provision coverage ratio $X_{11}$, the loan loss reserve adequacy ratio $X_{12}$, the net profit growth rate $X_{13}$ and the earnings per share $X_{14}$ have high loads on the third common factor $F_3$ which are 0.860, 0.635, 0.785 and 0.601, respectively.

Among them, the provision coverage ratio $X_{11}$ reflects the adequacy of the loan loss reserve accrued by the financial holding group. If the provision coverage ratio is enough, the asset quality risk is within the controllable range. This variable has the highest load among common factor $F_3$. The loan loss reserve adequacy ratio $X_{12}$ reflects the ratio between the actual provision and the required provision for loans of financial holding groups.

The net profit growth rate $X_{13}$ reflects the profit growth of financial holding groups and the expected future profit trend. Earnings per share $X_{14}$ shows the earning level of common shares of listed financial holding groups and reflects the earning ability of common shares in a certain operating period and the corresponding risk level of investment. The profits of domestic commercial banks are closely related to the quality of loan assets, and the quality of assets directly erodes profits. The provision for asset impairment loss accrued due to loan asset quality problems directly deducts profits.

Common factor $F_3$ is called "asset quality factor". The third common factor can reflect 9.07% of the information in all sample data, which can explain the asset quality of financial holding groups to a greater extent. The higher the common factor score, the better the asset quality of the financial holding group, on the contrary, the lower the common factor score, the worse the asset quality of the financial holding group.

4. Common factor $F_4$

Original variables such as cost-income ratio $X_{15}$ have higher load on the fourth common factor $F_4$, which is 0.739. Cost-income ratio reflects the amount of operating expenses that a financial holding group needs to spend per unit of operating income. With the gradual decline of domestic economic growth, the market-oriented reform of interest rates such as loans and deposits has been accelerated, and the pace of capital market reform such as the reform of enterprise listing registration system and the issuance of credit bonds has been accelerated. The competition among financial institutions, especially commercial banks, has become more intense and the cost has increased. The importance of cost management of financial holding groups has become more prominent (Cheng and Zhou 2012).

Common factor $F_4$ is called "cost control factor". The fourth factor $F_4$ can reflect the information in 7.81% of all sample data, which can explain the cost management ability and level of financial holding groups to a greater extent. The higher the common factor score, the better the cost control ability of the financial holding group, on the contrary, the lower the common factor score, the weaker the cost control ability of the financial holding group.

Through the above analysis of the four common factors and the explanation of their economic significance, four common factors have basically covered the main contents in the performance evaluation of financial holding groups, such as solvency status, profitability status, asset quality status, cost control capability status and embodied the principles of comprehensiveness, importance, hierarchy, and operability in the evaluation of financial holding groups. It conforms to the three principles of safety, liquidity and profitability in the operation and management of commercial banks and embodies the principle of combining financial information and non-financial information evaluation to evaluate business performance. The cumulative ratio of the above four factors to the information of the 15 indicators reaches 84.19%, which has high credibility.

The rotation component load matrix generated by factor rotation shows that these four common factors can establish four linear functional relationships with the 15 original variables, and the linear functions are independent to each other. The transformation matrix table after the varimax procedure generated by statistical software is as follows:

**Table 5.7** The transformation matrix table

| Component | 1 | 2 | 3 | 4 |
|---|---|---|---|---|
| 1 | – 0.662 | 0.522 | 0.538 | – 0.009 |
| 2 | 0.720 | 0.627 | 0.280 | 0.097 |
| 3 | – 0.161 | 0.236 | – 0.414 | 0.864 |
| 4 | 0.129 | – 0.528 | 0.679 | 0.494 |

According to the transformation matrix after the varimax procedure listed in Table 5.7 and four common factors, the expressions of factor variables $A_1$, $A_2$, $A_3$, $A_4$ can be obtained, which is shown as follows.

$$\mathbf{A_1= -0.662F_1+0.522F_2+0.538F_3-0.009F_4} \tag{5.1}$$

$$\mathbf{A_2= 0.720F_1+0.627F_2+0.280F_3+0.097F_4} \tag{5.2}$$

$$\mathbf{A_3= -0.161F_1+0.236F_2-0.414F_3+0.864F_4} \tag{5.3}$$

$$\mathbf{A_4= 0.129F_1-0.528F_2+0.679F_3+0.494F_4} \tag{5.4}$$

### 5.4.3 *Score Coefficient Matrix of Common Factors*

Based on factor extraction and rotation of component load matrix, the 13 financial holding groups need to be comprehensively evaluated after establishing the factor analysis model. And the original data can be analyzed furtherly.

The four common factors extracted by eigenvalue criterion can respectively explain the linear combination relationship among the 15 original variables, which can be expressed by factor score function. For example, the factor score function between the common factor and the original variable is as follows.

$$\mathbf{F_j= a_{j1}x_1+a_{j2}x_2+\cdots+a_{jp}x_p} \tag{5.5}$$

$$\mathbf{j = 1, 2, \ldots, m} \tag{5.6}$$

The scores of the four common factors of the 13 financial holding groups can be calculated by the factor score function. The coefficient in the score function comes from the matrix table of component score coefficient, which can be generated by the factor analysis function in the statistical analysis software. See Table 5.8 for details.

According to the matrix of components score coefficient shown in Table 5.8, a scoring model of the four factors is obtained, and the calculation formulas are as follows:

$$\begin{aligned}\mathbf{F_1} &= \mathbf{0.231x_1 + 0.215x_2 - 0.208x_3 + 0.164x_4 + 0.172x_5} \\ &\quad \mathbf{- 0.045x_6 + 0.071x_7 - 0.059x_8 + 0.026x_9 - 0.050x_{10}} \\ &\quad \mathbf{+ 0.090x11 + 0.040x_{12} + 0.020x_{13} - 0.052x_{14} - 0.008x_{15}}\end{aligned} \tag{5.7}$$

**Table 5.8** Matrix table of component score coefficient

| Operational indicators | Variables | Components | | | |
|---|---|---|---|---|---|
| | | 1 | 2 | 3 | 4 |
| Capital adequacy rate | $X_1$ | 0.231 | − 0.115 | 0.184 | 0.012 |
| Tier-one leverage capital | $X_2$ | 0.215 | − 0.063 | 0.103 | 0.021 |
| Asset-liability ratio (after normalization) | $X_3$ | − 0.208 | 0.144 | − 0.131 | 0.041 |
| Net profit (after normalization) | $X_4$ | 0.164 | 0.133 | − 0.11 | − 0.029 |
| Non-interest income (after normalization) | $X_5$ | 0.172 | 0.088 | − 0.085 | 0.007 |
| Rate of return on economic added value | $X_6$ | − 0.045 | 0.315 | − 0.143 | 0.082 |
| Return on equity | $X_7$ | 0.071 | 0.276 | − 0.1 | − 0.005 |
| Return on total assets | $X_8$ | − 0.059 | 0.298 | − 0.113 | 0.059 |
| Non-performing loan ratio (after normalization) | $X_9$ | 0.026 | 0.142 | 0.072 | − 0.362 |
| Growth rate of total operating revenue | $X_{10}$ | − 0.05 | 0.101 | 0.068 | − 0.259 |
| Provision coverage ratio (after normalization) | $X_{11}$ | 0.09 | − 0.128 | 0.428 | 0.053 |
| Provisions for loan losses (after normalization) | $X_{12}$ | 0.04 | 0.054 | 0.21 | 0.088 |
| Year-on-year growth rate of net profit | $X_{13}$ | 0.02 | − 0.107 | 0.366 | − 0.176 |
| Earnings per share | $X_{14}$ | − 0.052 | − 0.149 | 0.302 | 0.46 |
| Income-cost ratio (after normalization) | $X_{15}$ | − 0.008 | 0.051 | − 0.052 | 0.542 |

$$\begin{aligned} \mathbf{F_2} &= \mathbf{0.115x_1 - 0.063x_2 + 0.144x_3 + 0.133x_4 + 0.088x_5} \\ &\quad \mathbf{+ 0.315x_6 + 0.276x_7 + 0.298x_8 + 0.142x_9 + 0.101x_{10}} \\ &\quad \mathbf{- 0.128x_{11} + 0.054x_{12} - 0.107x_{13} - 0.149x_{14} + 0.051x_{15}} \end{aligned} \tag{5.8}$$

$$\begin{aligned} \mathbf{F_3} &= \mathbf{0.184x_1 + 0.103x_2 - 0.131x_3 - 0.110x_4 + 0.085x_5} \\ &\quad \mathbf{- 0.143x_6 - 0.100x_7 - 0.113x_8 + 0.072x_9 + 0.068x_{10}} \\ &\quad \mathbf{+ 0.428x_{11} + 0.210x_{12} + 0.366x_{13} + 0.302x_{14} - 0.005x_{15}} \end{aligned} \tag{5.9}$$

$$\begin{aligned} \mathbf{F_4} &= \mathbf{0.012x_1 + 0.021x_2 + 0.041x_3 - 0.029x_4 + 0.007x_5} \\ &\quad \mathbf{+ 0.082x_6 - 0.005x_7 + 0.059x_8 - 0.362x_9 - 0.259x_{10}} \\ &\quad \mathbf{+ 0.053x_{11} + 0.088x_{12} - 0.176x_{13} + 0.460x_{14} + 0.542x_5} \end{aligned} \tag{5.10}$$

Annex AC is the covariance matrix of components scoring generated by statistical software. From the table, we can know that the relationship among the four common factors $F_1$、$F_2$、$F_3$、$F_4$ is not linear and interdependent, but independent of each other. It also shows that the extracted main factor information does not overlap, which can achieve the goal of factor analysis.

### 5.4.4 Scoring of Common Factors

When the score coefficient matrix of common factors is confirmed, the score models of the factors can be used to calculate the factor score function of the 13 financial holding groups. The four common factor variables replace the 15 original variables for modeling and analysis, to evaluate the 13 financial holding groups and achieve the purpose of further simplification. The scores of the four common factors, from 2014 to 2018, were calculated by statistical software.

The scoring tables of the common factors $F_1$, $F_2$, $F_3$ and $F_4$, for the 13 financial holding groups, from 2014 to 2018, are presented in Annexes AD, AE, AF and AG, respectively.

### 5.4.5 Ranking of Comprehensive Performance Evaluation Scores

After calculating the score of each factor by the formulas presented previously, and to facilitate the evaluation and analysis of the overall business performance of the financial holding groups, the overall operating performance score of the financial holding groups can be calculated. The comprehensive scoring model of the financial holding group uses the contribution ratio of the variance of the initial eigenvalue of the factor as the weight and calculates the weighted total value of the factor score. The calculation formula is as follows:

$$\mathbf{F} = (\mathbf{36.570F_1 + 30.723F_2 + 9.076F_3 + 7.817F_4})/\mathbf{84.186} \tag{5.11}$$

F our factors weights are 36.570%, 30.723%, 9.076%, 7.817%, respectively.

Among them, $F_1$ factor of solvency weighted 36.57%, is the reflection of principle of liquidity. The liquidity principle describes the solvency of financial holding groups which is the ability to meet customer demand for deposit withdrawals and loan drawdowns. It serves as a fundamental of the profitability principle.

$F_3$ factor of asset quality weighted 9.07% and is the reflection of security principle that indicates the sound operation of a financial holding group. As a financial institution, a financial holding group itself should control any risks and needs to avoid the impact of various uncertainties on its day-to-day operations to ensure sound operations.

Both $F_2$ factor of profitability and $F_4$ factor of cost control reflect the "profitability" principle in the "three principles" of operation and management, with a total weight of 38.54%. It occupies a core position in the management of financial holding groups and shows that financial holding groups can make profits by carrying out business activities and doing a good job in cost control (Cheng and Zhou 2012)). The total weight of $F_2$ and $F_4$ is the highest in the "three principles", which is 1.97 percentage points higher than that of solvency factor $F_1$, and 29.464 percentage points higher than that of asset quality factor $F_3$.

The calculation formula of the net profit of a financial holding group is the operating income minus the cost. $F_2$ includes five original variables, such as economic value-added rate of return $X_6$, but does not include cost-income ratio $X_{15}$, which is listed as cost control factor $F_4$ separately. Cost control is an important part of financial management of financial holding groups, and it is also an important basis for achieving profit targets. The excessive cost of financial holding groups will lead to an increase in the price of external use of funds, which may lose the advantage of price competition and reduce profitability in the market competition of the financial industry. Especially, with the acceleration of interest rate marketization reform in recent years, the cost of financial holding groups, especially commercial banks, has increased rapidly. Whether the cost can be managed and controlled reasonably has become the main aspect restricting profitability. Financial holding groups have more financial costs to obtain financial licenses and carry out integrated operations through new construction, mergers and acquisitions and so forth Therefore, financial holding groups should pay more attention to fine management and strict control of costs and list their cost control as a separate public factor.

By using the IBM SPSS® statistical software, the business performance scores of each firm-year in the sample were obtained and are presented in the Annex AH and Annex II.

The average operating performance scores of each sample in the five years from 2014 to 2018 are calculated. See Annex JJ for the ranking according to comprehensive scores.

## 5.5 Verification of Empirical Results of Performance Evaluation

To verify the accuracy of the above factor analysis results, this research uses IBM SPSS® statistical software to conduct cluster analysis.

### 5.5.1 Introduction to Cluster Analysis

Cluster analysis is a statistical method that classifies samples according to the index data of samples or variables, and aggregates samples with more similar indexes into one class, which is convenient for analysis. After cluster analysis, samples of same types are more similar than other samples Liu (2015).

According to classified objects, cluster analysis can be divided into two types, the first is sample cluster that is Q clustering, and the second is variable cluster, that is R clustering. In this book, sample cluster is adopted. In other words, the data of the 13 financial holding groups are classified according to their common characteristics, and the 13 financial holding groups are divided into different categories and then the analysis is conducted.

Sample cluster (Q cluster) mainly tests the degree of familiarity of the 13 financial holding groups. There are two methods to measure it. One is to measure the degree of dependence between the data of each financial holding groups. The other is to classify the 13 financial holding groups into several small categories according to certain attributes, and then measure the degree of dependence among different categories. The main indicators to measure the data dependence of the 13 financial holding groups are the distance and the correlation coefficient of data. In this book, the first method is selected for calculation. Sample clustering (Q clustering) is carried out on the data of financial holding groups through the clustering analysis function of IBM SPSS® statistical analysis software. There are many methods in the statistical analysis software to measure the degree of closeness between financial holding groups, which are mainly determined according to the relevant data types.

According to the data types of the 13 financial holding groups, this research uses the Euclidean Distance function of statistical software to measure the distance of financial holding groups. In the process of clustering, financial holding groups with similar distance are classified into one category, while financial holding groups with far distances are classified into different categories. Euclidean Distance refers to the square root of the sum of the squares of the differences between the relevant original variable data in the 13 financial holding groups. The calculation step is to sum squares first, and then square root and the calculation formula is the following:

$$\mathbf{EUCLID} = \sqrt{\sum_{\mathbf{i=1}}^{\mathbf{k}} (\mathbf{x_i} - \mathbf{y_i})^2} \tag{5.12}$$

In the process of cluster analysis, the close relationship between samples and subclasses, and inter-sub-classes is calculated by statistical analysis software there are many analytical methods for measuring tightness in statistical analysis software, and this book uses Ward's Method. In the process of clustering analysis, the deviation sum of squares method combines two subcategories with the smallest distance into one category, and the criterion of judging the smallest distance is the smallest added value of the sum of squares of the Euclidean distance between financial holding groups.

## 5.5.2 *Evaluation Indicators and Sample Data Adopted*

### 5.5.2.1 Evaluation Indicators

In this verification method, the annual financial accounting reports of 13 banking financial holding groups in 2018 are selected as the research objects. The data come from financial and accounting reports disclosed by banking financial holding groups according to the requirements of CSRC, annual reports of listed companies.

The data of financial holding groups used in this verification method include five categories and 13 indicators, such as profitability, business growth, solvency, asset quality and management. The indicators of financial holding groups selected in 2018 and used for the cluster analysis in this book are consistent with the sample indicators used for the factor analysis above.

### 5.5.2.2 Processing Sample Data

The dimensional difference of variables in cluster analysis has a great influence on the results obtained. In the process of cluster analysis, variables need to be treated positively and standardly, to avoid getting inaccurate results and compare the results of cluster analysis with those of factor analysis.

For the convenience of comparative analysis, the selected 15 indicators can be divided into three categories, namely, positive indicators, negative indicators, and moderate indicators. Based on the directional difference of the selected indicators, the negative indicators and moderate indicators are treated in the same direction.

Based on the forward processing of the original data value of the variable, the standardization processing is carried out. Annex KK shows the processing methods of the original data. To verify the results of factor analysis, the standardized index data of 2018 used in cluster analysis in this research is consistent with the operational index data used in the factor analysis above.

## 5.5.3 *Results of the Cluster Analysis*

### 5.5.3.1 Classification Results

In this book, cluster analysis of the financial holding groups' data in 2018 is performed using IBM SPSS® statistical software. Based on the deviation sum of squares method, the European distance is used for analysis. The clustering results are shown in Fig. 5.1.

According to Fig. 5.1, the cluster analysis results can be divided into two categories, three categories or four categories, and the cluster analysis results' table of financial holding group performance data in 2018 is formed after sorting out (see Annex KK).

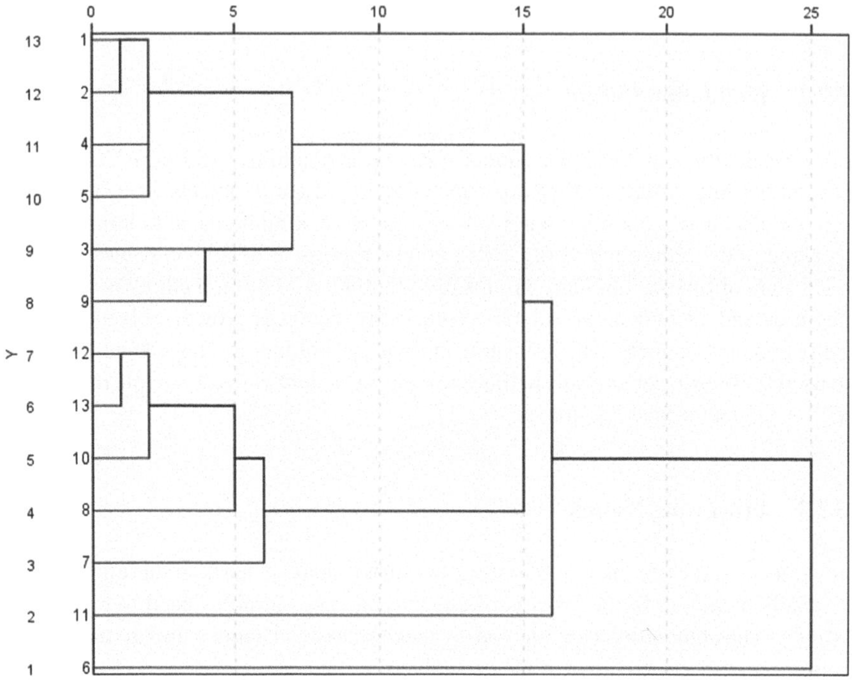


**Fig. 5.1** Cluster analysis results of performance data of financial holding groups in 2018

According to the results of clustering analysis of the financial holding group performance data in 2018 (Annex GG), the results generated by clustering analysis can be divided into three situations:

If the results are divided into two categories, Bank I constitutes the first category and the others belong to the second category;

If the results are divided into three categories, Bank I alone constitutes the first category, Bank G constitutes the second category and the others belong to the third category;

And if the results are divided into four categories, Bank I constitutes the first category, Bank G constitutes the second category, Bank D, Bank C, Bank B, Bank A, Bank J and Bank E represent the third category and the others belong to the fourth category.

#### 5.5.3.2 Results Comparison of Cluster Analysis and Factor Analysis

The comparison between the 2018 financial holding groups operating performance score table (Annex DD) and the 2018 financial holding groups' performance data cluster analysis results' table (Annex HH) shows that the classification of the 2018, 13 financial holding groups operating performance data cluster analysis results is very similar to the ranking of operating performance scores calculated through the factor analysis method. According to the classification results, the financial holding groups are sorted. The comparison of the results of the two methods is shown in Annex MM.

From Annex MM, we can have the following findings:

The cluster analysis results are divided into two categories. By comparison, the classification results of the cluster analysis are consistent with the business performance scores ranking calculated by the factor analysis.

The cluster analysis results are divided into three categories. According to the results of cluster analysis, the first category includes Bank I, the second category includes Bank G, and the third category includes 11 financial holding groups such as Bank D. By comparing the results of cluster analysis and the ranking of business performance scores calculated by factor analysis, it is found that the similarity between them is very high. Firstly, bank I belongs to the first category in cluster analysis results and ranks first in factor analysis results, which are consistent with each other; Secondly, 11 financial holding groups, such as Bank D, belong to the third category in the cluster analysis results, ranking between the 2nd and 13th in the factor analysis results, and their similarities are also consistent. Thirdly, Bank G belongs to the second category in cluster analysis results and ranks ninth in factor analysis results, and there are some differences in similarity between them. To sum up, the classification results of cluster analysis and factor analysis scores rank with a consistent rate of 92.30%, and the similarity is very high.

The cluster analysis results are divided into four categories. According to the results of cluster analysis, the first category includes Bank I, the second category includes Bank G, the third category includes six financial holding groups such as Bank D, and the fourth category includes five financial holding groups such as Bank K. By comparing the results of cluster analysis and the ranking of business performance scores calculated by factor analysis, it is found that the similarity between them is still very high. Firstly, the results of cluster analysis and factor analysis of Bank I are consistent. Secondly, six financial holding groups, such as Bank D, belong to the third category in the cluster analysis results, ranking between the 2nd and 7th in the factor analysis results, and their similarities are also consistent. Thirdly, five financial holding groups, such as Bank K, belong to the fourth category in the cluster analysis results, ranking between 8 and 13th in the factor analysis results, and their similarity is also consistent. Fourthly, Bank G belongs to the second category in cluster analysis results and ranks ninth in factor analysis results, and there are some differences in similarity between them. To sum up, the classification results of cluster analysis and factor analysis scores rank with a consistent rate of 92.30%, and the similarity is also very high.

Next, we analyze the reasons for the difference between the cluster analysis result and the factor analysis score ranking result. When the cluster analysis results are divided into three categories and four categories, the second category (Bank G) is inconsistent with the business performance scores calculated by the factor analysis. The main reasons for the difference are as follows:

1. Various calculating methods

Although cluster analysis and factor analysis are both statistical methods to reduce the dimension of variables, the two methods have different calculation methods. Cluster analysis is to quantitatively calculate the degree of familiarity between the 13 financial holding groups according to the actual values of multiple original variables and classify the 13 financial holding groups into different categories according to the similarity of variables, to reflect the inherent and inevitable connection among financial holding groups. Factor analysis is to condense many original variables of the 13 financial holding groups into a few common factors, which comprehensively reflect the main information of the original variables and evaluate the financial holding groups by calculating factor scores. The difference of the specific calculation methods between cluster analysis and factor analysis also causes the difference on the performance evaluation results.

2. High similarity between Bank I and Bank G.

Bank I and Bank G have the same shareholder background. "A Shares" of both are listed on the Shanghai Stock Exchange and their major shareholders are Group I and Group G, respectively (Bank I [BI] and Bank G [BG] 2018), which are large conglomerates spanning industry and finance, and domestic and overseas markets. While the main shareholder of the other banks is the Ministry of Finance.

Both Bank I and Bank G are national joint-stock banks and have branches outside the country.

Bank I and Bank G hold similar financial licenses. Bank I holds directly or indirectly six major financial licenses in banking, securities, insurance, funds, leasing, futures, and Bank G holds directly or indirectly seven major financial licenses such as banking, securities, insurance, trust, fund, leasing, futures. Both own many financing licenses.

Bank I and Bank G have similar rankings for some of the indicator variables. Of the 15 indicator variables included in the financial holding group's business performance evaluation indicators, Bank I and Bank G ranked similarly among the 13 bank-based financial holding group in 2018 in terms of growth rate of operating income ($X_{10}$), growth rate of net profit ($X_{13}$), and growth rate of intermediate business income. For example, in 2018, Bank I and Bank G's operating income growth rate ($X_{10}$) was 12.52% and 20.03%, ranking third and first respectively, among the 13 bank-based financial holding groups, with Bank J ranking second. In 2018, Bank I and Bank G's net profit growth rate ($X_{13}$) was 14.41% and 6.67%, ranked first and third respectively, among the 13 financial holding groups, with Bank H ranking second. Bank I and Bank G intermediate income growth rate in 2018 was 7.50% and 13.37%, ranked fourth and second respectively, among the 13 financial holding groups, with Bank E ranking first.

According to cluster analysis, Bank I and Bank G have a high degree of similarity in four aspects, such as shareholder background, geographic scope of operation, financial license holding, and ranking of indicator variables. According to the calculation principle of cluster analysis method, the classification of I bank and G bank is very close.

Through the above comparative analysis of clustering and factor analysis results, it can be concluded that the classification of the clustering results of the business performance data of the 13 financial holding groups in 2018 is very similar to the ranking of the business performance scores calculated through the factor analysis method. Therefore, it can be said that the ranking of business performance scores calculated by factor analysis method is accurate and can be used.

## 5.6 Conclusions and Implications of the Study on Performance Evaluation of Financial Holding Groups

In the previous section, the accuracy of the empirical results of the factor analysis method is validated through cluster analysis. In this section, the four factor scores, composite scores and rankings will be analyzed, with a focus on the 2018 scores, the average scores over the last five years and the change in scores from 2014 to 2018.

### *5.6.1 Grouping of Performance Evaluation of Financial Holding Groups*

For comparative analysis, the 13 financial holding groups are divided into three groups based on the number of financial licenses held directly or indirectly by them, as follows (see Table 5.9).

The first group is the bank-owned financial holding groups. Bank C, Bank D, Bank B, Bank A, Bank E, Bank I, Bank K, Bank L, and Bank J all hold four or more major financial licenses, and they are all financial holding groups initiated by traditional banks. The above nine financial holding groups are classified as bank-owned financial holding groups.

The second group is the bank-type financial holding groups owned by a financial holding group. Bank F, Bank G, and Bank H own two financial licenses. They should belong to financial holding groups according to the provisions in the Trial Measures for the Supervision and Administration of Financial holding groups. At the same time, the three banks belong to CITIC Group, Everbright Group and Ping An Group, respectively. Also, these groups hold more than 7 financial licenses and are financial holding groups. Therefore, Bank F, Bank G, and Bank H are classified into bank-type financial holding groups owned by a financial holding group.

The third group is the traditional bank-type financial holding groups. At present, most of the national commercial banks hold more than two financial licenses, while Bank M only holds two financial licenses. Besides, 98% of the net profit of Bank M comes from traditional banking. Therefore, Bank M is classified as a traditional bank-type financial holding group.

**Table 5.9** Groups of the 13 financial holding groups

| Serial number | Companies | Group | Number of financial licenses held directly or indirectly |
|---|---|---|---|
| 1 | Bank C | Bank-owned financial holding groups | 6 |
| 2 | Bank D | | 7 |
| 3 | Bank B | | 6 |
| 4 | Bank A | | 6 |
| 5 | Bank E | | 7 |
| 6 | Bank I | | 6 |
| 7 | Bank K | | 5 |
| 8 | Bank L | | 4 |
| 9 | Bank J | | 6 |
| 10 | Bank F | Bank-type financial holding groups owned by a financial holding group | 7 |
| 11 | Bank G | | 7 |
| 12 | Bank H | | 7 |
| 13 | Bank M | Traditional bank-type financial holding groups | 2 |

## *5.6.2 Analysis of Comprehensive Performance Evaluation Scores of Financial Holding Groups*

### 5.6.2.1 Comprehensive Scoring in 2018

In this section, the comprehensive scores of financial holding business performance in 2018 are analyzed according to the grouping ranking and single ranking of the financial holding groups. The analysis is as follows:

1. Grouping analysis

According to the comprehensive scores of the groups operating performance in 2018 (as shown in Table 5.10), the comprehensive score of bank-owned financial holding groups in 2018 was the highest, which was 6.65, 1.30 points higher than that of bank-type financial holding groups owned by financial holding group and 1.37 points higher than that of traditional bank-type financial holding groups.

2. Analysis on single group

From the comprehensive score in 2018, the top three financial holding groups are Bank I, Bank D and Bank C, with scores of 7.76, 7.67 and 7.36, respectively. The financial holding groups ranked the last three in comprehensive scores are Bank H, Bank M and Bank F, with scores of 5.11, 5.28 and 5.28, respectively. Annex NN shows the comprehensive score chart of financial holding groups' operating performance in 2018.

**Table 5.10** Grouping analysis on comprehensive scoring of business performance in 2018

| Group | Type | Comprehensive score | Ranking |
|---|---|---|---|
| 1 | Bank-owned financial holding groups | 6.65 | 1 |
| 2 | Bank-type financial holding groups owned by financial holding group | 5.34 | 2 |
| 3 | Traditional bank-type financial holding groups | 5.28 | 3 |
| 4 | Average | 6.24 | – |

These financial holding groups ranked ahead hold enough financial licenses. For instance, Bank I and Bank C each has six financial licenses, while Bank D has seven financial licenses.

These financial holding groups ranked behind are experiencing slow development. For instance, Bank M, ranked 12th, has a comprehensive performance score of 5.28, and only has a leased financial license. The 13th-ranked Bank H was originally Bank H1, which only had the financial license of the bank. In April 2012, Group H acquired Bank H1 and changed its name to Bank H. Although Bank H belongs to Group H which has complete financial licenses, it is still in running-in period. So, it ranks behind.

There is a big gap between financial holding groups ranked ahead and financial holding groups ranked behind. Bank I, which ranked first in the comprehensive score, scored 2.66 points higher than Bank H, which ranked last, and 2.49 points higher than Bank M, which ranked 12th.

#### 5.6.2.2 Average Overall Scoring from 2014 to 2018

In this section, the comprehensive scores of financial holding business performance from 2014 to 2018 are analyzed according to the grouping ranking of financial holding groups. The analysis is as follows:

According to the average scores of business performance from 2014 to 2018 (shown in Table 5.11), they are ranked as bank-owned financial holding groups, traditional bank-type financial holding groups, and bank-type financial holding groups owned by financial holding group. Among them, the average score of bank-owned financial holding groups is the highest, which is 6.84, 1 point higher than that of bank-type financial holding groups owned by financial holding group and 0.85 higher than that of traditional bank-type financial holding groups. The average score of traditional bank-type financial holding groups is 5.99, which is higher than that of bank-owned financial holding groups by 0.15, but lower than the overall average of the 13 financial holding groups by 0.55. The average score of bank-type financial holding groups owned by financial holding group is 5.84, which is lower than that of traditional banks by 0.15 and that of the overall average of the 13 financial holding groups by 0.70.

**Table 5.11** Group scores from 2014 to 2018

| Group | Type | Average score | Rank |
|---|---|---|---|
| 1 | Bank-owned financial holding groups | 6.84 | 1 |
| 2 | Bank-type financial holding groups owned by financial holding group | 5.84 | 3 |
| 3 | Traditional bank-type financial holding groups | 5.99 | 2 |
| 4 | Average | 6.54 | – |

#### 5.6.2.3 Changes of Comprehensive Score Ranking from 2014 to 2018

1. Group analysis

The gap between bank-owned financial holding groups score and the average score is widening. In 2014, bank-owned financial holding groups scored 7.88, which was higher than the average score of the 13 financial holding groups by 0.26 points. In 2018, bank-owned financial holding groups scored 6.65, which was higher than the average score of the 13 financial holding groups by 0.41 points, an increase in 0.14 points when compared with the difference in 2014. It shows that the competitiveness of bank-owned financial holding groups is enhanced rapidly.

The overall scores and ranking of bank-type financial holding groups owned by financial holding group are superior to those of traditional bank-type financial holding groups. In 2014, the comprehensive score of the bank-type financial holding groups owned by financial holding group was 6.91, which was lower than the comprehensive score of traditional bank-type financial holding groups by 0.43, ranking third in the group. In 2018, the comprehensive score of the bank-type financial holding groups owned by financial holding group was 5.34, which was 0.07 higher than that of traditional bank-type financial holding groups, ranking second in the group. It shows that the comprehensive advantages of bank-type financial holding groups owned by financial holding group are gradually reflected.

The comprehensive scores and rankings of traditional bank-type financial holding groups gradually declined. In 2014, the comprehensive score of traditional bank-type financial holding groups was 7.34, which was higher than the average score of the 13 financial holding groups by 0.27, ranking second. And in 2018, the comprehensive score of traditional bank-type financial holding groups was 5.28, which was lower than the average score of the 13 financial holding groups by 0.96, ranking third. With the deepening of interest rate marketization and the narrowing of bank interest margin space, the competitiveness of traditional banks has declined rapidly, and the competitiveness of comprehensive operations has become prominent. Table 5.12 presents the details.

2. Analysis on single group

The comprehensive scores and rankings of financial holding groups with relatively complete licensed are better than those with single licensed financial institutions. For

**Table 5.12** Overall group scores from 2014 to 2018

| Group | Type | 2014 | 2015 | 2016 | 2017 | 2018 |
|---|---|---|---|---|---|---|
| 1 | Bank-owned financial holding groups | 7.88 | 6.79 | 6.42 | 6.45 | 6.65 |
| 2 | Bank-type financial holding groups owned by financial holding group | 6.91 | 6.04 | 5.48 | 5.41 | 5.34 |
| 3 | Traditional bank-type financial holding groups | 7.34 | 6.18 | 5.73 | 5.43 | 5.28 |
| 4 | Average | 7.62 | 6.57 | 6.15 | 6.13 | 6.24 |

example, the top three financial holding groups with comprehensive scores are Bank D, Bank C and Bank B (see Annex OO), which hold 7, 6 and 6 financial licenses, respectively. Bank F, Bank G and Bank H ranked the last three in the comprehensive score, all of which are traditional banks and hold a single financial institution license.

The ranking of most financial holding groups with complete licenses has continuously improved. For instance, the comprehensive scores of Bank B, Bank E and Bank I, which have relatively complete financial licenses, increased by 5 places, 4 places and 3 places, respectively, when compared to 2014. Among them, the comprehensive score ranking of Bank I gradually improved from the 4th place in 2014 to the 1st place in 2018.

The comprehensive score and ranking of the financial holding group with a single financial license has a downward trend. For example, the comprehensive score of Bank M from 2014 to 2018 were 7.34 points, 6.18 points, 5.73 points, 5.44 points and 5.28 points, respectively, and the scores gradually decreased. In 2018, the comprehensive score decreased by 2.06 points when compared with 2014, a decrease of 28%. From 2015 to 2018, the comprehensive scores ranked 8th, 10th, 10th, and 12th respectively, and the comprehensive scores in 2018 decreased by 4 places compared with that in 2015.

The comprehensive scores and rankings of traditional banks may not be improved after being merged by financial holding groups. For example, after Bank H was acquired by Group H, the comprehensive scores from 2014 to 2018 were 6.96, 5.91, 5.36, 6.14 and 5.11 respectively, showing a downward trend. From 2014 to 2018, the comprehensive scores ranked 12th in 2014 and 13th in the remaining years. Compared with 2014, the comprehensive score in 2018 decreased by one place, ranking last among the 13 banking financial holding groups.

### 5.6.3 Analysis of Solvency Evaluation Index Scores

This section will analyze three aspects, namely the scores of factor $F_1$ in 2018, and the average scores and the ranking changes from 2014 to 2018.

#### 5.6.3.1 Solvency Scores in 2018

In 2018, the scores of the factor $F_1$ of bank-owned financial holding groups, traditional bank-type financial holding groups, and bank-type financial holding groups owned by financial holding group are 6.54, 5.24 and 4.84, respectively (see Annex PP). Among them, the score of $F_1$ of bank-type financial holding groups owned by financial holding group in 2018 increased by 0.71 when compared with that in 2017, mainly because M Bank replenished capital of 20 billion yuan in the second half of 2018, which led to a short-term and rapid improvement of risk offsetting ability. If the impact of replenished capital of 20 billion yuan is excluded, the score of factor $F_1$ in 2018 of bank-owned financial holding groups is higher than that of bank-type financial holding groups owned by financial holding group which in turn is higher than that of traditional bank-type financial holding groups.

#### 5.6.3.2 Average Score of Solvency Scores from 2014 to 2018

According to the average scores of $F_1$ (solvency) from 2014 to 2018 (see Annex QQ), bank-owned financial holding groups rank first, bank-type financial holding groups owned by financial holding group rank second and traditional bank-type financial holding groups rank last. Among them, the average score of bank-owned financial holding groups in recent five years is 5.82, which is 1.41 higher than that of bank-type financial holding groups owned by financial holding group and 1.63 higher than that of traditional bank-type financial holding groups. The average score of traditional bank-type financial holding groups is 4.19, which is 0.22 lower than that of bank-type financial holding groups owned by financial holding group and 1.18 points lower than that of 13 financial holding groups.

#### 5.6.3.3 Ranking and Scores Changes of Solvency Scores from 2014 to 2018

From the changes of factor $F_1$ scores and rankings from 2014 to 2018 (see Annex RR), we find that the scores of bank-owned financial holding groups, traditional bank-type financial holding groups, and bank-type financial holding groups owned by financial holding group have generally improved in recent five years. To be more specific, the factor $F_1$ scores of bank-owned financial holding groups in 2018 increased by 1.23 when compared with 2014, and the factor $F_1$ scores of bank-type financial holding groups owned by financial holding group in 2018 increased by 0.99 when compared with 2014 and the factor $F_1$ score of traditional bank-type financial holding groups in 2018 increased by 1.60 when compared with 2014. If the impact of capital increase of 20 billion yuan in 2018 is excluded, the factor $F_1$ score in 2017 increased by 0.89 when compared with 2014.

In addition, the average score of bank-owned financial holding groups has increased more than that of traditional bank-type financial holding groups and bank-type financial holding groups owned by financial holding group. The score of factor $F_1$ in 2018 increased by 1.23 compared with that in 2014, which is 0.24 higher than that of bank-type financial holding groups owned by financial holding group and 0.34 higher than that in the traditional bank-type financial holding groups. It shows that bank-owned financial holding groups have the best solvency.

## *5.6.4 Analysis of Profitability Evaluation Index Scores*

This section will analyze three aspects, namely the scores of factor $F_2$ in 2018, the average scores and the ranking changes from 2014 to 2018.

### 5.6.4.1 Profitability Scores in 2018

Annex SS shows that the scores of factor $F_2$ in 2018 of bank-owned financial holding groups is higher than that of bank-type financial holding groups owned by financial holding group which in turn is higher than that of traditional bank-type financial holding groups. The $F_2$ score of the bank-owned financial holding groups is 13.54, which is 1.52 higher than that of bank-type financial holding groups owned by financial holding group and 2.72 higher than that of traditional bank-type financial holding groups. The $F_2$ score of bank-type financial holding groups owned by financial holding group is 12.03, which is lower than that of the average of the 13 financial holding groups, and 1.20 points higher than that of the traditional bank-type financial holding groups. The $F_2$ score of traditional bank-type financial holding groups is 10.82, which is lower than that of bank-type financial holding groups owned by financial holding group by 1.20 points and lower than that of the 13 financial holding groups average by 2.16.

### 5.6.4.2 Average Score of Profitability Scores from 2014 to 2018

According to the average scores of $F_2$ (profitability) from 2014 to 2018 (see Annex TT), bank-owned financial holding groups rank first, traditional bank-type financial holding groups rank second and bank-type financial holding groups owned by financial holding group rank last.

Among them, the average score of bank-owned financial holding groups in recent five years is 15.06, which is 0.40 higher than that of bank-type financial holding groups owned by financial holding group and 0.61 higher than that of traditional bank-type financial holding groups. The average score of traditional bank-type financial holding groups is 15.06, which is 0.40 lower than that of bank-type financial holding groups owned by financial holding group and 0.05 lower than that of the 13 financial holding groups. The average score of bank-type financial holding groups owned by financial holding group is 14.66, which is 0.45 lower than that of 13 financial holding groups and 0.40 higher than that of traditional bank-type financial holding groups. It shows that from the average data in recent five years, the profitability of bank-owned financial holding groups is better than that of traditional bank-type financial holding groups, and the profitability of traditional bank-type financial holding groups is better than that of bank-type financial holding groups owned by financial holding group.

The main reason why the profitability of traditional bank-type financial holding groups is better than that of bank-type financial holding groups owned by financial holding group is the lack of interest rate marketization in China from 2014 to 2016, and the financial industry still takes the deposit and loan spreads as the main source of profit. With the deepening of interest rate marketization, the profit gap between bank-type financial holding groups owned by financial holding group and traditional bank-type financial holding groups gradually narrowed. And the year of 2018 becomes an inflection point. In 2018, the factor $F_2$ score of the bank-type financial holding groups owned by financial holding group was 12.03, which was higher than that of the traditional bank-type financial holding groups by 1.20. It shows that since 2018, the advantages of comprehensive management have gradually emerged.

#### 5.6.4.3 Ranking and Scores Changes of Profitability Scores from 2014 to 2018

From the score of the factor $F_2$ (profitability) from 2014 to 2018, the overall score of $F_2$ shows a downward trend, but there is a big gap in the decline of different types of financial holding groups (see Annex UU).

Influenced by the deepening of interest rate marketization and capital marketization reform in recent years, the profitability of these three types financial holding groups has declined.

The decrease in the profit factor score of financial control banks is smaller than that of financial control banks, and the decrease in the profit factor score of financial control banks is smaller than that of traditional banks. In 2018, the profit factor scores of bank-owned financial holding groups, bank-type financial holding groups owned by financial holding group, and traditional bank-type financial holding groups decreased by 6.62, 7.82 and 10.31, respectively, when compared with 2014. The decline of bank-owned financial holding groups score was 84.70% of the decline of bank-type financial holding groups owned by financial holding group and 64.23% of the decline of traditional bank-type financial holding groups. The decrease in scores of bank-type financial holding groups owned by financial holding group is 75.83% of that of traditional bank-type financial holding groups. It shows that after the marketization of interest rate, comprehensive management can play the role of "stabilizer" of profit.

### *5.6.5 Analysis of Asset Quality Evaluation Index Scores*

Financial holding groups have operational risks, especially in recent years, when China's economic growth slows down and hidden risks in some regions and industries increase. The importance of strengthening asset quality management of financial holding groups is highlighted. The previous section focused on the profitability score, while this section focuses on the asset quality score.

#### 5.6.5.1 Asset Quality Scores in 2018

Annex VV shows that the scores of factor $F_3$ in 2018 of bank-owned financial holding groups is higher than that of bank-type financial holding groups owned by financial holding group, which in turn is higher than that of traditional bank-type financial holding groups. The $F_3$ score of the bank-owned financial holding groups is 8.78, which is 0.24 higher than that of bank-type financial holding groups owned by financial holding group and 0.8 higher than that of traditional bank-type financial holding groups. The $F_3$ score of bank-type financial holding groups owned by financial holding group is 8.54, which is higher than that of the average of the 13 financial holding groups by 0.12, and 0.56 higher than that of the traditional bank-type financial holding groups. It shows that developing comprehensive finance is conducive to improving asset quality.

#### 5.6.5.2 Average Score of the Asset Quality Scores from 2014 to 2018

According to the average scores of $F_3$ (asset quality) from 2014 to 2018 (see Annex WW), bank-type financial holding groups owned by financial holding group rank first, traditional bank-type financial holding groups rank second and bank-owned financial holding groups rank last.

The average score of bank-type financial holding groups owned by financial holding group is 8.35, which is 0.27 higher than that of traditional bank-type financial holding groups and 0.97 higher than that of bank-owned financial holding groups. The scores of bank-owned financial holding groups is 7.84, which is 0.14 lower than that of 13 financial holding groups' average. It shows that after the implementation of comprehensive management, the difficulty of asset management increases and the safety of assets decreases.

#### 5.6.5.3 Ranking and Scores Changes of Asset Quality Scores from 2014 to 2018

From the score of the factor $F_3$ (asset quality) from 2014 to 2018, the overall score of $F_3$ shows a downward trend first and then rises with the development of Integrated finance.

In the past five years, the $F_3$ (asset quality) scores of bank-owned financial holding groups, bank-type financial holding groups owned by financial holding group and traditional bank-type financial holding groups show a "V" distribution. In other words, it has gradually decreased from 2014 to 2016, and gradually increased from 2016 to 2018.

From the improvement situation in 2018 compared with 2016, the improvement of $F_3$ (asset quality) scores of bank-owned financial holding groups, bank-type financial holding groups owned by financial holding group and traditional bank-type financial holding groups were 2.80, 2.76 and 1.31, respectively. The improvement score of bank-owned financial holding groups was 0.04 more than that of bank-type financial holding groups owned by financial holding group, which was 101.45% of the improvement of bank-type financial holding groups owned by financial holding group. The score improvement of bank-type financial holding groups owned by financial holding group is 1.45 more than that of traditional bank-type financial holding groups, which is 210.69% of that of traditional bank-type financial holding groups (see Annex XX).

### 5.6.6 *Analysis of Cost Control Evaluation Index Scores*

With the acceleration of interest rate market reform and the intensification of competition among financial institutions, it has become an important issue for financial holding groups to improve their profitability by effectively controlling costs. The previous section focused on the profitability score, while this section focuses on the cost management ability score.

#### 5.6.6.1 Cost Control Scores in 2018

Annex YY shows that the scores of factor $F_4$ in 2018 of traditional bank-type financial holding groups is higher than that of bank-type financial holding groups owned by financial holding group, which in turn is higher than that of bank-owned financial holding groups.

The $F_4$ score of the traditional bank-type financial holding groups is − 19.05, which is 2.8 higher than that of bank-type financial holding groups owned by financial holding group and 0.23 higher than that of bank-owned financial holding groups. The $F_4$ score of bank-type financial holding groups owned by financial holding group is − 21.85, which is 0.06 higher than that of bank-owned financial holding groups and 0.17 higher than that of the average of the 13 financial holding groups. It shows that in the short term, the development of integrated finance requires a certain amount of resources and high costs. For example, newly established or acquired other professional financial institutions need to pay a large amount of capital, pay a certain amount of mergers and acquisitions expenses, and pay new labor costs and so forth; The newly established branches of financial institutions need to increase the rental fees and labor costs of their business premises.

#### 5.6.6.2 Average Score of the Cost Control Scores from 2014 to 2018

According to the average scores of $F_4$ (cost control) from 2014 to 2018 (see Annex ZZ), bank-owned financial holding groups rank first, traditional bank-type financial holding groups rank second and bank-type financial holding groups owned by financial holding group rank last.

Among them, the average score of bank-owned financial holding groups is − 22.17, which is 0.99 points higher than that of bank-type financial holding groups owned by financial holding group and 2.4 points higher than that of traditional bank-type financial holding groups. The average score of bank-type financial holding groups owned by financial holding group is − 24.57, which is 1.41 points lower than that of traditional bank-type financial holding groups and 1.77 lower than that of the 13 financial holding groups. It shows that in the long run, the development of comprehensive management is conducive to improving the ability of cost management and reducing costs.

#### 5.6.6.3 Ranking and Scores Changes of Cost Control Scores from 2014 to 2018

According to the change of the factor $F_4$ (cost control) score from 2014 to 2018, developing comprehensive finance can promote cost reduction.

Compared with 2014, the scores of the cost control factor of bank-owned financial holding groups, bank-type financial holding groups owned by financial holding group and traditional bank-type financial holding groups increased by 9.03, 14.44 and 17.57, respectively, which shows that the development of comprehensive finance is conducive to reducing costs. However, the score of bank-owned financial holding groups increased less than bank-type financial holding groups owned by financial holding group and the score of bank-type financial holding groups owned by financial holding group increased less than the traditional bank-type financial holding groups. The scores increase in bank-owned financial holding groups is 62.51% of the increase in bank bank-type financial holding groups owned by financial holding group and 54.41% of the increase in traditional bank-type financial holding groups. The score increase of bank-type financial holding groups owned by financial holding group is 82.23% of the increase of traditional bank-type financial holding groups (see Annex AAA). It shows that the development of integrated finance, new establishment or acquisition of other professional financial institutions require certain investment in capital, acquisition costs, labor costs, business premises leasing, information system management and application.

## 5.7 Verification of Hypotheses in Performance Evaluation Research

To further analyze the influence of integrated operation on, solvency, profitability, cost control and operating performance, this section will further verify the hypobook of the relationship between integrated operation and solvency, profitability, cost control and operating performance of the 13 financial holding groups using IBM SPSS® Chi-square test model. According to the number of financial licenses held or indirectly held by the 13 financial holding groups, the companies are divided into three groups, including bank-owned financial holding groups, bank-type financial holding groups owned by financial holding group and traditional bank-type financial holding groups.

Chi-square test model is a hypobook testing method, and it is also a widely used statistical application of classified data. Chi-square test model types include the Chi-square test of four-grid data and the Chi-square test of row list data (Bi et al. 2019). This research adopts the Chi-square test of row list data.

### *5.7.1 Analysis on the Chi-Square Test Model of Integrated Management and Solvency*

Through chi-square test model, this book analyzes the solvency factor $F_1$ scores of the three groups of financial holding groups in recent five years from 2014 to 2018.

The precision test function of cross-table test in chi-square test model is used to judge the differences of each group. Chi-square test table is generated by chi-square test model, see Annex BBB for details.

The chi-square test model is used to test the scores of solvency factor $F_1$. The chi-square value $X^2$ is 143.437, and the corresponding *p value* is less than.001. The difference is statistically significant. Different financial licenses held or indirectly held by financial institutions have different impacts on profitability. According to chi-square test results, there are significant differences in the scores of solvency factor $F_1$ corresponding to the three groups of bank-owned financial holding groups, bank-type financial holding groups owned by financial holding group and traditional bank-type financial holding groups in recent five years. It can be considered that comprehensive operation and solvency factor $F_1$ have statistical significance.

Through grouping and the cross tabulation of solvency factor scores (see Annex CCC), we can see the correlation difference between grouping and solvency factor scores. Among the three sub-groups, the solvency score of bank-owned financial holding groups is 28.96, accounting for 40.40% of the total, the solvency score of bank-type financial holding groups owned by financial holding group is 21.87, accounting for 30.50% of the total, and the solvency score of traditional bank-type financial holding groups' group is 20.89, accounting for 29.10% of the total. To sum up, the solvency of bank-type financial holding groups owned by financial holding group is better than that of bank-owned financial holding groups, and the solvency of bank-owned financial holding groups' group is better than that of traditional bank-type financial holding groups' group. The conclusion about solvency obtained by Chi-square test model analysis is consistent with the conclusion of solvency score calculated by factor analysis, as shown in the average score table of solvency factor from 2014 to 2018 (Table 5.12).

### *5.7.2 Analysis on the Chi-Square Test Model of Integrated Management and Profitability*

Through IBM SPSS® chi-square test model, the profitability factor $F_2$scores of three groups of financial holding groups in recent five years from 2014 to 2018 were analyzed.

According to the chi-square test model in the chi-square test table of profitability factor scores (see Annex DDD), the chi-square value is 449.875, and the corresponding is less than 0.001, which is statistically significant. According to the chi-square test results, there are significant differences in the scores of profitability factor corresponding to the three groups of bank-owned financial holding groups, bank-type financial holding groups owned by financial holding group and traditional bank-type financial holding groups in recent five years. It can be considered that the scores of comprehensive operation and profitability factor have statistical significance.

Through the grouping and cross tabulation of profitability factor scores (see Annex EEE), we can see the correlation difference between grouping and profitability factor scores. Among the three sub-groups, the profitability score of bank-owned financial holding groups is 76.37, accounting for 34% of the total, the profitability score of bank-type financial holding groups owned by financial holding group is 73.28, accounting for 32.60% of the total, and the profitability score of traditional bank-type financial holding groups is 75.29, accounting for 33.50% of the total. To sum up, the profitability of the bank-owned financial holding groups is better than that of the traditional bank-type financial holding groups, and the solvency of the traditional bank-type financial holding groups is better than that of the bank-type financial holding groups owned by financial holding group. The conclusion about profitability obtained by chi-square test model analysis is consistent with the conclusion of proftability scores calculated by factor analysis, as shown in the table of average scores of profitability factors from 2014 to 2018 (Annex QQ).

### 5.7.3 Analysis on the Chi-Square Test Model of Integrated Operation and Cost Control

Through IBM SPSS® chi-square test model, this book analyzes the scores of the cost control factor $F_4$ of three groups of financial holding groups from 2014 to 2018. Because the enhancement variable value of chi-square test model should be positive, it is necessary to positively process the scores of cost control factors before chi-square test.

The chi-square test model is used to test the score of the cost control factor $F_4$ (see Annex FFF). The chi-square value $X^2$ is 698.922, and the corresponding *p value* is less than.001, which denotes statistical significance. According to the chi-square test results, the scores of the cost control factor $F_4$ corresponding to the three groups of bank-owned financial holding groups, bank-type financial holding groups owned by financial holding group and traditional bank-type financial holding groups are different in recent five years. It can be considered that the scores of comprehensive operation and cost control factor $F_4$ have statistical significance.

Through the cross tabulation of grouping and cost control ability factor scores (see Annex GGG), we can see the relevant differences between grouping and cost control ability scores. Among the three sub-groups, the profitability score of bank-owned financial holding groups is 110.83, accounting for 31.70% of the total, the cost control ability score of bank-type financial holding groups owned by financial holding group is 122.86, accounting for 35.20% of the total, and the cost control ability score of traditional bank-type financial holding groups is 115.78, accounting for 33.10% of the total. Because the scores of cost control ability factors are all negative, the positive treatment of negative numbers is carried out before Chi-square test. To sum up, the cost control ability of the bank-owned financial holding groups is better than that of the traditional bank-type financial holding groups, and the solvency of the traditional bank-type financial holding groups is better than that of the bank-type financial holding groups owned by financial holding group. The conclusion about cost control ability obtained by Chi-square test model analysis is consistent with the conclusion of cost control ability score calculated by factor analysis, as shown in the table of average score of cost control ability factor from 2014 to 2018 (Annex WW).

### 5.7.4 Analysis on Chi-Square Model Test of Integrated Operation and Business Performance

Through chi-square test model, the operating performance scores of the three groups of financial holding groups in recent five years from 2014 to 2018 were analyzed (see Annex HHH).

The chi-square test model shows that the chi-square value $X^2$ is 222.540, and the corresponding *p value* is less than 0.001, denoting statistical significance. According to the chi-square test results, there are significant differences in scores of comprehensive operation performance corresponding to three groups of bank-owned financial holding groups, bank-type financial holding groups owned by financial holding group and traditional bank-type financial holding groups in recent five years, so it can be considered that the scores of comprehensive operation and operation performance have statistical significance.

Through the cross-table (see Annex III), we can see the correlation difference between grouping and comprehensive operating performance scores. Among the three sub-groups, the score of comprehensive operating performance of bank-owned financial holding groups is 40.43, accounting for 36.30% of the total, while that of bank-type financial holding groups owned by financial holding group is 35.26, accounting for 31.70% of the total, while that of traditional bank-type financial holding groups is 35.59, accounting for 32.0% of the total. To sum up, the comprehensive operating performance of the bank-owned financial holding groups is better than that of the traditional bank-type financial holding groups, and the comprehensive operating performance of the traditional bank-type financial holding groups is better than that of the bank-type financial holding groups owned by financial holding group. This is also consistent with the conclusion of comprehensive operating performance scores calculated by factor analysis, as shown in the table of comprehensive average scores of groups from 2014 to 2018 (Table 5.11).

### *5.7.5 Summary of Performance Evaluation Research Hypotheses*

The statistical analysis software IBM SPSS® is used in the study of 13 financial holding groups that are divided into three groups, and the study focuses on solvency factors, profitability factors, asset quality factors, cost control factors and operating performance factor. On this basis, four research hypotheses on integrated operation and solvency, integrated operation and profitability, integrated operation and cost control and integrated operation and business performance are verified by the chi-square test model, and Table 5.13 shows the details. Through the above analysis and verification, we can see that the four research hypotheses put forward in this book are supported by the empirical tests.

## 5.8 Summary

This chapter sets the research hypotheses, and analyzes the reliability and validity of the data based on normalization and standardization. Through the KMO test and the Bartlett sphere test on it, it shows that factor analysis is suitable.

**Table 5.13** Summary of research hypotheses and test results

| Number | Hypotheses | Test results |
|---|---|---|
| 1 | The implementation of integrated management has a positive impact on the profitability of China's financial holding groups | True |
| 2 | The implementation of integrated management has a positive impact on the solvency of China's financial holding groups | True |
| 3 | The implementation of integrated management has a positive impact on the cost control of China's financial holding groups | True |
| 4 | The implementation of integrated management has a positive impact on the business performance of China's financial holding groups | True |

The empirical analysis is carried out. Common factors are extracted through the eigenvalue criterion and the scree test. Rotating component load matrix and common factor score coefficient matrix are used to calculate the common factor score, business performance score and ranking. The empirical results are then verified by cluster analysis. The comprehensive score and ranking of business performance and the ranking and scores of factors $F_1$, $F_2$, $F_3$ and $F_4$ are analyzed and summarized.

At last, based on the analysis of the comprehensive score of business performance and the scores and rankings of four factors, four research hypotheses, such as integrated operation and solvency, integrated operation and profitability, integrated operation and cost control ability, integrated operation, and business performance, are validated by the chi-square test model, and supported by the empirical tests.

# Chapter 6
# Conclusions and Suggestions for Performance Evaluation Research of Financial Holding Groups

Taking China's bank-type financial holding groups as research subjects, this book draws lessons from the latest research on financial holding groups based on the relevant theories and adopts the factor analysis method as the research method of operating performance while carrying out modeling and data analyses. This chapter summarizes the main conclusions of the research on the performance evaluation of China's financial holding groups, discusses the contribution and meaning of this book, sums up the practical significance for management, points out the limitations of this research, and gives an outlook on the direction for future research.

## 6.1 Conclusions of Performance Evaluation Research on Financial Holding Groups

Supported in the review of literature, we discuss and clarify the definition of financial holding groups, summarize the main types and characteristics of financial holding groups, and summarize and review the supporting theories of financial holding groups, including economies of scale, economies of scope, synergy effect and decentralized risk effect. In this book, the current research situation of domestic and foreign scholars on financial holding groups is discussed and the recent research on the operating performance of financial holding groups are introduced.

In this book, the data regression analysis of solvency factor, profitability factor, asset quality factor, cost control factor, comprehensive operating performance, is carried out by IBM SPSS® statistical software. On the basis of summarizing the contents of each chapter, the main conclusions are as follows. First, the operating performance evaluation model of Chinese banking financial holding groups is established. The second is to analyze the impact of diversification on business performance. Diversification has a positive impact on the improvement of operating performance, solvency, profitability and cost control ability, and also has a positive impact on



X. Ning, *Performance Evaluation of Financial Holding Companies*,
https://doi.org/10.1007/978-981-97-8128-7_6

the improvement of asset quality. Third, the transformation of traditional banks has become an urgent choice at present, and the transformation of traditional banks to integrated operation is the direction. Fourth, classify and evaluate financial holding groups. According to the classification of diversification degree of financial holding operation, the book evaluates and compares the operating performance of banks owned by financial holding groups, financial holding banks and traditional banks, and finds that the operating performance of individual traditional banks may not improve after being merged by financial holding groups.

## 6.2 Academic Significance of Performance Evaluation of Financial Holding Groups

In the previous section, research conclusions are summed up. This book has consistent findings with some previous literature and promotes and perfects the related theories. The academic significance of this study is as follows.

1. China's financial holding groups have various effects including the economies of scale.

Some foreign scholars have made empirical studies on financial holding groups in the United States, and they draw a conclusion that there are economies of scale (Gao 2021) and economies of scope in financial holding groups Clark (1988), synergy effect (Holzhauser 2010) and decentralized risk effect in relevant countries (Wall 1993). However, no scholars have studied whether there are economies of scale and so forth in China's financial holding groups. This book fills this gap.

Based on previous literature research and from the perspective of performance evaluation, this research collects the operating performance data of 13 listed banking financial holding groups from 2014 to 2018 and conducts an empirical analysis of operating performance through factor analysis. It shows that the integrated operation of China's financial holding groups in recent years has a positive effect on improving operating performance and profitability, enhancing risk compensation ability, and strengthening cost control ability.

China's financial holding groups have economies of scale. The expansion of asset scale, integrating resources, sharing fixed costs, promoting various financial products, and realizing customer information sharing, have a positive effect on improving business performance, improving profitability, enhancing risk compensation ability, and strengthening cost control ability.

China's financial holding groups have economies of scope. Financial holding groups have multiple financial institutions, whose business scope is wider than traditional commercial banks, and their business structure and profit-making channels are more diversified than traditional banks. Diversification of operations has a positive effect on business performance.

China's financial holding groups have synergy effects in terms of R&D, products, marketing, and information technology. For example, China Merchants Bank makes use of its good customer base in developing retail financial business to sell life insurance, public offering of fund, and asset management products for its subsidiaries. Based on providing diversified financial products and services to customers, it also further consolidated the customer base of retail financial business and promoted the continuous improvement of the business performance of China Merchants Bank in recent years.

China's financial holding groups have a decentralized risk effect. China's financial holding groups have promoted risk offsetting ability by implementing diversified operations. From the operating performance data from 2014 to 2018, it can be concluded that the risk offsetting ability of bank-owned financial holding groups is better than that of bank-type financial holding groups owned by financial holding group, and the risk offsetting ability of bank-type financial holding groups owned by financial holding group is better than that of traditional bank-type financial holding groups.

2. This book explores the methods of evaluating the operation performance of China's financial holding groups.

In China, research on financial holding groups started relatively late. Financial holding groups are still in the early stages of development in the country. In recent years, although there has been an increase in the literature on financial holding groups in China, many of them focus on the necessity of reforming the operation system of China's financial industry, the choice of models, and the reform of the regulatory system. There is very little literature on the theory and methods of integrated operation and management of China's financial holding groups, especially on performance evaluation, due to the short history of their development. The research results provide new ideas and new perspectives for related research and make up for the shortcomings of related previous research.

3. Conducting evaluation research in accordance with degrees of diversification of financial holding groups.

In this research, the innovation point is that we divide financial holding groups into bank-owned financial holding groups, bank-type financial holding groups owned by financial holding group and traditional bank-type financial holding groups. Each type of banks owns different number of financial licenses. In addition, the operating performance of the three types of financial holding groups is compared and analyzed.

In the analysis of business performance, it is mainly evaluated from four dimensions, namely, comprehensive business performance, risk compensation ability, profitability, and cost control ability. In the evaluation process, the degree of business diversification, performance and risk are comprehensively analyzed, and the score of business performance evaluation is calculated. To a certain extent, it enriches the theory of financial holding group's performance evaluation.

4. Diversification of financial holding groups promotes the improvement of business performance evaluation.

Several scholars (Barth et al. 2000) support that there is a positive correlation between business diversification and performance. With the deepening of interest rate marketization reform, the spread between deposits and loans which is the main source of traditional bank profits, has narrowed. Realizing integrated operation can expand capital marketization business and gain profit growth point. Diversified operation, diversified business structure and diversified profit methods of financial institutions can maintain the stability of the business performance of financial holding groups. The implementation of integrated management can increase the economies of scale and scope, strengthen the risk control management of commercial banks, expand the sources of profits, and enhance the competitiveness of banks. From the comprehensive scores and ranking trends of business performance in recent five years, diversified banking financial holding groups are more competitive than companies that do not implement integrated operation. The business performance of bank-owned financial holding groups is better than that of bank-type financial holding groups owned by financial holding group and the competitiveness of bank-type financial holding groups owned by financial holding group has gradually increased, while the business performance of bank-type financial holding groups owned by financial holding group is better than traditional bank-type financial holding groups. In response to the reform of interest rate marketization and the acceleration of financial disintermediation, there is a transition from traditional banks to financial holding groups to improve their income structure, realize economies of scale and scope, reduce operating costs, and improve their operating performance.

## 6.3 Suggestions for Performance Evaluation Management of Financial Holding Groups

Based on the results and conclusions of the previous research, this book will provide valuable recommendations for financial holding groups, such as bank-owned financial holding groups, bank-type financial holding groups owned by financial holding group, traditional bank-type financial holding groups and traditional banks, which have important practical management implications.

1. It is an important strategic choice for traditional banks to implement integrated operation.

With the gradual opening of the financial industry, the reform of interest rate marketization has been deepened, the capital market has undergone prosperous development, the proportion of direct financing has increased, and fin-tech has gained fast development. The pace of financial disintermediation has accelerated. The interest difference between loans and deposits of traditional commercial banks is decreasing day by day, which brings great pressure on the banking industry to make profits and survive. The trend of financial disintermediation is accelerating, which brings obvious impact to the traditional financing intermediary led by banks, and the traditional customer base of banks is facing significant diversion pressure.

Implementing integrated management enables commercial banks to enter non-bank financial fields such as trust, insurance, securities, futures, investment. When macroeconomic policies and situations change, and the market operating environment changes, implementing integrated operation enables customers to choose more financial services and helps to adjust business development priorities in a timely manner and rationally optimize business structure. It will help commercial banks and ensure the overall stability of bank operations to go ahead with the transformation from relying on single deposit and loan spread income to relying on diversified income such as investment banking business, trust business and investment business, reduce profit volatility, and obtain stable and sustainable growth of profit.

Implementing integrated management, commercial banks can promote the transformation from holding customer assets to entrusting investment and management of customer assets and provide one-stop integrated financial services. By carrying out integrated operation, commercial banks can promote the continuous improvement of investment management and asset allocation capabilities in various ways such as deposit and loan business, trust business and investment banking business, and constantly meet the diversified investment and asset allocation needs of customers. Satisfying the diversified needs of customers can broaden the business scope, increase the profitable income sources, promote stable and sustainable development, and continuously enhance the core advantages in the market competition. Using deposit and loan business, trust business, investment banking business and other ways, commercial banks can improve the efficiency of customer service, reduce the cost of customer service and business operation, improve customer adhesion, promote the realization of economies of scale and scope, promote the further dispersion and reduction of business risks, and continuously improve profitability.

To sum up, commercial banks should take integrated management as the main direction of future strategic development, promote diversified business scope and common development of multiple functions, and promote the implementation and implementation of intensive management.

2. It helps to promote corporate governance at both group and subsidiary levels.

In recent years, with the rapid development of commercial banks' consolidation and conglomeration, financial holding groups have become large institutions with complex management, which requires continuous optimization of corporate governance and to clarify the division of responsibilities between the group and subsidiary levels of financial holding groups and stimulate vitality through institutional innovation.

At the group level, the focus is to promote the establishment and improvement of corporate governance system and strengthen the construction of integrated financial service system.

Establish and improve the corporate governance system. The group and its subsidiaries have established corporate governance structures of stockholders' meeting, board of directors, administrative committee and senior management and formulated the book of association of the group and its subsidiaries. According to the book of association, the management performs their duties and checks and balances effectively. Under the board of directors, there are professional management committees for strategic management, senior management nomination, business audit, investment decision-making, salary management, risk management, related party transactions, to review relevant major issues and put forward professional opinions. A clear and forward-looking strategic plan for the group's development should be made to establish a corporate culture with prominent brand and characteristics, maintain steady operation and promote sustainable development.

Promote the construction of an integrated financial service system. Financial holding groups need to promote the construction of an integrated financial service system which requires financial holding groups to accurately grasp the development trend of the financial industry, actively face the changes in the market environment, adhere to the customer-centered and market-oriented policies, promote the construction of the group's integrated financial and technological services system, and continuously improve its profitability. By establishing an integrated financial service model, financial holding groups will provide customers with comprehensive financial service solutions, create various types of financial products covering the whole life cycle, and establish and improve a one-stop integrated financial service system, continuously promote financial empowerment through technology, ecological empowerment through technology and ecological empowerment through finance, strive to build a financial ecosystem, provide financial products and services for corporate customers, individual customers and financial peers, and continuously enhance the ability of value creation.

At the subsidiary level, the emphasis is on promoting the establishment of a unified authorization management system, promoting the implementation of the group's strategic planning in subsidiaries, and creating a distinctive business development model.

Financial holding groups need to enhance the establishment of a unified authorization management system. According to the development stages, industry rules and business characteristics faced by different subsidiaries, a unified authorization management system is established, and a differentiated management model is implemented. These companies should establish the management structure of subsidiaries and subsidiaries dynamically adjust the organizational structure post setting and market-oriented salary incentive mechanisms according to the business needs and the needs of specialization and marketization.

The strategic plans should be implemented. The group has set up a strategic development management department, which is responsible for the preparation and implementation of the Group's overall strategic plan, and guides and supervises subsidiaries in the preparation of strategic development plans to promote the implementation of the plan; The board of directors of the subsidiary shall prepare the strategic development plan of the subsidiary according to the strategic development direction of the subsidiary specified in the group strategic plan. In the daily management of subsidiaries, the group reviews the major development strategies, major business activities, appointment and dismissal of important personnel and important risk management policies of subsidiaries and evaluates the implementation of the strategic plan formulated by the group in accordance with the agenda of shareholders' meeting, board of directors and board of supervisors, which will lay a solid foundation on the stable operation of subsidiaries and enhance the coordinated development of quality, efficiency and speed of subsidiaries.

What is more, it helps promote each business segment to form a distinctive development model. In terms of banking business, financial holding groups adhere to the priority strategy of scientific and technological development, promote the digital transformation of operations, and improve the refined level of service and management. Expanding retail business requires to focus on the living ecosystem and improving wealth management capabilities. To strengthen the business to the public, financial holding groups should focus on the financial ecosystem, and provide integrated financial services for enterprises. Commercial banks are taken as the basic platform of integrated financial services, which provides carriers of customer recommendation and marketing channels for other subsidiaries and accelerates the transformation of companies. In terms of insurance business, agility and experience feeling of services are improved due to the overall advantages of the group and the driving forces of technology, products, and channels. By constructing multi-level product systems such as life insurance, property insurance, pension insurance and health insurance, the group provides insurance services for different age groups and different customer groups. By strengthening the construction of insurance brokers, insurance agents, bank insurance and internet insurance, the group will provide customers with exclusive insurance products and services. In terms of investment business, the group will give full play to the advantages of securities, trust, fund, leasing and asset management, implement a development strategy focusing on core business to provide wealth management, equity investment, enterprise securities services, investment, and loan linkage. The group will also broaden and deepen the business growth channels and build a leading asset management brand in the industry.

3. Establishing business collaboration mechanism within the group and among subsidiaries.

By promoting the establishment of management mechanisms such as business collaboration and benefit distribution among subsidiaries of the group, the cross-selling and business collaboration among subsidiaries are strengthened, the integration and utilization of resources within the group are deepened, and the effect of integrated financial services is promoted.

A collaborative management mechanism is established in the group. Various measures are taken to promote business collaboration among subsidiaries of the group and promote the rapid growth of business collaboration. At the group level, the strategic development management department is responsible for coordinating the business collaboration among subsidiaries, focusing on promoting collaborative work in three aspects: integrating sales channels, integrating financial product research and development, and integrating information sharing. Integration of sales channels refers to integrate banking, securities, insurance, trust, and other sales channels, carry out unified business activities including channel marketing, customers, joint promotion of channel application, and reduction of sales costs. Integrating financial product research and development means developing integrated products and services covering the whole life cycle of enterprises for major clients and taking advantages of the protection function of credit products, investment products, private placement products and insurance products, under the condition that subsidiaries can develop products on their own. Integrating information sharing means that various subsidiaries will share information about customer demand, business development forecast, and risk monitoring, which will enhance the sensitivity of information, improve the speed of information acquisition, and reduce the cost of information acquisition. Establishing a management mechanism such as benefit distribution of business collaboration among subsidiaries within the group promotes the provision of integrated financial services. Business collaboration is brought into the business performance evaluation of subsidiaries and business departments and evaluation will be regularly carried out to promote the business collaboration among subsidiaries. When carrying out business collaboration among subsidiaries, the collaborative business shall be handled according to market-oriented management, such as adopting market-oriented business access and exit mechanism, pricing management mechanism and risk management mechanism, to realize the benefit distribution accounting of each subsidiary, promote resource sharing and complementary advantages, and ensure the effectiveness of collaborative development.

The cross-selling and business synergy should be strengthened. The first thing is to build an integrated financial service platform. Establishing a group data sharing center aims to manage the customer and business data of each subsidiary within the group and form a centralized data platform. Financial holding groups need to promote the construction of One Connect, an integrated financial services platform. Through this platform, customers can enjoy various financial services and products with an account, thus improving the level of one-stop integrated financial services. The second thing is to carry out business cooperation. Financial holding groups need to promote cross-selling among different financial subsidiaries and business lines and implement a "package" of integrated financial services. For example, banks can cooperate with trust companies to provide family trust services to private banking customers. Banks can cooperate with security companies to jointly develop enterprise investment and loan business and sell direct financing services such as issuing credit bonds and listing counseling. In addition, financial holding groups need to promote customers migration. In other words, they strive to recommend insurance, trust financing and asset management products to bank customers, sell banking financing, trust investment and asset management services to insurance customers, and provide integrated financial services. They should encourage offline customers to use various online services, for example, recommending mobile applications to customers of community banks to handle business quickly, which will improve operation and service efficiency and reduce operating costs.

4. Establish an Enterprise Risk Management system for the group and its subsidiaries.

Form an Enterprise Risk Management culture. Financial holding groups have many different types of specialized financial subsidiaries, which carry out many kinds of business and face different types and complex risks. To ensure that the overall risk management and control requirements of financial holding groups can be truly implemented among the holding financial institutions within the group, an Enterprise Risk Management policy system is formulated, and the overall risk policies of the group and each holding financial institution are clarified to ensure that the whole group has a clear and unified understanding of risk management and control business risks. Establishing the risk preference and risk limits of the group and its holding financial institutions and transmitting the group's risk management strategies to the holding financial institutions, helps to maintain the stability of the overall risk boundary of the group. In addition, the universal risk management system is internalized into an organizational culture, and the risk management culture is transformed into guidelines that are generally accepted and pursued by all employees.

Adhere to the Five Principles and do a good job in risk management of the group and its subsidiaries. The Five Principles mainly include the principle of matching risk management with business development, the principle of full coverage of risk management scope, the principle of independent operation of risk management between parent group and subsidiary group, the principle of effective risk management and the principle of classified risk management.

Financial holding groups need to adhere to the principle of matching risk management with business development, establish and improve an Enterprise Risk Management system, strengthen internal compliance management and prevention and control, match the degree of risk management with the speed and scale of business development, and avoid shortcomings in risk management, which is slower than the speed of business development.

Financial holding groups must adhere to the principle of full coverage of risk management. Horizontally, an Enterprise Risk Management system needs to cover all business departments, positions, and all personnel, and cover various risk areas such as market risk, operational risk, and transaction risk. Vertically, the risk management system should cover the group and its subsidiaries, covering all business lines such as asset management, financial market, and investment. In addition, the Enterprise Risk Management system should cover the whole process, that is, covering decision-making, implementation, and supervision, while risk management and business development should be carried out simultaneously.

The group must adhere to the principle of independent operation of risk management between the parent group and the subsidiary group and set up an Enterprise Risk Management mechanism that is separate and restricted from business operation mechanism in the group and subsidiaries. Risk management mechanism includes organizational structure, reporting route, risk disposal, and supervision, which promotes mutual checks and balances between risk management and business development, risk management institutions and business departments.

Financial holding groups must stick to the principle of effectiveness of risk management. The construction of a risk management system is combined with daily operation and management. The result of risk management is applied into the process of business access, examination and approval, and monitoring, and it is an evaluation index of business performance of the group and its subsidiaries, which will effectively prevent various risks such as market risk, operational risk, and liquidity risk, while promoting risk management.

Financial holding groups must adhere to the principle of risk classified management. The scope and boundaries of risk management responsibilities between the group and subsidiaries should be clarified, which helps to avoid gaps in risk management. The group is mainly responsible for the overall construction of a risk management system, supervising and managing major risks of subsidiaries and managing cross-business risks among subsidiaries. Subsidiaries carry out their own risk management according to the regulatory requirements of their respective industries, to match risk management with business development and promote the implementation of an Enterprise Risk Management system.

Strengthen the management of credit risk and market risk, and formulate specific risk-resistance strategies. Strengthening credit risk management refers to effectively integrate the distribution of credit risks of financial holding groups, master the situation of credit risks, establish an internal credit evaluation system of financial holding groups, implement credit risk grading and early warning system, and effectively improve the timeliness of credit risk response. Also, financial holding groups should strengthen credit risk concentration management and credit risk monitoring and establish a risk quantification mechanism.

Strengthening market risk management means to establish an early warning risk index system, set risk tolerance and related risk limits of financial holding groups, and effectively control market risks.

Strengthen liquidity risk management. Combined with the characteristics of the financial industry, based on the establishment of liquidity index monitoring systems for banks, securities and insurance subsidiaries, the liquidity risk monitoring system of the whole group is gradually established, the management of maturity mismatch and amount mismatch is strengthened, the liquidity risk emergency plan is established, and emergency drills are conducted in a timely manner to improve the liquidity risk management ability.

Establish a risk big data management system to improve the risk management ability in the whole course of business. With the rapid development of financial science and technology, through the combination of scientific and technological development and scenarios, risk data and risk information systems are created, and risk management Informa ionization and digitalization are well built. In view of market risk, credit risk, and operational risk, technology such as digitalization and intelligent management will be used in risk management and control of business front office, middle office of management and back office of support. Establishing a big data risk model and analysis system will help to timely and quickly judge the risk status according to the risk indicators. Combined with risk quantitative indicators, the risk situation undertaken by subsidiaries can be measured. Combined with qualitative indicators, the impact of risks on the group and subsidiaries can be monitored and evaluated, which promptly triggers risk early warning and quickly handles risks.

Improve the management level of financial technology and digital intelligence. With the deep integration of technology and finance, cutting-edge technologies such as blockchain, cloud computing and artificial intelligence have intensified the innovation of the financial industry and promoted the efficiency of the financial industry. At the group's level, financial holding groups need to improve the group's digital intelligent management level in an all-round way, and design and operate the digital mode of enterprise organization and daily business by implementing the digital management strategy. Firstly, business processing is digitalized. Centered on clients, digital transformation of business processes is implemented to improve customer's experience and increase customer fidelity. Secondly, the process of product design is digitalized. Financial holding groups design and provide targeted financial products according to the quantitative results of customers that is obtained by quantifying the financial status and personal preferences of customers. Thirdly, the service channel is digitalized. Financial holding groups strive to create an ecological circle of financial services, focus on customers' basic necessities of life, cooperate with large shopping malls, hotels, buses, cinemas, and provide targeted integrated financial services such as payment, credit loans and wealth management products. Fourthly, risk management is digitalized. Using big data, artificial intelligence, Internet of Things, 5G and other technologies, companies can accurately know customers' preferences, and using cloud computing and blockchain we can track customers' credit, thus improving the efficiency and accuracy of risk identification. Fifthly, talents in digitalization field are cultivated. Financial holding groups set up a financial technology team, strengthen research on artificial intelligence and mobile internet, and vigorously cultivate talents in these fields.

At the subsidiaries' level, subsidiaries can carry out customer management, precision marketing, intelligent risk control and operation management based on big data technology. For instance, in the banking business, relying on advanced technologies such as artificial intelligence and cloud services, financial holding groups will establish a new core banking cloud platform, blockchain trade financing, intelligent robot customer service, smart mobile banking, digital credit, smart investment and financial advisor, multi-channel recommendation and sales to greatly improve the efficiency of serving customers, enhance user experience and reduce operating costs. In terms of insurance business, advanced technologies such as big data are applied to four important directions, namely customer service, agency, underwriting and claims settlement, and various applications such as intelligent double recording, intelligent underwriting, product risk pricing and big data anti-fraud are promoted. In terms of securities business, with the help of the existing basic data such as customer information, transaction records and research reports of securities companies, it helps securities firms to carry out digital transformation, and applies artificial intelligence to intelligent investment, intelligent customer service, intelligent risk control, intelligent stock selection and intelligent mobile applications.

5. Accelerating the growth of financial talents.

For modern financial industry, whether it is commercial bank, securities group, insurance group, trust group, futures group or investment group, its production factors include capital, information, and entrepreneurial ability. With the deepening of interest rate marketization and capital market reform, financial technology is developing rapidly, new formats, new markets and new environment bring new challenges, and the role of financial talents is becoming increasingly prominent. In view of the separate operation in China in the early stage, the financial talents are only engaged in one kind of business such as commercial banks, securities companies and insurance companies, and the all-rounders who are proficient in the business of commercial banks, securities companies and insurance companies are very scarce. It is of great significance to speed up the training of integrated talents and accelerate the establishment of an integrated talent training system with different categories, full coverage, and specialization.

Establish a team of integrated financial experts with multiple levels. According to the needs of the existing financial business development, financial holding groups will establish a team of experts at three levels: high-end, middle-level and grass-roots level. Among them, the high-end expert team focuses on cultivating integrated financial innovation awareness, improving group leadership, and solving major integrated financial problems, and the middle-level expert team focuses on cultivating strong integrated financial management professional ability and ability to analyze and solve integrated financial problems, while grass-roots expert team focuses on training integrated financial business and product knowledge, professional ethics and safety, and meeting the needs of integrated financial service posts.

Establish a regular evaluation and training mechanism for integrated financial talents. A multi-dimensional evaluation model of integrated financial talents is built, and an integrated financial expert evaluation library is set up. Through group review and panel discussion of judges, financial holding groups regularly carry out evaluation and professional improvement of expert teams at all levels of integrated finance, and link with individual performance to promote the professional ability of talents at all levels. According to the characteristics of personal growth, the group establishes professional talent and management talent cultivation systems. The group needs to open the transition channel between the group and its subsidiaries. Vertically, promotions can be carried out smoothly according to levels. Horizontally, the professional talents cultivation system and the management talent cultivation system are transformed. Among the subsidiaries, cross-sectional part-time positions can be carried out to build a three-dimensional talent development overpass. The group has accelerated the transformation of personnel structure and intensified the selection and reserve of financial technology talents. Financial holding groups will stablish a talent pool training system for core positions, increase the training of group management talents, comprehensive financial talents, international development talents and financial science and technology talents, and promote the group's strategic planning.

Establish an integrated financial hierarchical training and market-oriented incentive mechanism. The group will focus on personnel training in key positions in comprehensive finance, foster people through various training brands, promote the construction of talent training bases, online learning platforms, and overseas rotation training programs, accelerate strategic planning and corporate culture dissemination, and promote the improvement of organizational efficiency and professional quality of personnel. Adhere to the market-oriented incentive mechanism, attract and motivate outstanding talents, establish a selection and training mechanism for "horse racing" based on performance, and select outstanding young talents according to the market-oriented principle; Strengthen the tracking of market salary, continuously optimize the salary management mechanism, and continuously optimize the salary structure of front office, middle office and back office, so as to provide strong human capital support for building an integrated financial service brand.

## 6.4 Research Limitations

This chapter summarizes the results of the previous empirical study and analysis of the results of business performance evaluation of 13 bank-type financial holding groups, discusses the contributions of the theory of business performance evaluation and summarizes the managerial implications of improving business performance evaluation of financial holding groups in practice. However, because the development of China's financial holding groups is in its initial stage, and the research problem itself has a certain degree of complexity, and is limited by many objective and subjective factors, such as limited public operation data of financial holding groups and the fact that management information is a commercial secret, there are certain shortcomings in the research process of this book, which require further in-depth discussion.

1. Limitations of the research sample

In terms of governing body of financial holding groups, they can be divided into five categories, including financial institutions, central enterprises, financial holding groups established by local governments, financial holding groups established by private enterprises and the Internet financial holding groups. In view of the current development status of China's financial holding groups and the availability of data, we only conduct research on 13 listed national banking financial holding groups. Although the total assets of the above 13 banking financial holding groups at the end of 2018 are 146.60 trillion yuan, accounting for 69.82% of the total assets of the national banking industry, and they obtained a net profit of 1.40 trillion yuan, accounting for 76.50% of the net profit of the national banking industry, the selected samples may not completely represent the overall banking financial holding groups. Therefore, whether the research conclusions are applicable to all financial holding groups remains to be further tested.

2. Limitations of the research model

According to the three principles of safety, liquidity and profitability of commercial bank management, the principle of combining financial information with non-financial information evaluation, and the principle of evaluating financial holding groups, we select 15 evaluation indicators including solvency, profitability, and asset quality, and use the EVA model. Compared with the main evaluation indicators of traditional commercial banks, the non-interest income indicator is added as the main evaluation indicator of financial holding groups, and the non-interest income is regarded as an important indicator reflecting the diversified development degree and level of banking financial holding groups. Considering the confidentiality and limited access of listed companies' information, most of the indicators selected in this book are financial and risk indicators, and a certain amount of qualitative indicators such as corporate governance are not quantified and included in the performance evaluation method, so the research on this aspect needs to be deepened.

3. Limitations of data analysis

According to the diversification degree of financial holding groups, that is, the number of financial licenses they hold, the banking financial holding groups are divided into three categories, namely bank-owned financial holding groups, bank-type financial holding groups owned by financial holding group and traditional bank-type financial holding groups. In this book, we make a comparative analysis on business performance and a data regression analysis from four dimensions, such as risk offset factor, profitability factor, cost control factor and comprehensive operating performance score. This book analyzes the comprehensive performance scores and rankings of 13 financial holding groups, and only analyzes the scores and rankings of risk offset factors, profitability factors and cost control factors of some financial holding groups. The scores and rankings of risk offset factors, profitability factors and cost control factors of 13 financial holding groups were not analyzed one by one. In the next step, we will do further discussion and analysis.

## 6.5 Prospects for Future Research

This book carries out an exploratory study on the business performance evaluation of financial holding groups, which is only the starting point of the research work, and it will be necessary to carry out continuous research on this in the future to further expand the theoretical contribution and practical significance.

1. Extend the sample selection

In this book, 13 national banking financial holding groups are selected as research objects. Expanding sample coverage and sample size can help us better analyze financial holding groups, improve the representativeness and universality of the research results, and facilitate comparative analysis, to do a better job in data analysis and summarization. With the rapid development of financial holding groups in China, and with more and more standardized management and richer disclosure of data, it is believed that the theoretical research and practical application of business performance evaluation of financial holding groups will be further deepened in the future.

2. Expanding the theoretical model of business performance evaluation

In this book, 15 evaluation indicators of solvency, profitability, and asset quality are selected, and most of the performance evaluation indicators are financial indicators and risk indicators, which are basically quantitative indicators. Not only quantitative indicators but also qualitative indicators will make an impact on business performance. In further research, some qualitative indicators will be added, and they will be quantified. Further improving and perfecting the evaluation method will make the evaluation system of financial holding groups comprehensive and scientific.

Factor analysis method and EVA model are used in this research. In the follow-up stage, we will try to use other methods or combine the factor analysis method and other analysis methods, which can improve the theoretical model. Conducting comparative analysis on these two situations will enable us to draw conclusions that are closer to the actual situation.

3. In-depth data analysis

The research on individual financial holding groups is not deep and comprehensive enough, the influence of each indicator on comprehensive business performance has not been analyzed in depth, and the data analysis is not sufficient. Each financial holding group has its own operating characteristics, and there is no in-depth analysis of the differences between them. In fact, it needs to be discussed in depth and objectively, which is also a topic worthy of further research.

# Annexes

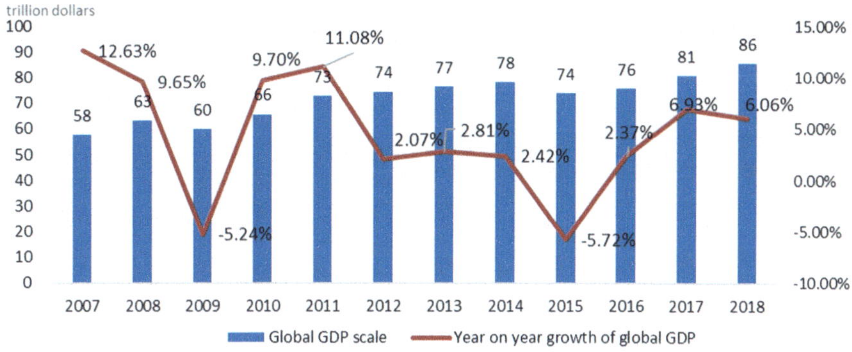


**Annex A**—Global GDP from 2007 to 2018. *Source* The website of World Bank

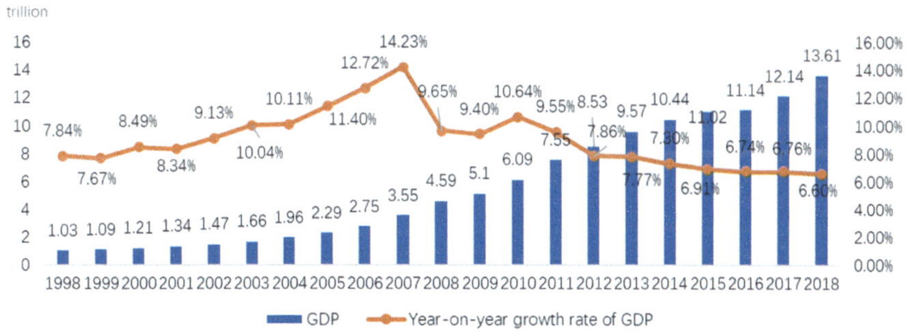


**Annex B**—China's GDP from 1998 to 2018. *Source* The website of National Bureau of Statistics



X. Ning, *Performance Evaluation of Financial Holding Companies*,
https://doi.org/10.1007/978-981-97-8128-7

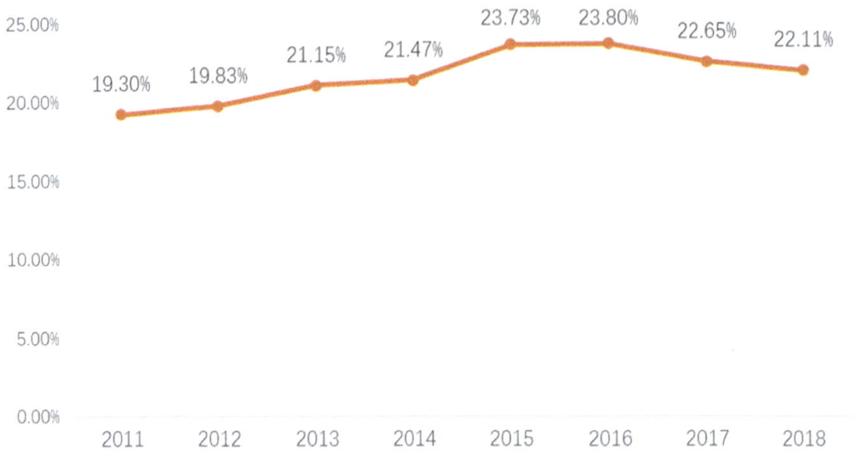


**Annex C**—Non-interest income in China's banking industry from 2011 to 2018. *Source* Website of China Banking and Insurance Regulatory Commission

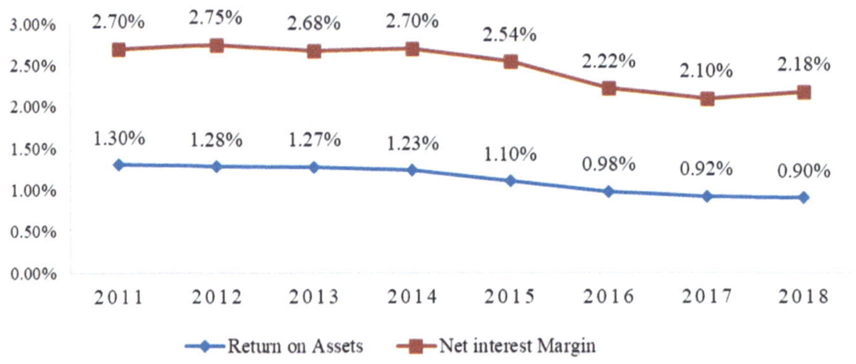


**Annex D**—Net interest margin of banking industry in China. *Source* Website of China Banking and Insurance Regulatory Commission

**Annex E**—Types of financial holding groups in China

| No | Types | Examples |
|---|---|---|
| 1 | Financial holding group dominated by a financial institution | The Bank of China, the China Construction Bank, the Agricultural Bank of China, the Industrial and Commercial Bank of China, the Bank of Communications, the National Development Bank, the China Merchants Bank, the Ping An Bank, the Industrial Bank, the Everbright Bank, the Pudong Development Bank, the China Huarong Asset Management Group, the China Great Wall Asset Management Group, the China Cinda Asset Management Group, the China Orient Asset Management Group, China Ping An Insurance (Group) Group, the People's Property Insurance Group of China, China Life Insurance (Group) Group, China Taiping Life Insurance Group |
| 2 | Financial holding group dominated by a central enterprise | China Merchant Group, CNPC Capital Group, State Grid Yingda Group, Huaneng Capital Group, Minmetals Capital and AVIC Capital Group |
| 3 | Financial holding group dominated by the local government | Beijing Financial Holding Group, Shanghai International Group, Guangzhou Yuexiu Group, TEDA Investment Holding Group, Chongqing Yufu Asset Management Group, Jiangsu Guoxin Investment Group |
| 4 | Financial holding group dominated by a private enterprise | FOSUN International Group, Lenovo, Evergrande Group, and Wangxiang Group |
| 5 | Financial holding group dominated by an Internet giant | Alibaba, Tencent Financial Technology, JD Finance, and Baidu Finance |

*Source* China Financial Stability Report issued by the People's Bank of China in 2018 (PBC 2019)

**Annex F**—Classification of major financial holding groups dominated by financial institutions

| Classification | Examples |
|---|---|
| Banking financial holding groups | The Bank of China, the China Construction Bank, the Agricultural Bank of China, the Industrial and Commercial Bank of China, the Bank of Communications, the China Development Bank, the China Merchants Bank, the Ping An Bank, the Industrial Bank, the China Everbright Bank and the Shanghai Pudong Development Bank |
| Insurance financial holding groups | China Ping An Insurance (Group) Group, People's Insurance Group of China, China Life Insurance (Group) Group |
| Asset management companies | China Huarong Asset Management Group, China Great Wall Asset Management Group, China Cinda Asset Management Group, China Oriental Asset Management Group |

*Source* China Financial Stability Report (PBOC, 2019)

**Annex G**—The financial licenses held by some bank-based financial holding groups

| Bank | Banking | Securities | Insurance | Trust | Fund | Leasing | Futures | Total number of licenses |
|---|---|---|---|---|---|---|---|---|
| A | √ | √ | √ | | √ | √ | √ | 6 |
| B | √ | √ | √ | | √ | √ | √ | 6 |
| C | √ | √ | √ | | √ | √ | √ | 6 |
| D | √ | √ | √ | √ | √ | √ | √ | 7 |
| E | √ | √ | √ | √ | √ | √ | √ | 7 |
| F | √ | √ | √ | √ | √ | √ | √ | 7 |
| G | √ | √ | √ | √ | √ | √ | √ | 7 |
| H | √ | √ | √ | √ | √ | √ | √ | 7 |
| I | √ | √ | √ | | √ | √ | √ | 6 |
| J | √ | √ | | √ | √ | √ | √ | 6 |
| K | √ | √ | | √ | √ | √ | | 5 |
| L | √ | √ | | | √ | √ | √ | 5 |
| M | √ | | | | | √ | | 2 |

*Source* The annual Reports of the 13 Listed Banks (2014–2018)

**Annex H**—Development course of the integrated finance of I Bank

| 1993 | 2002 | 2003 | 2008 | 2009 | 2015 |
|---|---|---|---|---|---|
| I Bank International Financial Holding (Securities) Group was established in1993, with a registered capital of HK$ 4129 million | I Bank Fund was established on December 27, 2002, with a registered capital of 1.31 billion yuan | I Bank Life Insurance, established in August 2003, is the first life insurance group jointly funded by domestic and foreign companies after China became a member of the World Trade Organization, with a registered capital of 2.8 billion yuan | I Bank Leasing was established in March 2008 with a registered capital of 6 billion yuan | In 2009, I Bank completed the acquisition of the equity of P Bank, and P Bank became a subsidiary of I Bank | In March 2015, I Bank Consumer Finance Group was established with a registered capital of 3.8 billion yuan |

*Source* Annual report of I Bank from 2014 to 2018

**Annex I**—Integrated financial organization structure of I Bank

<table>
<tr><th>Market category</th><th>Bank</th><th>Insurance</th><th>Others</th></tr>
<tr><td rowspan="4">Domestic market</td><td rowspan="4">I Bank</td><td rowspan="4">I Bank Life Insurance</td><td>I Bank Fund</td></tr>
<tr><td>I Bank Financing Leasing</td></tr>
<tr><td>I Bank consumer Finance</td></tr>
<tr><td>I Bank Financing Leasing</td></tr>
<tr><td rowspan="2">Overseas market</td><td>P Bank</td><td rowspan="2"></td><td rowspan="2">I Bank International Financial Holding Group</td></tr>
<tr><td>6 overseas branches</td></tr>
</table>

*Source* Annual reports of I Bank from 2014 to 2018

**Annex J**—Major operating indicators of I Bank from 2014 to 2018

| Indicator | 2014 | 2015 | 2016 | 2017 | 2018 |
|---|---|---|---|---|---|
| Total assets | 4,731,829 | 5,474,978 | 5,942,311 | 6,297,638 | 6,745,729 |
| Operating revenue | 165,863 | 201,471 | 209,025 | 220,897 | 248,555 |
| Net profits | 56,049 | 58,018 | 62,380 | 70,638 | 80,819 |
| ROE (%) | 19.28 | 17.09 | 16.27 | 16.54 | 16.57 |
| ROA (%) | 1.28 | 1.14 | 1.09 | 1.15 | 1.24 |
| Non-performing loans ratio (%) | 1.11 | 1.68 | 1.87 | 1.61 | 1.36 |
| LLRA (%) | 540.68 | 425.57 | 332.39 | 430.75 | 597.64 |
| Capital adequacy ratio (%) | 12.38 | 12.57 | 13.33 | 15.48 | 15.68 |
| Cost-income ratio (%) | 30.54 | 27.67 | 28.01 | 30.23 | 31.02 |
| NIIR (%) | 32.47 | 32.13 | 35.61 | 34.43 | 35.47 |

*Source* The annual reports of I Bank (2014–2018)
*Note* The unit of total assets, operating revenue and net profits is million yuan

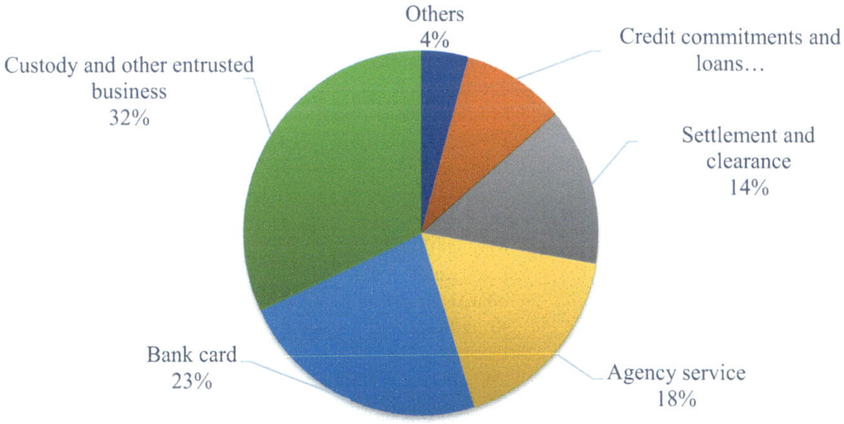


**Annex K**—The proportion of charges and commission income of I Bank. *Source* Annual report for 2018 of I Bank

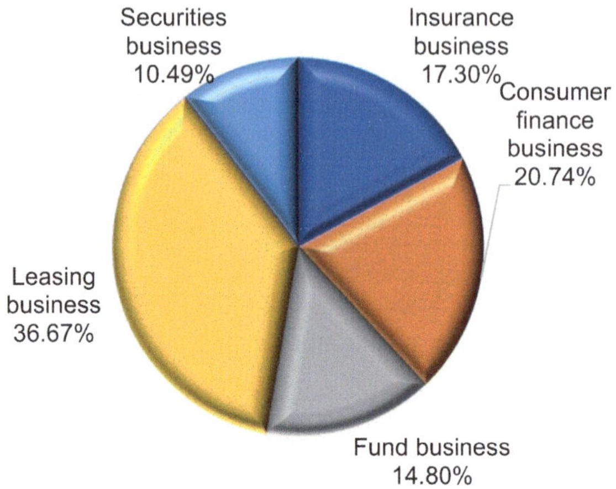


**Annex L**—The proportion of net profits of major subsidiaries of I Bank. *Source* Annual report for 2018 of I Bank

**Annex M**—Comprehensive financial development process of E Bank

| 2000 | 2005 | 2007 | 2010 | 2017 |
|---|---|---|---|---|
| E Bank Insurance Group was established in November 2000 with a registered capital of HK$ 400 million yuan | E Bank Fund Insurance was established in August 2005 with a registered capital of 200 million yuan | E Bank International Trust Group was officially opened in October 2007 with a registered capital of 5765 million yuan<br>E Bank Leasing Group was officially opened in December 2007 with a registered capital of 8.5 billion yuan<br>E Bank International Holding Group was established in May 2007 and listed on the main board of Hong Kong Stock Exchange in May 2017 | Insurance Group was established in January 2010 with a registered capital of 5.1 billion yuan | E bank Investment Group was established in December 2017 with a registered capital of 10 billion yuan |

*Source* The annual reports from 2014 to 2018 of E Bank

**Annex N**—Comprehensive financial organizational structure of E Bank

| Market type | Bank | Insurance | Investment |
|---|---|---|---|
| Domestic market | E Bank | E Bank Insurance Group | E Bank Financial Asset Investment Group |
| | R Bank | E Bank Life Insurance Group | E Bank Fund Group |
| | S Rural Commercial Bank | | E Bank International Trust Group |
| | Four rural banks | | E Bank Financial Leasing Group |
| Overseas market | E Bank (Hong Kong) Branch Office | | E Bank Financial Holding Group |
| | E Bank (Britain) Branch Office | | |
| | E Bank (Luxembourg) Branch | | - |
| | E Bank (Brazil) Branch | | |
| | 23 overseas subsidiaries and branches | | |

*Source* The annual report from 2014 to 2018 of E Bank
*Remarks* Domestic market refers to the market in Chinese mainland. Overseas market refers to the market outside Chinese mainland, including the Hongkong, the Macau, and UK.

**Annex O**—Major operating indicators of E Bank in recent years

| Indicator | 2014 | 2015 | 2016 | 2017 | 2018 |
|---|---|---|---|---|---|
| Total assets | 62,682.99 | 71,553.62 | 84,031.66 | 90,382.54 | 95,311.71 |
| Operating revenue | 1774.01 | 1938.28 | 1931.29 | 1960.11 | 2126.54 |
| Net profits | 660.35 | 668.31 | 676.51 | 706.91 | 741.65 |
| ROE (%) | 14.87 | 13.46 | 12.22 | 11.40 | 11.17 |
| ROA (%) | 1.08 | 1.00 | 0.87 | 0.81 | 0.80 |
| Non-performing loan ratio (%) | 1.25 | 1.51 | 1.52 | 1.50 | 1.49 |
| LLRA (%) | 328.31 | 290.56 | 245.43 | 231.48 | 272.92 |
| Capital adequacy ratio (%) | 14.04 | 13.49 | 14.21 | 14.00 | 14.37 |
| Cost-income ratio (%) | 30.29 | 30.36 | 31.60 | 31.85 | 31.50 |
| NIIR (%) | 24.03 | 25.62 | 30.17 | 35.02 | 38.44 |

*Source* The annual reports of E Bank (2014–2018)
*Note* The unit of total assets, operating income and net profits is one hundred million yuan

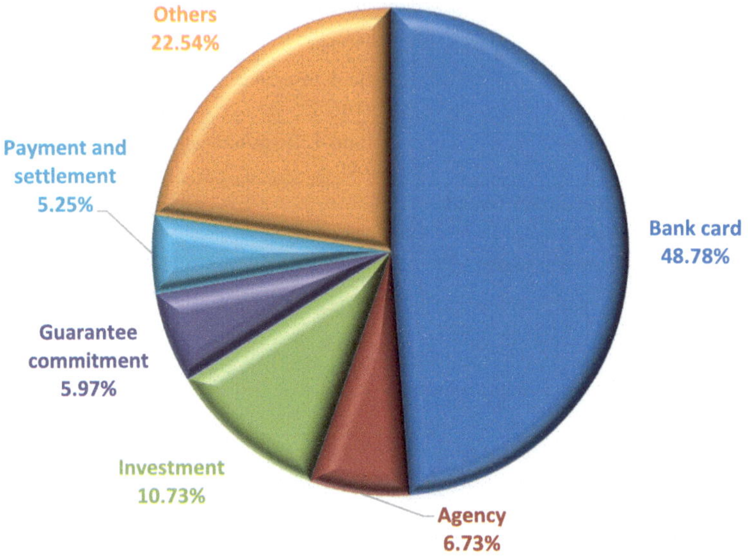


**Annex P**—The proportion of E Bank's service charge sources. *Source* The annual report for 2018 of E Bank

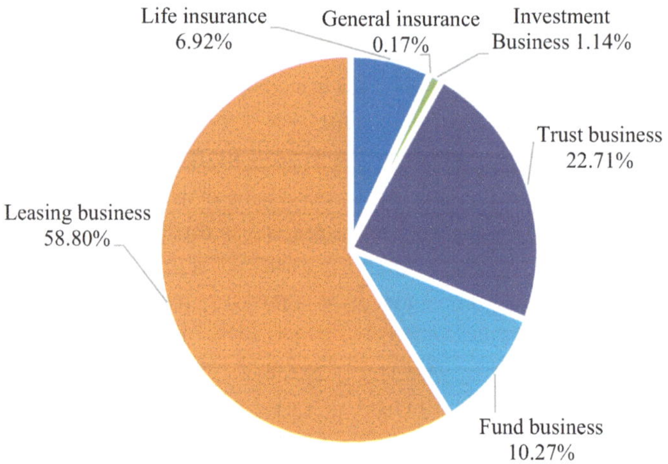


**Annex Q**—The proportion of net profits of major subsidiaries of E Bank in 2018. *Source* The annual report for 2018 of E Bank

**Annex R**—The main operating indicators of M Bank from 2014 to 2018

| Indicator | 2014 | 2015 | 2016 | 2017 | 2018 |
|---|---|---|---|---|---|
| Total assets | 18,516.28 | 20,206.04 | 23,562.35 | 25,089.27 | 26,805.80 |
| Operating revenue | 548.85 | 588.44 | 640.25 | 663.84 | 722.27 |
| Net profits | 180.23 | 189.52 | 197.56 | 199.33 | 209.86 |
| ROE (%) | 19.31 | 17.18 | 15.75 | 13.54 | 12.67 |
| ROA(%) | 1.02 | 0.98 | 0.90 | 0.82 | 0.81 |
| Non-performing loan ratio (%) | 1.09 | 1.52 | 1.67 | 1.76 | 1.85 |
| LLRA (%) | 389.27 | 293.06 | 295.16 | 277.74 | 263.88 |
| Capital adequacy ratio (%) | 11.03 | 10.85 | 11.36 | 12.37 | 13.19 |
| Cost-income ratio (%) | 37.57 | 35.01 | 34.50 | 32.96 | 32.58 |
| NIIR (%) | 15.75 | 21.69 | 23.48 | 28.72 | 28.64 |

*Source* The annual reports of M Bank (2014–2018)
*Note* The unit of total assets, operating income and net profits is one hundred million yuan

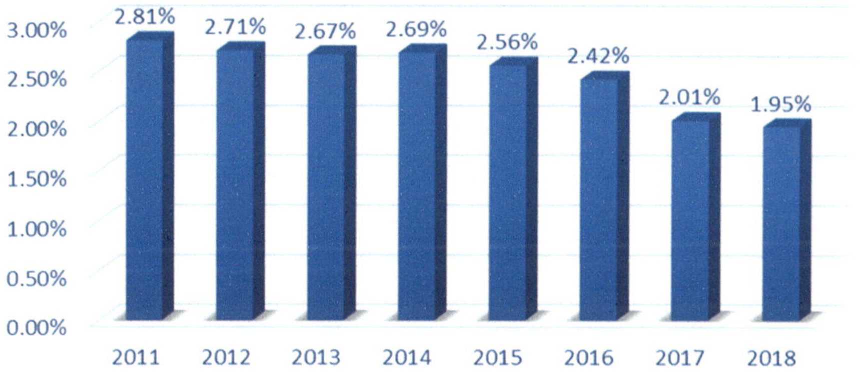


**Annex S**—Net interest margin from 2011 to 2018 of M Bank. *Source* The annual reports of M Bank (2011–2018)

**Annex T**—Indexes system of the Wole Scoring Method in the performance evaluation of commercial banks

| Number | Classification | Operation Indicators |
|---|---|---|
| 1 | Profitability | Return on equity |
| 2 | | Return on total assets |
| 3 | | Cost-to-income ratio |
| 4 | Solvency | Capital adequacy ratio |
| 5 | | Core capital adequacy ratio |
| 6 | | Loan-to-deposit ratio |
| 7 | | Provision coverage |

(continued)

(continued)

| Number | Classification | Operation Indicators |
|---|---|---|
| 8 | | NPL ratio |
| 9 | Growth capacity | Total assets growth rate |
| 10 | | Net profit growth rate |
| 11 | | Fees and commissions net income |

*Source* Wang Xiuzhen (2016)

**Annex U**—Main indicators and evaluation criteria of CAMELSS

| Number | Classification | Main indicators | Criteria |
|---|---|---|---|
| 1 | Capital adequacy | Capital adequacy ratio, degrees of reserves adequacy; | Level 1: Extremely higher than the regulatory requirements |
| | | | Level 2: Significantly higher than the regulatory requirements |
| | | | Level 3: Slightly higher than the regulatory requirements |
| | | | Level 4: Fail to meet the regulatory requirements |
| | | | Level 5: Unable to repay the debt |
| 2 | Asset quality | Overdue asset ratio, NPL ratio, provision coverage; | Level 1: Asset with high quality and strong risk control and management |
| | | | Level 2: Asset with relatively high quality and risk management |

(continued)

(continued)

| Number | Classification | Main indicators | Criteria |
|---|---|---|---|
| | | | Level 3: Asset with low quality and risk management |
| | | | Level 4: Lower asset quality and risk management |
| | | | Level 5: Poor asset quality and risk management |
| 3 | Management | Management mechanism such as group operation, risk control level, internal control management and implementation, information system construction and management level, and compliance of daily business operation with laws and regulations; | Level 1: Management is in good condition |
| | | | Level 2: Management is in satisfactory condition |
| | | | Level 3: Management status needs to be further improved |
| | | | Level 4: There are detailed defects in risk management |
| | | | Level 5: Poor risk management |
| 4 | Profitability | Return on assets, return on equity, cost income ratio; | Level 1: Profitability is extraordinarily high |
| | | | Level 2: Profitability is strong |
| | | | Level 3: The level of profitability is acceptable |

(continued)

(continued)

| Number | Classification | Main indicators | Criteria |
|---|---|---|---|
| | | | Level 4: The level of profitability is dissatisfied |
| | | | Level 5: The level of profitability is negative |
| 5 | Liquidity | Current ratio, Loan-to-deposit ratio | Level 1: Liquidity is strong |
| | | | Level 2: Liquidity is adequate |
| | | | Level 3: Liquidity is at common level |
| | | | Level 4: Liquidity is not sufficient |
| | | | Level 5: Liquidity is in seriously shortage |

*Source* Luo Gangfei and Pan Jiashun (2013)

**Annex V**—Comparison and analysis of advantages and disadvantages of major evaluation methods

| Number | Evaluation method | Advantages | Disadvantages |
|---|---|---|---|
| 1 | DuPont method | 1. The rate of return on equity is converted into the product of three operating indicators to form a relatively complete evaluation system<br>2. The level and organization are relatively clear | 1. It is not possible to explain the completion of all operation and management performance of a financial institution in a multi-dimensional, relatively complete and realistic way<br>2. The key point of guiding senior managers is to care about and attach importance to the recent performance of business management, but not to the future governance development of financial institutions, the changing trend of customer demand and the realization of risk prevention and control value<br>3. Lack of prediction of future business development of the financial enterprise<br>4. Lack of evaluation on the management capability of financial institutions such as risk management |

(continued)

(continued)

**Annex V**—Comparison and analysis of advantages and disadvantages of major evaluation methods

| Number | Evaluation method | Advantages | Disadvantages |
|---|---|---|---|
| 2 | Wole Scoring Method | 1. The combination of financial indicators and non-financial indicators provides strong support for the strategic management of enterprises<br>2. Pay more attention to team cooperation and have better incentive effect on employees and management | 1. Some indicators are subjective and not easy to determine objectively<br>2. The design cost is relatively high, which needs to spend more on the determination of index value and important level<br>3. The cost of later adjustment is relatively high. If there is a big change, it needs to be redesigned<br>4. The impact of a single indicator may be greater. When a serious abnormality occurs in one of the evaluation indexes, it may lead to a great change in the calculated evaluation results of business performance |
| 3 | Factor Analysis Method | 1. Hidden representative factors and influence can be found<br>2. The number of variables can be reduced and the relationship between variables can be tested<br>3. The proportion of each factor in the factor score is not determined according to human factors, but is obtained by quantitative analysis, which can ensure that the evaluation results accord with the actual situation<br>4. The whole process can be carried out conveniently and quickly with computer software and has strong operability | If the factor load is not all positive or negative, or the dimension difference of the original variable data value is large, the significance of performance evaluation by this method is not significant |

(continued)

(continued)

**Annex V**—Comparison and analysis of advantages and disadvantages of major evaluation methods

| Number | Evaluation method | Advantages | Disadvantages |
|---|---|---|---|
| 4 | CAMELSS | 1. There are many indicators involved<br>2. The evaluation aspect is relatively extensive<br>3. It can show the performance of commercial banks comprehensively and objectively | 1. The weights of indicators are set artificially, and the evaluation methods and results are subjective to some extent<br>2. The degree of differentiation is not high, which is not conducive to distinguishing the performance evaluation of the same type of commercial banks<br>3. The evaluation output mode is limited. The evaluation results are mainly output through reporting, which may increase subjective judgment and cannot reflect the actual situation |
| 5 | GYROSCOPE | | |

*Source* Ministry of Finance (2021)

**Annex W**—Evaluation indicators of business performance

| S. No. | Classification | Business indicators | Item character |
|---|---|---|---|
| 1 | Profitability | Return on equity | Positive index |
| 2 | | Return on total assets | Positive index |
| 3 | | Net profit | Positive index |
| 4 | | Non-interest income | Positive index |
| 5 | Business growth | Rate of return on economic added value | Positive index |
| 6 | | The growth rate of operating income | Positive index |
| 7 | | The growth rate of net profit | Positive index |
| 8 | Solvency | The capital adequacy rate | Positive index |
| 9 | | Tier-one leverage capital | Positive index |
| 10 | | Asset-liability ratio | Moderate index |
| 11 | Asset quality | Provision coverage ratio | Positive indexes |
| 12 | | Provisions for loan losses | Positive index |
| 13 | | Non-performing loan ratio | Negative index |
| 14 | Business management | Cost-to-income ratio | Negative index |
| 15 | | Earnings per share | Positive index |

**Annex X**—Main advantages and disadvantages of statistical analysis software

| Name | Advantages | Disadvantages |
|---|---|---|
| SPSS | 1. The function is the same as Excel, which is very easy to use<br>2. The system is easy and fast to operate, and the database can be edited on the system page<br>3. It has a variety of functions such as variance analysis, factor analysis, regression analysis, chi-square test and so forth, which are relatively complete<br>4. The main advantage lies in the ability to test various special effects, such as analysis of variance, and analysis of multiple variables such as multivariate analysis of variance, factor analysis and regression analysis | The structure of the generated graph is relatively simple |
| Stata | 1. It has more software functions for analysis, and can simply operate the database<br>2. It has regression analysis, variance analysis, factor analysis and other quantitative analysis functions<br>3. The main advantage lies in being able to carry out regression analysis easily | Only one data file can be processed, and multiple data files cannot be operated at the same time |
| SAS | 1. The function of the system is various, and the user can use the computer language for programming, processing and operation<br>2. It has regression analysis, variance analysis, factor analysis, multivariate analysis and other statistical analysis functions<br>3. SQL programming language, such as the database processing, processing can be used<br>4. It can process multiple data files at the same time<br>5. The most important advantage lies in the analysis of variance and mixed model analysis | 1. It is very difficult to master programming<br>2. Only after a long period of training can users master the processing and processing methods of data |

*Source* Shengchu (2015), Wentong (2017) and Tiemei (2016)

**Annex Y**—Evaluation indicators of business performance

| S. No. | Classification | Business indicator | Variables | Quality of indicators |
|---|---|---|---|---|
| 1 | Solvency | Capital adequacy ratio | $X_1$ | Positive index |
| 2 | | Tier-one leverage capital | $X_2$ | Positive index |
| 3 | | Asset liability ratio | $X_3$ | Moderate index |
| 4 | Profitability | Return on total assets | $X_7$ | Positive index |
| 5 | | Return on equity | $X_8$ | Positive index |
| 6 | | Net profit | $X_4$ | Positive index |
| 7 | | Non-interest income | $X_5$ | Positive index |
| 8 | Business growth | Rate of return on economic added value | $X_6$ | Positive index |

(continued)

(continued)

| S. No. | Classification | Business indicator | Variables | Quality of indicators |
|---|---|---|---|---|
| 9 | | The growth rate of operating income | $X_{10}$ | Positive index |
| 10 | | The growth rate of net profit | $X_{13}$ | Positive index |
| 11 | Asset quality | Provision coverage ratio | $X_{11}$ | Positive index |
| 12 | | Provisions for loan losses | $X_{12}$ | Positive index |
| 13 | | Non-performing loan ratio | $X_{9}$ | Negative index |
| 14 | Business management | Cost-to-income ratio | $X_{15}$ | Negative index |
| 15 | | Earnings per share | $X_{14}$ | Positive index |

**Annex Z**—The data sources of evaluation indicators

| S. No. | Classification | Operational indicator | Annual disclosure report of listed companies | |
|---|---|---|---|---|
| | | | Financial statement information | Non-financial statement information |
| 1 | Profitability | Return on equity | √ | |
| 2 | | Return on total assets | √ | |
| 3 | | Net profit | √ | |
| 4 | | Non-interest income | √ | |
| 5 | Business growth | Rate of return on economic added value | √ | √ |
| 6 | | The growth rate of operating income | √ | |
| 7 | | The growth rate of net profit | √ | |
| 8 | Solvency | The capital adequacy rate | | √ |
| 9 | | Tier-one leverage capital | | √ |
| 10 | | Asset-liability ratio | √ | |
| 11 | Asset quality | Provision coverage ratio | √ | √ |
| 12 | | Provisions for loan losses | √ | √ |
| 13 | | Non-performing loan ratio | | √ |
| 14 | Business management | Cost-to-income ratio | √ | |
| 15 | | Earnings per share | | √ |

**Annex AA**—Test table of KMO and Bartlett

| Type | | Value |
|---|---|---|
| Bartlett test of sphericity | Sufficient Kaiser–Meyer–Olkin measure of sampling | 0.712 |
| | Approximate chi-square | 1350.517 |
| | df | 105.000 |
| | Sig | 0.000 |

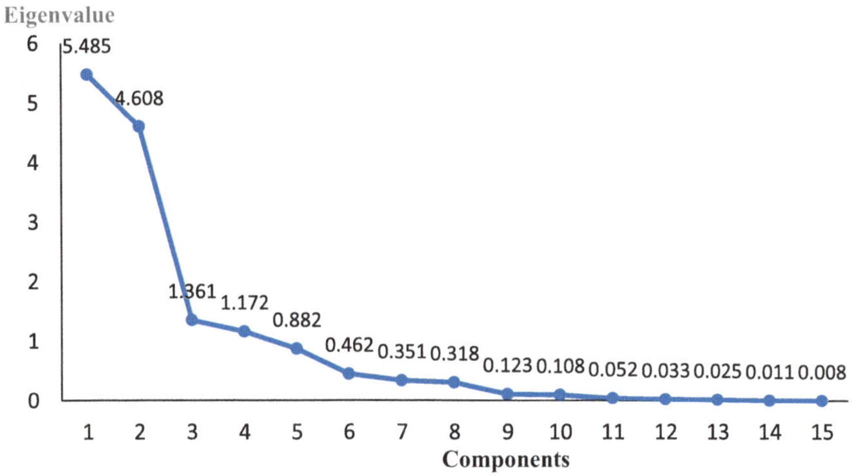


**Annex BB**—Crushed stone diagram

**Annex CC**—The covariance matrix of components scoring

| Components | 1 | 2 | 3 | 4 |
|---|---|---|---|---|
| 1 | 1.000 | 0.000 | 0.000 | 0.000 |
| 2 | 0.000 | 1.000 | 0.000 | 0.000 |
| 3 | 0.000 | 0.000 | 1.000 | 0.000 |
| 4 | 0.000 | 0.000 | 0.000 | 1.000 |

**Annex DD**—Score of the common factor $F_1$ for each financial holding group

| S. No. | Companies | 2014 | | 2015 | | 2016 | | 2017 | | 2018 | |
|---|---|---|---|---|---|---|---|---|---|---|---|
| | | Score | Ranking | Score | Ranking | Score | Ranking | Score | Ranking | Score | Ranking |
| 1 | A Bank | 6.5404 | 3 | 6.8161 | 3 | 7.3039 | 3 | 7.2053 | 3 | 7.4342 | 3 |
| 2 | B Bank | 4.9159 | 5 | 5.1609 | 5 | 5.6606 | 5 | 5.8135 | 7 | 6.7747 | 5 |
| 3 | C Bank | 6.9096 | 1 | 7.3017 | 1 | 7.637 | 1 | 7.4512 | 2 | 7.8655 | 2 |
| 4 | D Bank | 6.7124 | 2 | 6.873 | 2 | 7.3074 | 2 | 7.7774 | 1 | 8.5451 | 1 |
| 5 | E Bank | 6.1815 | 4 | 5.6162 | 4 | 6.5443 | 4 | 6.508 | 5 | 6.432 | 6 |
| 6 | F Bank | 4.0787 | 9 | 4.0159 | 6 | 4.6065 | 7 | 5.0248 | 9 | 5.2026 | 9 |
| 7 | G Bank | 4.028 | 10 | 4.0119 | 7 | 4.4009 | 9 | 5.9766 | 6 | 4.8717 | 10 |
| 8 | H Bank | 3.4607 | 13 | 3.0643 | 13 | 4.0906 | 11 | 4.7822 | 11 | 4.4546 | 12 |
| 9 | I Bank | 4.5681 | 6 | 3.9813 | 8 | 5.2288 | 6 | 6.8078 | 4 | 7.1561 | 4 |
| 10 | J Bank | 4.2545 | 7 | 3.1485 | 12 | 4.3731 | 10 | 5.5909 | 8 | 4.6978 | 11 |
| 11 | K Bank | 4.0787 | 8 | 3.7098 | 10 | 3.7899 | 13 | 4.4216 | 13 | 5.5634 | 7 |
| 12 | L Bank | 3.6412 | 11 | 3.8605 | 9 | 4.4221 | 8 | 5.0035 | 10 | 4.4087 | 13 |
| 13 | M Bank | 3.6333 | 12 | 3.5704 | 11 | 3.9887 | 12 | 4.5256 | 12 | 5.2362 | 8 |

**Annex EE**—The score of the common factor $F_2$ for each financial holding group

| S. No. | Companies | 2014 | | 2015 | | 2016 | | 2017 | | 2018 | |
|---|---|---|---|---|---|---|---|---|---|---|---|
| | | Score | Ranking | Score | Ranking | Score | Ranking | Score | Ranking | Score | Ranking |
| 1 | A Bank | 18.5462 | 11 | 15.2497 | 11 | 13.8011 | 7 | 13.5559 | 3 | 13.4168 | 6 |
| 2 | B Bank | 17.4286 | 12 | 12.6369 | 13 | 10.9674 | 13 | 13.1772 | 4 | 13.7317 | 5 |
| 3 | C Bank | 21.2921 | 4 | 16.578 | 7 | 14.0736 | 4 | 14.7 | 1 | 14.1806 | 3 |
| 4 | D Bank | 20.3731 | 8 | 16.2066 | 9 | 15.0007 | 1 | 14.3243 | 2 | 13.9995 | 4 |
| 5 | E Bank | 16.3059 | 13 | 14.4829 | 12 | 12.3707 | 12 | 12.0431 | 9 | 12.6515 | 9 |
| 6 | F Bank | 18.7689 | 10 | 16.8257 | 5 | 12.9157 | 11 | 11.7215 | 11 | 11.0169 | 12 |
| 7 | G Bank | 19.9229 | 9 | 15.9244 | 10 | 13.5726 | 8 | 11.6038 | 12 | 13.4038 | 7 |
| 8 | H Bank | 20.8481 | 7 | 17.2491 | 3 | 13.1169 | 10 | 11.2876 | 13 | 11.6582 | 10 |
| 9 | I Bank | 21.9496 | 2 | 16.9218 | 4 | 13.1761 | 9 | 13.0208 | 5 | 15.0558 | 1 |
| 10 | J Bank | 21.2586 | 5 | 18.7763 | 1 | 14.6139 | 2 | 12.4187 | 7 | 14.3692 | 2 |
| 11 | K Bank | 22.4003 | 1 | 17.3852 | 2 | 14.0167 | 5 | 11.8045 | 10 | 11.1195 | 11 |
| 12 | L Bank | 21.9423 | 3 | 16.6269 | 6 | 13.8629 | 6 | 12.1654 | 8 | 13.3559 | 8 |
| 13 | M Bank | 21.1362 | 6 | 16.4876 | 8 | 14.2804 | 3 | 12.5613 | 6 | 10.823 | 13 |

**Annex FF**—The score of the common factor $F_3$ for each financial holding group

| S. No. | Companies | 2014 | | 2015 | | 2016 | | 2017 | | 2018 | |
|---|---|---|---|---|---|---|---|---|---|---|---|
| | | Score | Ranking | Score | Ranking | Score | Ranking | Score | Ranking | Score | Ranking |
| 1 | A Bank | 9.1667 | 10 | 3.5745 | 13 | 3.4447 | 13 | 7.0975 | 5 | 9.4144 | 4 |
| 2 | B Bank | 9.1099 | 11 | 5.5444 | 11 | 4.5143 | 12 | 6.8057 | 7 | 7.815 | 10 |
| 3 | C Bank | 9.598 | 8 | 5.2427 | 12 | 5.5291 | 8 | 7.8512 | 2 | 9.4177 | 3 |
| 4 | D Bank | 9.3929 | 9 | 6.6479 | 5 | 6.4043 | 6 | 7.8259 | 3 | 8.8999 | 6 |
| 5 | E Bank | 8.4994 | 12 | 6.58 | 6 | 5.2214 | 11 | 6.4201 | 8 | 7.6796 | 11 |
| 6 | F Bank | 10.0429 | 7 | 6.561 | 7 | 5.4387 | 9 | 6.9352 | 6 | 9.7087 | 2 |
| 7 | G Bank | 20.915 | 1 | 10.7795 | 1 | 6.6761 | 4 | 5.6248 | 10 | 8.2293 | 8 |
| 8 | H Bank | 12.1058 | 5 | 7.4662 | 4 | 7.5412 | 2 | 12.3582 | 1 | 15.613 | 1 |
| 9 | I Bank | 13.196 | 4 | 9.0462 | 3 | 7.798 | 1 | 7.3237 | 4 | 9.2408 | 5 |
| 10 | J Bank | 14.4132 | 2 | 9.2288 | 2 | 6.3823 | 7 | 4.6473 | 13 | 5.9902 | 12 |
| 11 | K Bank | 8.418 | 13 | 6.1509 | 9 | 5.38 | 10 | 5.4059 | 11 | 4.3729 | 13 |
| 12 | L Bank | 13.9789 | 3 | 6.4859 | 8 | 6.6621 | 5 | 5.3034 | 12 | 7.9757 | 9 |
| 13 | M Bank | 9.1667 | 10 | 3.5745 | 13 | 3.4447 | 13 | 7.0975 | 5 | 9.4144 | 4 |

**Annex GG**—The score of the common factor $F_4$ for each financial holding group

| S. No. | Companies | 2014 | | 2015 | | 2016 | | 2017 | | 2018 | |
|---|---|---|---|---|---|---|---|---|---|---|---|
| | | Score | Ranking | Score | Ranking | Score | Ranking | Score | Ranking | Score | Ranking |
| 1 | A Bank | 10.3116 | 6 | 6.1442 | 10 | 6.8318 | 3 | 6.0341 | 9 | 8.2784 | 7 |
| 2 | B Bank | 9.1667 | 10 | 3.5745 | 13 | 3.4447 | 13 | 7.0975 | 5 | 9.4144 | 4 |
| 3 | C Bank | 9.1099 | 11 | 5.5444 | 11 | 4.5143 | 12 | 6.8057 | 7 | 7.815 | 10 |
| 4 | D Bank | 9.598 | 8 | 5.2427 | 12 | 5.5291 | 8 | 7.8512 | 2 | 9.4177 | 3 |
| 5 | E Bank | 9.3929 | 9 | 6.6479 | 5 | 6.4043 | 6 | 7.8259 | 3 | 8.8999 | 6 |
| 6 | F Bank | 8.4994 | 12 | 6.58 | 6 | 5.2214 | 11 | 6.4201 | 8 | 7.6796 | 11 |
| 7 | G Bank | 10.0429 | 7 | 6.561 | 7 | 5.4387 | 9 | 6.9352 | 6 | 9.7087 | 2 |
| 8 | H Bank | 20.915 | 1 | 10.7795 | 1 | 6.6761 | 4 | 5.6248 | 10 | 8.2293 | 8 |
| 9 | I Bank | 12.1058 | 5 | 7.4662 | 4 | 7.5412 | 2 | 12.3582 | 1 | 15.613 | 1 |
| 10 | J Bank | 13.196 | 4 | 9.0462 | 3 | 7.798 | 1 | 7.3237 | 4 | 9.2408 | 5 |
| 11 | K Bank | 14.4132 | 2 | 9.2288 | 2 | 6.3823 | 7 | 4.6473 | 13 | 5.9902 | 12 |
| 12 | L Bank | 8.418 | 13 | 6.1509 | 9 | 5.38 | 10 | 5.4059 | 11 | 4.3729 | 13 |
| 13 | M Bank | 13.9789 | 3 | 6.4859 | 8 | 6.6621 | 5 | 5.3034 | 12 | 7.9757 | 9 |

**Annex HH**—Operating performance scores for each financial holding group

| S. No. | Companies | 2014 | | 2015 | | 2016 | | 2017 | | 2018 | |
|---|---|---|---|---|---|---|---|---|---|---|---|
| | | Score | Ranking | Score | Ranking | Score | Ranking | Score | Ranking | Score | Ranking |
| 1 | A Bank | 7.7916 | 6 | 7.0368 | 3 | 6.8535 | 3 | 6.6937 | 4 | 6.7744 | 5 |
| 2 | B Bank | 7.2399 | 9 | 6.0846 | 11 | 5.8293 | 8 | 6.3311 | 5 | 6.82 | 4 |
| 3 | C Bank | 8.8166 | 1 | 7.804 | 1 | 7.2789 | 2 | 7.2892 | 2 | 7.3583 | 3 |
| 4 | D Bank | 8.5699 | 2 | 7.5643 | 2 | 7.3619 | 1 | 7.4036 | 1 | 7.6669 | 2 |
| 5 | E Bank | 7.0036 | 11 | 6.2879 | 8 | 6.1116 | 6 | 5.9955 | 7 | 6.1193 | 7 |
| 6 | F Bank | 6.7738 | 13 | 6.188 | 9 | 5.4631 | 12 | 5.3632 | 12 | 5.2795 | 11 |
| 7 | G Bank | 7.0108 | 10 | 6.0335 | 12 | 5.6004 | 11 | 5.7325 | 8 | 5.6466 | 9 |
| 8 | H Bank | 6.9569 | 12 | 5.9081 | 13 | 5.3617 | 13 | 5.1354 | 13 | 5.106 | 13 |
| 9 | I Bank | 7.9886 | 4 | 6.5884 | 6 | 6.3265 | 5 | 7.063 | 3 | 7.7639 | 1 |
| 10 | J Bank | 7.9223 | 5 | 6.7456 | 4 | 6.3852 | 4 | 6.242 | 6 | 6.1696 | 6 |
| 11 | K Bank | 8.0628 | 3 | 6.7441 | 5 | 5.8174 | 9 | 5.4034 | 11 | 5.6678 | 8 |
| 12 | L Bank | 7.536 | 7 | 6.2879 | 7 | 5.8389 | 7 | 5.6636 | 9 | 5.4764 | 10 |
| 13 | M Bank | 7.3444 | 8 | 6.1794 | 10 | 5.7251 | 10 | 5.435 | 10 | 5.276 | 12 |

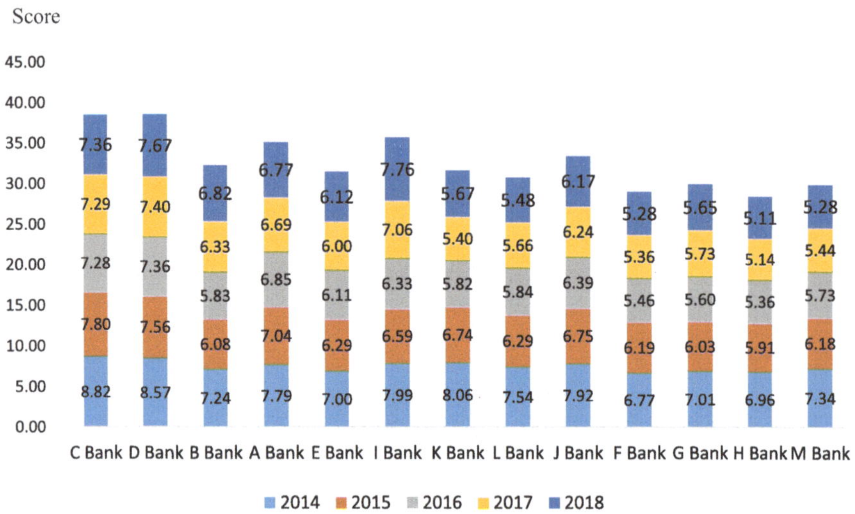


**Annex II**—Operating performance score for each financial holding group

**Annex JJ**—The average operating performance scores for each financial holding groups by factor and for the overall sample period

| S. No. | Group | $F_1$ score | $F_2$ score | $F_3$ score | $F_4$ score | Overall score | Overall rank |
|---|---|---|---|---|---|---|---|
| 1 | Bank C | 7.4330 | 16.1649 | 6.7578 | − 22.5037 | 7.7094 | 2 |
| 2 | Bank D | 7.4431 | 15.9808 | 7.5277 | − 22.6789 | 7.7133 | 1 |
| 3 | Bank B | 5.5484 | 16.0248 | 11.0169 | − 24.1938 | 7.1461 | 3 |
| 4 | Bank A | 5.6651 | 13.5883 | 6.5396 | − 17.3987 | 6.4610 | 6 |
| 5 | Bank E | 4.3127 | 15.3452 | 8.1323 | − 21.1487 | 6.3391 | 7 |
| 6 | Bank I | 7.0600 | 14.9139 | 7.5200 | − 24.0988 | 7.0300 | 4 |
| 7 | Bank K | 4.2672 | 15.5907 | 5.9455 | − 21.2990 | 6.1605 | 9 |
| 8 | Bank L | 4.4130 | 16.2873 | 9.3209 | − 22.8611 | 6.6930 | 5 |
| 9 | Bank J | 6.2564 | 13.5708 | 7.8342 | − 23.3071 | 6.3036 | 8 |
| 10 | Bank F | 3.9705 | 14.8320 | 10.4450 | − 27.2193 | 5.6936 | 13 |
| 11 | Bank G | 4.5857 | 14.2497 | 6.8801 | − 22.3688 | 5.8135 | 12 |
| 12 | Bank H | 4.1908 | 15.0577 | 8.0812 | − 23.1556 | 5.9920 | 11 |
| 13 | Bank M | 4.6578 | 14.8855 | 7.7373 | − 24.1251 | 6.0048 | 10 |

**Annex KK**—Evaluation indexes for the cluster analysis

| S. No. | Classification | Business indicator | Variables | Quality of indicators | Standardization process |
|---|---|---|---|---|---|
| 1 | Profitability | Capital adequacy ratio | $X_1$ | Positive indicator | —— |
| 2 | | Tier-one leverage capital | $X_2$ | Positive indicator | —— |
| 3 | | Asset liability ratio | $X_3$ | Positive indicator | Yes |
| 4 | | Return on total assets | $X_4$ | Positive indicator | Yes |
| 5 | Business growth | Return on equity | $X_5$ | Positive indicator | —— |
| 6 | | Net profit | $X_6$ | Positive indicator | —— |
| 7 | | Non-interest income | $X_7$ | Positive indicator | —— |
| 8 | Solvency | Rate of return on economic added value | $X_8$ | Positive indicator | —— |
| 9 | | Growth rate of operating income | $X_9$ | Positive indicator | —— |
| 10 | | Growth rate of net profit | $X_{10}$ | Moderate indicator | —— |
| 11 | Asset quality | Provision coverage ratio | $X_{11}$ | Positive indicator | Yes |
| 12 | | Provisions for loan losses | $X_{12}$ | Positive indicator | Yes |
| 13 | | Non-performing loan ratio | $X_{13}$ | Reverse indicator | —— |
| 14 | Business management | Cost-to-income ratio | $X_{14}$ | Reverse indicator | —— |
| 15 | | Earnings per share | $X_{15}$ | Positive indicator | —— |

**Annex LL**—Cluster analysis on performance data of financial companies in 2018

| S. No. | Group | Divided into two categories | Divided into three categories | Divided into four categories |
|---|---|---|---|---|
| 1 | Bank I | 1 | 1 | 1 |
| 2 | Bank G | 2 | 2 | 2 |
| 3 | Bank D | 2 | 3 | 3 |
| 4 | Bank C | 2 | 3 | 3 |
| 5 | Bank B | 2 | 3 | 3 |
| 6 | Bank A | 2 | 3 | 3 |

(continued)

(continued)

| S. No. | Group | Divided into two categories | Divided into three categories | Divided into four categories |
|---|---|---|---|---|
| 7 | Bank J | 2 | 3 | 3 |
| 8 | Bank E | 2 | 3 | 3 |
| 9 | Bank K | 2 | 3 | 4 |
| 10 | Bank L | 2 | 3 | 4 |
| 11 | Bank F | 2 | 3 | 4 |
| 12 | Bank M | 2 | 3 | 4 |
| 13 | Bank H | 2 | 3 | 4 |

**Annex MM**—Results comparison of cluster analysis and factor analysis on performance of financial holding groups in 2018

| S. No. | Companies | Cluster analysis | | | Comprehensive score ranking of factor analysis |
|---|---|---|---|---|---|
| | | Two categories | Three categories | Four categories | |
| 1 | Bank I | 1 | 1 | 1 | 1 |
| 2 | Bank G | 2 | 2 | 2 | 9 |
| 3 | Bank D | 2 | 3 | 3 | 2 |
| 4 | Bank C | 2 | 3 | 3 | 3 |
| 5 | Bank B | 2 | 3 | 3 | 4 |
| 6 | Bank A | 2 | 3 | 3 | 5 |
| 7 | Bank J | 2 | 3 | 3 | 6 |
| 8 | Bank E | 2 | 3 | 3 | 7 |
| 9 | Bank K | 2 | 3 | 4 | 8 |
| 10 | Bank L | 2 | 3 | 4 | 10 |
| 11 | Bank F | 2 | 3 | 4 | 11 |
| 12 | Bank M | 2 | 3 | 4 | 12 |
| 13 | Bank H | 2 | 3 | 4 | 13 |

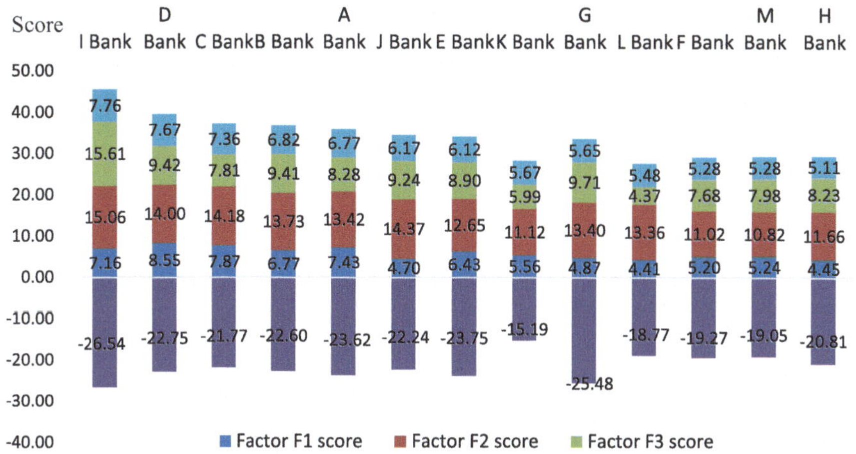


**Annex NN**—Business performance scoring of financial holding groups in 2018

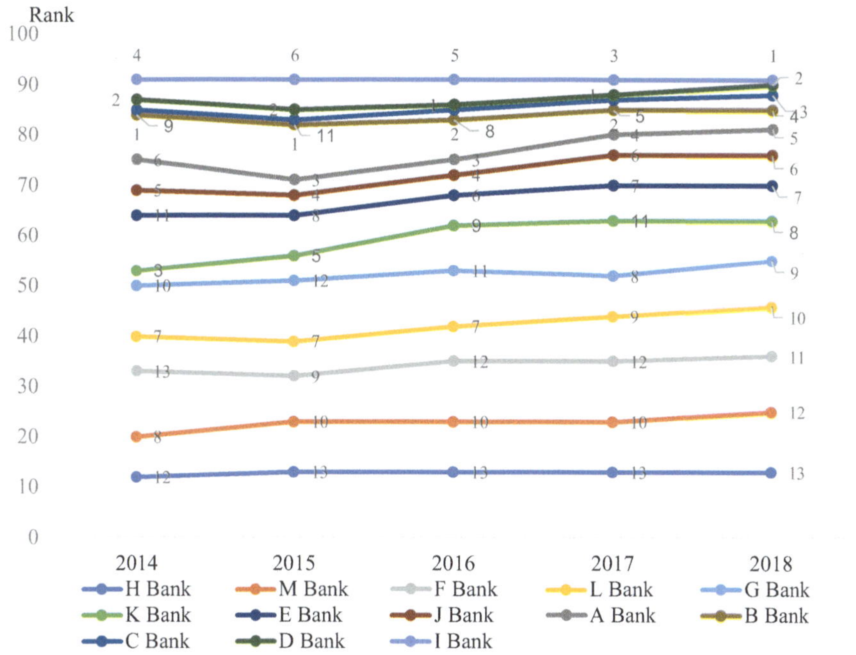


**Annex OO**—Ranking of operating performance of financial holding groups from 2014 to 2018

**Annex PP**—Scores of the factor $F_1$ in 2018

| Group | Type | Score | Rank |
|---|---|---|---|
| 1 | Bank-owned financial holding groups | 6.54 | 1 |
| 2 | Bank-type financial holding groups owned by financial holding group | 4.84 | 3 |
| 3 | Traditional bank-type financial holding groups | 5.24 | 2 |
| 4 | Average | 6.05 | —— |

**Annex QQ**—Scores of the factor $F_1$ from 2014 to 2018

| Group | Type | Average score | Rank |
|---|---|---|---|
| 1 | Bank-owned financial holding groups | 5.82 | 1 |
| 2 | Bank-type financial holding groups owned by financial holding group | 4.41 | 2 |
| 3 | Traditional bank-type financial holding groups | 4.19 | 3 |
| 4 | Average | 5.37 | —— |

**Annex RR**—Scores of grouping factor $F_1$ of financial holding groups

**Annex SS**—Scores of the factor $F_2$ in 2018

| Group | Type | Score | Rank |
|---|---|---|---|
| 1 | Bank-owned financial holding groups | 13.54 | 1 |
| 2 | Bank-type financial holding groups owned by financial holding group | 12.03 | 2 |
| 3 | Traditional bank-type financial holding groups | 10.81 | 3 |
| 4 | Average | 12.98 | —— |

**Annex TT**—Scores of the factor $F_2$ from 2014 to 2018

| Group | Type | Average score | Rank |
|---|---|---|---|
| 1 | Bank-owned financial holding groups | 15.27 | 1 |

(continued)

(continued)

| Group | Type | Average score | Rank |
|---|---|---|---|
| 2 | Bank-type financial holding groups owned by financial holding group | 14.66 | 3 |
| 3 | Traditional bank-type financial holding groups | 15.06 | 2 |
| 4 | Average | 15.11 | —— |

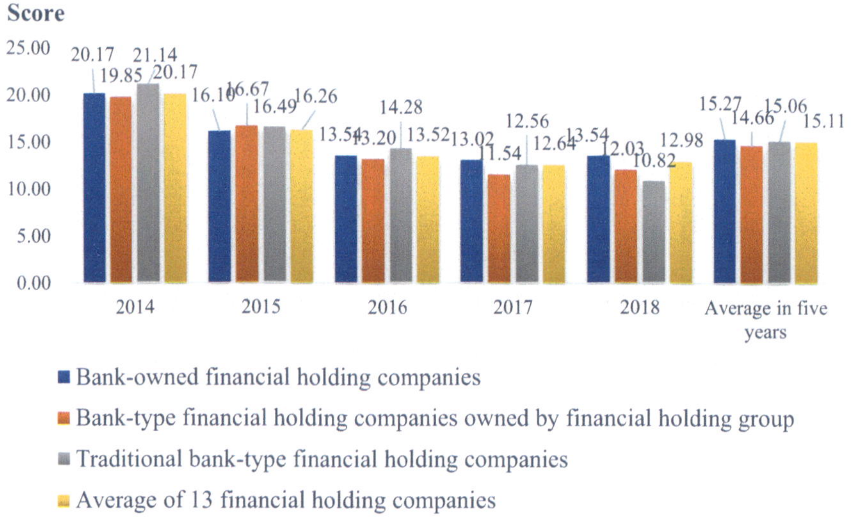


**Annex UU**—Scores of grouping factor $F_2$ of financial holding groups from 2014 to 2018

**Annex VV**—Scores of the factor $F_3$ in 2018

| Group | Type | Score | Rank |
|---|---|---|---|
| 1 | Bank-owned financial holding groups | 8.78 | 1 |
| 2 | Bank-type financial holding groups owned by financial holding group | 8.54 | 2 |
| 3 | Traditional bank-type financial holding groups | 7.98 | 3 |
| 4 | Average | 8.66 | —— |

**Annex WW**—Scores of the factor $F_3$ from 2014 to 2018

| Group | Type | Average score | Rank |
|---|---|---|---|
| 1 | Bank-owned financial holding groups | 7.84 | 1 |
| 2 | Bank-type financial holding groups owned by financial holding group | 8.35 | 2 |
| 3 | Traditional bank-type financial holding groups | 8.08 | 3 |
| 4 | Average | 7.98 | —— |

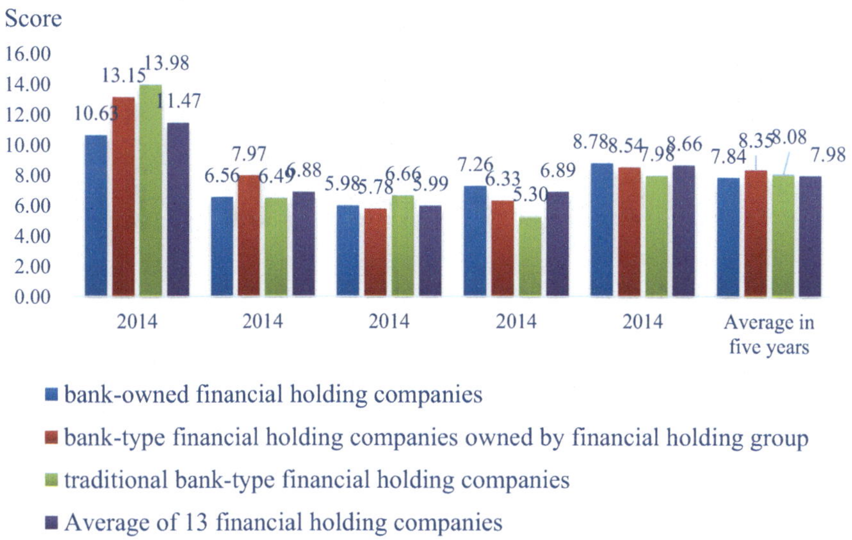


**Annex XX**—Scores of grouping factor $F_3$ of financial holding groups, by years

**Annex YY**—Scores of the factor $F_4$ in 2018

| Group | Type | Score | Rank |
|---|---|---|---|
| 1 | Bank-owned financial holding groups | – 21.91 | 3 |
| 2 | Bank-type financial holding groups owned by financial holding group | – 21.85 | 2 |
| 3 | Traditional bank-type financial holding groups | – 19.05 | 1 |
| 4 | Average | – 21.68 | —— |

**Annex ZZ**—Scores of the factor $F_4$ from 2014 to 2018

| Group | Type | Average score | Rank |
|---|---|---|---|
| 1 | Bank-owned financial holding groups | – 22.17 | 1 |
| 2 | Bank-type financial holding groups owned by financial holding group | – 24.57 | 3 |
| 3 | Traditional bank-type financial holding groups | – 23.16 | 2 |
| 4 | Average | – 22.80 | —— |

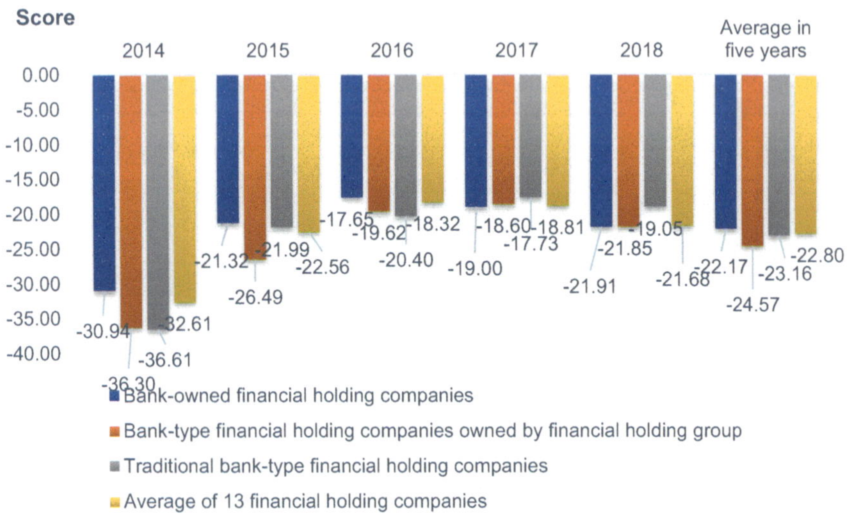


**Annex AAA**—Scores of the grouping factor $F_4$ of financial holding groups, by years

**Annex BBB**—Chi-square test table for solvency factor scores

| Type | Value | df | Progressive Sig. (bilateral) | Exact Sig. (bilateral) |
|---|---|---|---|---|
| Pearson chi-square | 143.437 | 22 | 0.0000 | 0.0000 |
| Likelihood ratio | 156.004 | 22 | 0.0000 | 0.0000 |
| Accurate test of Fisher | 108.241 | | | 0.0000 |
| N in the effective case | 72 | | | |

**Annex CCC**—Groups and cross tabulation of solvency factor scores

| | Type | Total score | |
|---|---|---|---|
| Group | Bank-owned financial holding groups | Count | 28.96 |
| | | Expected count | 29.00 |
| | | Percentage in group | 100.00% |
| | | Percentage in total | 40.40% |
| | Bank-type financial holding groups owned by financial holding group | Count | 21.87 |
| | | Expected count | 21.90 |

(continued)

(continued)

| | Type | Total score | |
|---|---|---|---|
| | | Percentage in group | 100.00% |
| | | Percentage in total | 30.50% |
| | Traditional bank-type financial holding groups | Count | 20.89 |
| | | Expected count | 20.90 |
| | | Percentage in group | 100.00% |
| | | Percentage in total | 29.10% |
| Total | | Count | 71.72 |
| | | Expected count | 71.70 |
| | | Percentage in group | 100.00% |
| | | Percentage in total | 100.00% |

**Annex DDD**—Chi-square test table for profitability factor scores

| Type | Value | df | Progressive Sig. (bilateral) | Exact Sig. (bilateral) |
|---|---|---|---|---|
| Pearson chi-square | 449.875 | 28 | 0.0000 | 0.0000 |
| Likelihood ratio | 494.173 | 28 | 0.0000 | 0.0000 |
| Accurate test of Fisher | 410.024 | | | 0.0000 |
| N in the effective case | 225 | | | |

**Annex EEE**—Groups and cross tabulation of probability factor scores

| Type | | | Total score |
|---|---|---|---|
| Group | Bank-owned financial holding groups | Count | 76.37 |
| | | Expected count | 76.40 |
| | | Percentage in group | 100.00% |
| | | Percentage in total | 34.00% |
| | Bank-type financial holding groups owned by financial holding group | Count | 73.28 |
| | | Expected count | 73.30 |

(continued)

(continued)

| Type | | | Total score |
|---|---|---|---|
| | | Percentage in group | 100.00% |
| | | Percentage in total | 32.60% |
| | Traditional bank-type financial holding groups | Count | 75.29 |
| | | Expected count | 75.30 |
| | | Percentage in group | 100.00% |
| | | Percentage in total | 33.50% |
| Total | | Count | 71.72 |
| | | Expected count | 71.70 |
| | | Percentage in group | 100.00% |
| | | Percentage in total | 100.00% |

**Annex FFF**—Chi-square test table for cost control factor scores

| Type | Value | df | Progressive Sig. (bilateral) | Exact Sig. (bilateral) |
|---|---|---|---|---|
| Pearson chi-square | 698.922 | 28 | 0.0000 | |
| Likelihood ratio | 767.218 | 28 | 0.0000 | 0.0000 |
| Accurate test of Fisher | 669.125 | | | 0.0000 |
| N in the effective case | 349 | | | |

**Annex GGG**—Groups and cross tabulation of cost control factor scores

| Type | | | Total score |
|---|---|---|---|
| Group | Bank-owned financial holding groups | Count | 110.83 |
| | | Expected count | 110.80 |
| | | Percentage in group | 100.00% |
| | | Percentage in total | 31.70% |
| | Bank-type financial holding groups owned by financial holding group | Count | 122.86 |

(continued)

(continued)

| Type | | | Total score |
|---|---|---|---|
| | | Expected count | 122.90 |
| | | Percentage in group | 100.00% |
| | | Percentage in total | 35.20% |
| | Traditional bank-type financial holding groups | Count | 115.78 |
| | | Expected count | 115.80 |
| | | Percentage in group | 100.00% |
| | | Percentage in total | 33.10% |
| Total | | Count | 71.72 |
| | | Expected count | 71.70 |
| | | Percentage in group | 100.00% |
| | | Percentage in total | 100.00% |

**Annex HHH**—Chi-square test table

| Type | Value | df | Progressive Sig. (bilateral) | Exact Sig. (bilateral) |
|---|---|---|---|---|
| Pearson chi-square | 222.540 | 28 | 0.000 | 0.000 |
| Likelihood ratio | 244.04 | 28 | 0.000 | 0.000 |
| Accurate test of Fisher | 176.173 | | | 0.000 |
| N in the effective case | 111 | | | |

**Annex III**—Cross tabulation

| Type | | | Total score |
|---|---|---|---|
| Group | Bank-owned financial holding groups | Count | 40.43 |
| | | Expected count | 40.40 |
| | | Percentage in group | 100.00% |
| | | Percentage in total | 36.30% |

(continued)

(continued)

| Type | | | Total score |
|---|---|---|---|
| | Bank-type financial holding groups owned by financial holding group | Count | 35.26 |
| | | Expected count | 35.30 |
| | | Percentage in group | 100.00% |
| | | Percentage in total | 31.70% |
| | Traditional bank-type financial holding groups | Count | 35.59 |
| | | Expected count | 35.60 |
| | | Percentage in group | 100.00% |
| | | Percentage in total | 32.00% |
| Total | | Count | 111.27 |
| | | Expected count | 111.30 |
| | | Percentage in group | 100.00% |
| | | Percentage in total | 100.00% |

# Bibliography

Allen, Jagtian (2000) The risk effects of combining banking, securities, and insurance activities. J Econ Bus 52(6):485–497
Arthur EW (2001) How should we respond to the growing risks of financial conglomerates? Electron J 12(11):283–294
Arthur EW (2002) The transformation of the United States financial services industry, 1975–2000: competition, consolidation and increased risks. Univ Ill Law Rev 215(153):225–240
Barth JR, Caprio JG, Levine R (2000) Banking systems around the globe: do regulation and ownership affect performance and stability. Policy Res Work Pap Ser 220(4):31–96
Barth JR, Caprio JG, Levine R (2001) Banking systems around the globe. University of Chicago Press
Berger AN, Hunter WC, Timme SG (1993) The efficiency of financial institutions: a review and preview of research past, present and future. J Bank Finance 17(17):221–249
Berry TR (2013) Property rights and the value of insurer product-line diversification: a cross-country analysis. J Risk & Insur 17(2):179–187
Benston GJ (1998) The federal safety net and the repeal of the glass Stesgall act's separation of commercial and investment banking. J Financ Serv Res 12(5):300–313
Bhargava R, Fraser DR (1989) On the wealth and risk effects of commercial bank expansion into securities underwriting: an analysis of section 20 subsidiaries. J Bank Finance 10(2):287–306
Boyd JH, Graham SL, Hewitt RS (1993) Bank holding group mergers with nonbank financial firms: effects on the risk of failure. J Bank Finance 17(1):43–63
Kahn, Winton (2004) Are bank holding companies a source of strength to their banking subsidiaries? Federal Reserve Bank of New York staff reports, (Report No. 189/2004)
Chen CJ, Zhou HW (2012) 商业银行财务管理学 [Financial management of commercial banks]. Xi'an Jiaotong University Press
Chen DS (2008) 商业银行参与证券投资基金的法律模型分析 [Research on the legal model of commercial banks' involvement in securities investment funds]. Jiangxi Univ Financ Econ 58(02):102–107
Chen JQ (2018) 央企并购地方国企绩效分析 [Performance analysis of central enterprises merging local state-owned enterprises]. Mod Mark 162(06):11–13
Chen L, Li YQ (2011) 中国农业上市公司绩效评价 [Performance evaluation of Chinese agricultural listed companies]. Chin Agric Sci Bull 27(04):416–422.
Chen QX, Yu J, Liu YF (2013) 企业并购财务协同效应影响因素研究 [Research on influencing factors of financial synergy effect of mergers and acquisitions]. Times Finance 809(17):175–178
Chen R (2014) On the scope economic effect of China's insurance industry and the choice of comprehensive operation mode [Master's book]. Yunnan University of Finance and Economics



X. Ning, *Performance Evaluation of Financial Holding Companies*, https://doi.org/10.1007/978-981-97-8128-7

Chen S (2020) 金融控股集团协同发展的路径与对策探讨 [Discussion on the path and countermeasures of coordinated development of financial holding groups]. Manag Obs 480(12):153–154
China Banking and Insurance Regulatory Commission (2019) 2018 annual report of China Banking Regulatory Commission
China Banking and Insurance Regulatory Commission (2019) List of legal persons of banking financial institutions in 2018
China Banking and Insurance Regulatory Commission (2019) Main regulatory indicators of commercial banks in 2018
China Banking Association (2016) Notice on carrying out the evaluation of GYROSCOPE evaluation system for steady development ability of commercial banks
China Banking Association (2021) 风险管理 [Risk management]. China Financial Publishing House
China Banking Regulatory Commission (2005) Core indicators of commercial bank risk supervision
China Security Regulatory Commission (2021) Measures for the administration of information disclosure of listed companies
Chronopoulos DK, Girardone C, Nankervis JC (2011) Are there any cost and profit efficiency gains in financial conglomeration? Evidence from the accession countries. Eur J Financ 15(4):385–404
Demsetz, Strahan (1997) Diversifcation, size, and risk at bank holding companies. J Money Credit Bank 29(29):300–313
Deng SH (2006) Integrated operation of commercial banks: international comparison and China's choice [Master's book]. Xiamen University
Ding SH (2008) Study on the synergy effect of financial holding group [Master's book]. University of Science and Technology of China
Ding YQ, Qiu DF (2010) Evaluation of the operating performance of city commercial banks based on factor analysis. Value Eng 29(16):55–56
E Bank (2019) Annual report of E Bank in 2018
Elsas R, Hackethal A, Holzhäuser M (2010) The anatomy of bank diversification. J Bank Finance 34(6):1274–1287
Ellul A, Yerra V (2013) Stronger risk controls, lower risk: evidence from U.S. Bank Holding Companies. J Financ 68(68):1757–1803
Fan YP, Yin ZT (2019) Research on the development and supervision of financial holding companies-from the perspective of international comparison. Financ Regul Res 19(12):38–53
Feng SL, Sun Y, Zhou WB (2015) Research on the performance and risk of Chinese financial holding companies. J Guizhou CollE Financ Econ 195(03):49–57
Gao HY (2021) Western economy. China Renmin University Press
Gao X, Zhang SQ (2012) Analysis of financial risk and financial synergy in cross-border M&A. Friends Account 725(29):80–82
Gao ZQ (2007) Research on the internal contradiction of insurance holding group [Master's book]. Nankai University
Guo M (2005) Organizational economics analysis of diversified financial groups. People's Publishing House
Guo Q, Zhang QQ, Li TG, Li WJ (2019) 金融控股公司监管问题研究 [Research on the supervision of financial holding companies]. Huabei Finance 482(02):10–16
Guo RX, Zhang PF, Yang MP (2015) 金融控股公司理论与实证研究综述 [A summary of theoretical and empirical research on financial holding companies]. Zhejiang Soc Sci 364(04):131–143
Han KC, Liu HB (2019) How to strengthen the supervision legislation of financial holding companies. Banker 422(02):47–49
Han XY (2019a) The effective boundary and normative suggestions of China's financial control supervision. Banker 408(03):96–99
Han XY, Dong Z (2019) International experiences of the development model of financial holding group. Banker 422(2):50–53
Han Y (2019b) Supervision logic of financial holding group. J Financ Dev Res 96(11):68–74

Herring, Litan (1995) Financial regulation in the global economy. Brookings Institution Press
He C, Fu JW, Wang LX (2018) Research on governance optimization of financial holding companies in China. Southwest Financ 466(10):58–65
Holzhauser M, Elsas R, Hackethal A (2010) The anatomy of bank diversification. J Bank Finance 34(6):1274–1287
Huang D (2021) 货币银行学 [Money and banking]. China Renmin University Press
Huang Q (2013) 中国金融控股公司发展模式研究 [Research on the development model of China's financial holding group]. China Financial House
Huang RQ (2013) Research on the performance evaluation of listed commercial banks in China [Master's book]. Southwestern University of Finance and Economics
Huo AY, Gao XH, Fan MM (2006) On the theoretical basis of the existence of financial holding companies. Financ Account Mon 644(20):71–73
I Bank (2019) Annual report of I Bank in 2018
Kwan SH (1997) Securities activities by commercial banking firms section 20 subsidiaries. Brookings-Wharton papers on financial services
Iman Van L, Arnold S (2003) Risk in financial conglomerates: management and supervision. Int Rev Econ Financ 27(2):171–182
Jia J (2014) Research on development strategy of founder financial holding group [Master's book]. Beijing Jiaotong University
Jiang D (2014) Research on the influence of mixed operation on systemic risk [Master's book]. Hunan University
Jiang H, Ye KW (2014) The design of regulatory mechanism for incentive compatibility of financial holding companies in China. Jinan J 36(07):32–42
Jiang H, Zhen DC (2018) Discussion on the performance of financial control and non-financial control-from the perspective of Taiwan Province banking industry. Mod Mark 166(10):37–39
Jin LL (2017) Financial synergy benefits of M&A of North-South cars [Master's book]. East China Jiaotong University
Joint Forum on Financial Conglomerates (2013) Supervision principle on financial group. China Financial Publishing House
Kanatas G, Qi J (2003) Integration of lending and underwriting: implications of scope economies. J Financ 58(3):1167–1191
Kang HP (2006) Research on risk control of financial holding group. Economy Press China
Kanter RM (2003) Challenge of organizational change: how companies experience it and leaders guide it. Simon and Schuster
Kwan SH (1997) Securities activities by commercial banking firms section 20 subsidiaries. Federal Reserve Bank of San Working Paper
Li HH (2019) Research on performance management of commercial banks based on EVA theory [Master's book]. Shandong University
Li R (2018) Research on synergy effect of financial holding groups in China [Master's book]. Capital University of Economics and Business
Li Y (2006) Risk-benefit analysis of commercial banks' investment banking. Financ Account Mon 916(30):32–33
Li YL (2016) The comparison and choice of business models of financial holding companies in China from the perspective of efficiency and risk [Master's book]. Southwestern University of Finance and Economics
Li ZL (2018) Research on the comprehensive management supervision system of commercial banks in China [Doctoral dissertation]. Southwest University of Political Science and Law
Lin JJ (2016) Research on the choice of development mode of China's financial holding group. J Tech Econ & Manag 239(06):78–82
Liu GQ, Dong YS, Li W (2018) Why should synergy create value? Organizing and cooperating to help the top 500 enterprises create value. Enterp Manag 465(09):92–96
Liu H (2010) Research on the development model and risk management of financial holding group [Doctoral dissertation]. Southwestern University of Finance and Economics

Liu P (2017) 金融集团发展与监管 [Financial group development and supervision]. China Financial Publishing House
Liu W, Hsu C-M (2014) Profit Performance of financial holding companies: evidence from Taiwan. Emerg Mark Financ Trade 50(3):190–200
Liu XJ (2015) Research on dynamic clustering and increment in data mining [Master's book]. Harbin University of Science and Technology
Liu YY (2009) Research on scope economy in mixed operation of banks [Master's book]. Nankai University
Liu Y (2018) Empirical research on performance evaluation of commercial banks in China based on factor analysis method [Master's book]. Central China Normal University
Lu MM (2015) Research on the correlation between diversification degree and performance of financial holding companies in China [Master's book]. Shandong Normal University
Luo GF, Pan JS (2013) Research on China's banking credit evaluation-based on the data of 16 listed banks from 2007 to 2011. Shanghai Financ 196(7):38–41
Lv H (2014) Research on the operating performance of financial holding companies in China [Master's book]. Shandong Normal University
M Bank (2019) Annual report of M Bank in 2018
Ma J (2002) A comparative study of financial holding group and universal bank —The choice of China's financial mixed operation mode. Wuhan University
Ministry of Finance of PRC (2016) Measures for financial enterprise performance evaluation
Ministry of Finance (2014) Accounting standards for business enterprises-basic standards
National Bureau of Statistics (2019) Statistical bulletin of national economic and social development in 2018
Nie F (2008) Research on risk management of financial holding group based on ANP [Master's book]. Wuhan University of Technology
Pan XC (2015) Econometrics. China Renmin University Press
Pan Y (2009) Research on the development of financial holding companies in China [Master's book]. Yunnan University
Pennacchi G (2010) Comments on Morgan and Stiroh. J Financ Serv Res 20(2):209
People's Bank of China (2012) 12th five-year plan for financial industry development and reform
People's Bank of China (2019) 11th five-year plan for financial industry development and reform
People's Bank of China (2019) China financial stability report 2018
People's Bank of China (2019) China monetary policy report
People's Bank of China (2020) China financial stability report 2019
People's Bank of China (2020) Trial measures for supervision and administration of financial holding companies
Qian DP (2016) Connotation, basic characteristics and subject supervision of financial holding group. Financ Perspect J 354(06):17–25
Rupert TJ, Sherman HD (2006) Do bank mergers have hidden or foregone value? Eur J Oper Res 12(1):253–268
Robert W (1997) A survey of corporate governance. J Financ 52(2):737–783
Santomero AW, Chung (1992) Evidence in support of broader banking powers. Financ Mark 12(1):1–69
Santomero AD, Eckles (2000) The determinants of success in the new financial services environment. FRBNY Econ Policy Rev 12(10):11–23
Saunders A, Walter I (1994) How risky would universal banks be. Oxford University Press
Schaeck (2008) On measuring concentration in banking systems. Financ Res Lett 5(01):59–67
Shao YY, Wu WH, Lin YP, Yu GH (2019) Practice and enlightenment of risk prevention and supervision of financial holding companies-based on typical cases of financial punishment in Taiwan. Fujian Finance 398(02):57–61
State Council of the PRC (2013) Inter-ministerial joint meeting system of financial supervision and coordination
Stiro KJ (2004) Do community banks benefit from diversification. J Financ Serv Res 425(1):135–160

Stiroh KJ, Rumble A (2006) The dark side of diversification: the case of US financial holding companies. J Bank Finance 30(8):2131–2161
Su ZQ, Wang S (2014) Disagreements and main obstacles in research on non-interest income of commercial banks—literature review on research on non-interest income of commercial banks. Financ Theory Pract 427(07):87–92
Sun XY (2015) A comparative study on the operating performance of cross-strait financial control banks [Master's book]. Jinan University
Tang JX, Yang L, Huang Q (2010) A comparative study on the operating performance of financial holding banks and non-financial holding banks in China. Commun Financ Account 726(06):73–76
The National People's Congress of the People's Republic of China Standing Committee (2015) Law of the People's Republic of China on commercial banks
The National People's Congress of the People's Republic of China (1995) Insurance law of the People's Republic of China
The National People's Congress of the People's Republic of China (1998) Securities law of the People's Republic of China
Vennet RV (1999) Cost and profit efficiency of financial conglomerates and universal banks in Europe. J Money Credit Bank 34(01):254–282
Wall LD, Eisenbeis RA (1984) Risk considerations in deregulating bank activities. Econ Rev 12(05):5–19
Wan W (2018) Research on the development and supervision of financial holding companies in China. Southwest Finance 443(06):9–17
Wang CY (2016a) Research on the application of Dupont analysis in commercial banks—taking ICBC as an example. Account Futur Ed 282(08):130–131
Wang H (2017) A case study of China Ping An comprehensive financial strategy [Master's book]. Hebei University
Wang JX, Yin ZT (2019) Research on the risk of China's financial holding group. View Financial 282(06):56–57
Wang MS, Liu XF (2013) 商业银行收入结构对盈利能力的影响研究 [Research on the influence of commercial bank's income structure on profitability]. Nankai Bus Rev 128(16):143–149
Wang O, Qi B (2007) 国际金融监管体制的演变及发展趋势 [Evolution and development trend of international financial supervision system]. ShangHai Securities News 5703(42)
Wang QF (2009) Research on the supervision of financial holding companies in China [Master's book]. Southwestern University of Finance and Economics
Wang ST (2008) On the choice of supervision mode of China's financial holding group [Master's book]. Fudan University
Wang XZ (2016) 我国上市商业银行财务绩效分析—沃尔评分法的应用 [Financial performance analysis of China's listed commercial banks-application of Wall Score Method.] J Nanchang Vocat Tech Techers 33(05):48–56
Wei P (2012) Analysis on the development of intermediary business income of listed banks in China—based on the annual report data of 11 listed banks from 2006 to 2011. Southwest Financ 395(11):51–54
World Bank (2020) World development report 2019
Wu YH (2017) Probe into the coordinated development of comprehensive financial services by financial holding groups. Financ Econ 450(06):63–67
Wu Z (2010) Financial development in transition economies: experience and reference. Financ Dev Rev 9(09):135–143
Xia B (2001) Research on financial holding group. China Financial Press
Xia Q (2007) Research on financial performance evaluation index system of commercial banks. On Econ Probl 344(08):111–113
Xiao WD, Jing X (2012) Integrated operation of China's banking industry: theory, present situation and prospect. Mod Manag Sci 362(02):3–5

Xiao YQ (1990) Camel rating system of credit rating of American financial institutions. Stud Int Financ 82(10):33–35

Xie P (2004) 金融控股公司的发展与监管 [Development and Supervision of Financial Holding Group]. CITIC Press Group

Xu J (2013) Research on the development of community banks in China based on financial symbiosis theory [Master's book]. Suzhou University

Xu PC (2008) Research on financial supervision under the trend of comprehensive operation of commercial banks in China [Doctoral dissertation]. Northwest University

Xu XP (2012) A comparative study on leverage effect of Chinese and foreign commercial banks-based on the case analysis of China Construction Bank and Bank of America. Financ Theory Pract 178(06):91–94

Yamori N, Harimaya K, Kondo K (2003) Are banks affiliated with bank holding companies more efficient than independent banks? The recent experience regarding Japanese regional BHCs. Asia-Pacific Finan Markets 10(4):359–376

Yan YM (2008) Synergistic effect of financial holding group investment projects: mechanism, system and management measures. Financ Theory Pract 360(12):18–20

Yang H, Tian T, Hua GQ (2004a) 中国金融控股公司立法若干问题研究 [Research on some problems of legislation of financial holding companies in China]. Jianghuai Tribune 278(02):48–55

Yang MH, Zhang XY, Shao ZQ (2002) Practice and operation of financial holding group. Economy and Management Publishing House

Yang MH, Zhang XY, Shao ZQ, Hong B (2004) 金融控股公司实务与操作 [Practice and operation of financial holding group]. CITIC Press Group

Yao FY (2007) Performance analysis of sub-banks and general banks of regional financial holding companies in Taiwan Province [Master's book]. Chung Hsing University

Ye ZY (2003) On the selection of index positive and dimensionless methods in multi-index comprehensive evaluation. Zhejiang Stat 112(04):25–26

Yeager, Harshma (2004) The financial modernization act: evolution or Revolution Working Paper

Yue LJ (2005) Research on the mode and efficiency of China's commercial banks in securities business [Doctoral dissertation]. Huazhong University of Science and Technology

Zhang CY (2005) Research on risk factors and control in mixed operation of commercial banks [Master's book]. Chongqing University

Zhang CZ, Zhang WC (2010) 金融控股集团管理实务 [Management practice of financial holding group]. Machinery Industry Press

Zhang DX, Deng B (2013) Operating performance of China's financial holding companies under the impact of financial crisis-from the perspective of risk control right allocation of micro-subjects. J Manag Sci China 16(07):66–79

Zhang RM, Zhao YQ (2012) Analysis of synergy effect of financial holding group. Mod Bus Trade Ind 24(10):97

Zhang WT (2017) SPSS统计分析基础教程 [Basic course of SPSS statistical analysis]. Higher Education Press

Zhang Y (2014) Empirical research on the influence of bank concentration and competition on bank stability from the perspective of supervision [Master's book]. Shandong University

Zhao MH (2009) Research on financial supervision of insurance group—based on the analysis of cash flow characteristics and risks [Doctoral Dissertation]. Xiamen University

Zhao WH (2017) Research on the influence of diversified operation of property insurance companies on group performance under different scales [Master's book]. Southwestern University of Finance and Economics

Zhao X, Dong JR (2008) Research on synergy effect of financial holding group and its enlightenment to China. Economy Forum 617(15):113–115

Zhen GM, Zhen XX (2011) Study on synergy effect of financial holding group. Productivity Research 311(11):52–53

Zhou CG (2016) 股份制商业银行经营绩效评价—基于骆驼评级体系的分析[Performance evaluation of joint-stock commercial banks-analysis based on camel rating system]. Fujian Finance 371(11):63–66

Zhou PF, Wang C (2003) 中国银行业规模经济与范围经济的实证研究 [An empirical study on economies of scale and scope in China's banking industry]. China Ind Econ 250(10):21–28

Zhu X (2011) An empirical study on performance differences between quasi-financial-controlled background banks and non-financial-controlled background banks in China [Master's book]. Xiamen University

**SPRINGER NATURE**

# GPSR Compliance

*The European Union's (EU) General Product Safety Regulation (GPSR) is a set of rules that requires consumer products to be safe and our obligations to ensure this.*

*If you have any concerns about our products, you can contact us on ProductSafety@springernature.com*

In case Publisher is established outside the EU, the EU authorized representative is:

Springer Nature Customer Service Center GmbH
Europaplatz 3
69115 Heidelberg, Germany

The manufacturer's authorised representative in the EU is Springer Nature Customer Service Centre GmbH, Europaplatz 3, 69115 Heidelberg, Germany. If you have any concerns regarding our products, please contact ProductSafety@springernature.com

Printed and bound by CPI Group (UK) Ltd, Croydon, CR0 4YY
01/10/2026
02225858-0002